Seasonal Music Insights: Vivaldi and Much More

by Betsy Schwarm

classical music historian and author of the
Classical Music Insights series

Copyright September 2018
by Elizabeth Schwarm Glesner

ISBN 978-0-9993051-1-9

Cover by Wayne Rigsby of Gearbox Creative

Vivaldi image by Wayne Rigsby;
seasonal nature photos by Betsy Schwarm

Chapter headers by RJ Miller
Author photo by Conor Glesner

Table of Contents

Chapter One: Seasonal Sounds 1-8

Chapter Two: Full Cycles 9-62

Antonio Vivaldi: *The Four Seasons* 11-14
Joseph Haydn: *The Seasons* 14-17
Louis Spohr: Symphony no. 9, "Jahrzeiten" 18-19
Fanny Mendelssohn-Hensel: *Das Jahr* 20-22
Giuseppe Verdi: *I Vespri Siciliani* –
    Four Seasons ballet music 22-24
Joachim Raff: Symphonies no. 8-11 24-27
Peter Tchaikovsky: *The Seasons* 28-30
Isaac Albeniz: *Les Saisons* 30-31
Edward German: *The Seasons* 32-33
Alexander Glazunov: *The Seasons* 34-36
Albert Roussel: Symphony no. 1,
    "Poeme de la forêt" 36-38
Henry Hadley: Symphony no. 2,
    "Four Seasons" 39-41
Charles Ives: *New England Holidays* 42-44
Gian Francesco Malipiero: Sinfonia no. 1,
    "... come quattro stagioni" 44-45
Astor Piazzolla:
    Quattro Porteño de Buenos Aires 46-48
Lawrence Ashmore: *The Four Seasons* 48-50
Peter Schickele: *A Year in the Catskills* 51-52
Philip Glass: Second Violin Concerto,
    "American Four Seasons" 53-54
Pēteris Vasks: *Gadalaiki (The Seasons)* 55-56
Mark O'Connor: *The American Seasons*,
    "Seasons of an American Life" 57-60

Chapter Three: Spring 63-103

    Beethoven: Violin Sonata no. 5, "Spring" ... 64-66
    R Schumann: Symphony no. 1, "Spring" ... 67-69
    JK Paine: Symphony no. 2, "In the Spring"
        "In the Spring" 69-72

Sir Arthur Sullivan: *Victoria and Merrie England* –
    May Day 72-75
Nicolai Rimsky-Korsakov:
    May Night Overture 75-76
Zdenek Fibich: *Vesna (Spring)* 77-78
Josef Foerster: Springtime and Desire ... 78-80
Mikhail Ippolitov-Ivanov: *Spring Overture,*
    "Yar-kmel" 80-81
Claude Debussy: *Printemps* 81-83
Jean Sibelius: *Spring Song* 84
Albert Roussel:
    Pour une fete de printemps 85
Josef Suk: *Jaro (Spring)* 86-87
Ottorino Respighi: *Three Botticelli Pictures*
    – I. Primavera (Spring) 87-89
Frank Bridge: *Enter Spring* 90-91
Igor Stravinsky: *The Rite of Spring* 91-94
Sir Arnold Bax: *Spring Fire* 94-95
Darius Milhaud:
    Concertino de printemps 95-97
Lili Boulanger:
    D'un matin de printemps 97-98
Aaron Copland: *Appalachian Spring* 98-100
Dmitri Kabalevsky: *Spring* 100-101

Chapter Four: Summer 104-138

    Beethoven: Symphony no. 6, "Pastorale" ... 105-107
    Mikhail Glinka: Spanish Overture no. 2,
        "Summer Night in Madrid" 107-108
    Felix Mendelssohn:
        Fantasia on Last Rose 108-109
    Heinrich Ernst: Etude on
        Last Rose of Summer 110-111
    Emil Waldteufel: *Soiree d'ete* 111-112
    Englebert Humperdinck: *Moorish Rhapsody* –
        I. Tarifa: Elegy at Summer 113-114
    Frederick Delius:
        Summer Night on the River 115
    Wilhelm Peterson-Berger: *Frösöblomster* ... 116-117
    Hugo Alfven: *Midsummer Vigil* 118-119
    Josef Suk: *A Summer's Tale* 120-122
    Zoltán Kodaly: *Summer Evening* 123-124
    Anton Webern: *Im Sommerwind* 124-125
    Rebecca Clarke: *Midsummer Moon* 125-126
    Sergei Prokofiev: *Summer Day* 127-128

Arthur Honegger: *Pastorale d'ete* 128-130
Walter Piston: *Three New England Sketches* –
    II. Summer Evening 130-131
Howard Hanson: *Bold Island Suite* –
    II. Summer Seascape 132-133
Samuel Barber: *Summer Music* 133-134
Joaquin Rodrigo: *Concierto de estio* 134-136
Libby Larsen: *Deep Summer Music* 136-137

Chapter Five: Autumn 139-176

    L Mozart: Sinfonia da caccia,
        "The Hunt" 140-141
    W Mozart: Quartet no. 17, "The Hunt" ... 141-143
    Napoléon Coste: *Feuilles d'autumne* 143-144
    Franz Liszt: two Transcendental Etudes –
        "Wilde Jagd"; "Ricordanza" 145-146
    Josef Strauss: *Herbstrosen* Walzer 147-148
    Edvard Grieg: *In Autumn* 149-150
    Cécile Chaminade: three Etudes de concert –
        Autumne; Fileuse; Tarantelle ... 150-152
    Sergei Lyapunov: *Chant d'Automne* 153-154
    Edward MacDowell: Orchestral Suite no. 1 –
        In a Haunted Forest;
        In October; Forest Spirits 154-156
    Frederick Delius: *North Country Sketches* –
        Autumn 157-158
    Joseph Marx: *Feste im Herbst* 159-160
    Sir Arnold Bax: *November Woods* 160-161
    Sergei Prokofiev: *Autumnal Sketch* 162
    Leo Sowerby: *Comes Autumn Time* 163-164
    Gerald Finzi: *The Fall of the Leaf* 165-166
    William Alwyn: *Autumn Legend* 166-167
    Peggy Stuart Coolidge:
        New England Autumn 168-169
    Einojuhani Rautavaara:
        Autumn Gardens 169-171
    Jennifer Higdon: *Autumn Music* 172-173
    Eric Whitacre: *October* 173-174

Chapter Six: Winter 177-216

James Oswald: *Airs for the Seasons* –
    four winter sonatas   178-179
L Mozart: *Musical Sleighride*   179-181
W Mozart: German Dance,
    "Sleigh Ride"   181-182
Emile Waldteufel: *Les Patineurs*
    (Skater's Waltz)   182-183
Peter Tchaikovsky: Symphony no. 1,
    "Winter Daydreams"   184-186
Peter Tchaikovsky: *The Nutcracker* –
    The Forest in Winter;
    Waltz of the Snow Flakes 187-188
Eugene Ysaÿe:
    Chant d'hiver (*Winter Song*) 189-190
Nicolai Rimsky-Korsakov:
    The Snow Maiden   190-192
Claude Debussy: piano suite for winter –
    Footsteps in the Snow,
    Feuilles mortes;
    Snow is Dancing;
    Wind on the Plains   193-195
Julius Fučik: *Winterstürme*   195-196
Gustav Holst: *A Winter Idyll*   196-197
Erno von Dohnányi: *Winterreigen* 198-200
Ernest Bloch:
    Hiver, from *Hiver-Printemps* 200-201
Erich Korngold: *The Snowman*   201-203
Gerald Finzi: *New Year Music*   203-204
Leroy Anderson: *Sleigh Ride*   205-206
Joan Tower: *Snow Dreams*   206-208
Michael Daughtery: *American Gothic* –
    II. Winter Dreams   208-209
Michael Torke: *December*   210-211
Conni Ellisor: *Blackberry Winter* 211-214

Chapter Seven: Seasonal Songs and Choral Works
.... 217-257

    Thomas Morley: three madrigals –
        It was a Lover and His Lass;
        April is in My Mistresses' Face;
        Now is the Month of Maying   218-220
    Vivaldi: *Dorilla in Tempe* –
        "Dell'aura sussurrar" chorus   220-221
    W Mozart: two vocal works for spring –
        Schon lacht der holde Frühling;
        Sehnsucht nach dem Frühling   222-224
    Franz Schubert: four seasonal songs –
        Frühlingsgesang; Ständchen;
        Mond in einer Herbstnacht;
        Winterabend   225-228
    Hector Berlioz: *Les Nuit d'été*   228-231
    Felix Mendelssohn: seasonal part songs –
        Sechs Lieder im Freien zu singen ..   231-233
    J Strauss Jr: *Voices of Spring*   234-235
    Gabriel Fauré: four seasonal songs –
        Autumne; Dans le forêt de septembre;
        Bonne chanson #7 & 9   235-238
    Gustav Mahler: *Das Lied von der Erde* –
        Der Einsame im Herbst;
        Der Trunkene im Frühling   238-240
    Frederick Delius: two summer part songs –
        Midsummer Song; Songs to be Sung
        of a Summer Night on the Water ...   241-242
    R Strauss: 4 Last Songs:
        Frühling; September   243-244
    Ralph Vaughan Williams: *Folk Songs*
        of the Four Seasons   245-247
    Carl Orff: *Carmina Burana* – Spring   247-248
    Samuel Barber:
        Knoxville: Summer of 1915   249-251
    Lori Laitman: three seasonal songs –
        Dear March; Apple Orchard;
        Early Snow   251-253
    Eric Whitacre: *Winter*   253-255

Chapter Eight: Shakespearean Diversions
.... 258-272

    Felix Mendelssohn: *A Midsummer Night's Dream*
                                        260-262
    Benjamin Britten: *A Midsummer Night's Dream*
                                        263-265
    Lars-Erik Larsson: *A Winter's Tale* 266-267
    Michael Torke: *A Winter's Tale* 267-269

Appendices:

I.	Vivaldi's Poems	....	274-277
II.	Selected Vocal Texts	....	278-324
III.	Pronunciation Guide	....	325-326
IV.	Glossary	....	326-333
V.	Sources	....	334-338
VI.	Acknowledgements and Author Information	....	338-339
VII.	Index	....	340-356

Author's Note

Vivaldi's *The Four Seasons* – particularly *Spring* – has been a *point d'entrée* to fine music for countless persons over many generations. However, it is far from the only example of seasonal expressions in music. Here is a collection of insights into many works of seasonal flavor. Some will be familiar, others less so, but all offer perspectives on seasonal moods and scenes, and all are compositions I think you'll enjoy exploring.

Happy listening!

Betsy

Seasonal Music Insights: | 1
Vivaldi and Much More

Chapter One:

Seasonal Sounds

Few works of great music are as widely familiar as Vivaldi's *Spring*, its opening moments above. Its mostly frolicking demeanor is simply fun, as well as easy to appreciate, even if the solo part is far from easy to play. Listeners love its high spirits, violinists love the time in the spotlight, and concert presenters love a work that will reliably attract audiences. Moreover, the notion of a world resembling that which Vivaldi's music suggests, having more sunshine than storms, is surely appealing. Certainly, a great many composers have turned their attention to crafting seasonal expressions.

The trick is sorting out visions and tales as opposed to meanings. In the very first of his Young People's Concerts, given January 8, 1958, Leonard Bernstein (1918 – 1990) observed, "Music is never *about* things. Music just *is*. It's a lot of beautiful notes and sounds put together so well that we get pleasure out of hearing them." He went on to add, "When you say, 'What does it mean?' you're really saying 'What is it trying to tell me?' or 'What ideas does it make me have?'" A century after Bernstein's birth, that's exactly the idea behind this seasonal survey.

Another American composer to consider the concept of musical meaning, in this case, specifically in the sense of seasonal moods, is Michael Torke (b. 1961), who agrees with Bernstein: "Music never literally represents things, but it does evoke feelings, impressions, and sometimes memories... This is something I discover as I'm writing; it is not that I set out intending to describe the last month of the year through music. Rather, the associations creep up on me as I'm composing."

Listeners and performers, too, can make associations; comparing those thoughts with composers' impressions or those of outside observers can trigger further ideas, as well as closer listening. What is it about the music that triggered that specific image or experience? Was it something the violas were doing? Was it the tempo of the music? Was it the combination of notes in that specific key? Was it how one moment differed from the very next moment? How did those impressions arise out of those little black dots on the page? Seeking out those connections brings one closer to the music itself, even if one can't read music or doesn't have the score at hand. The sounds are there, and they speak to those who listen with attention.

So this survey is, in part, an overview of music that relates in some manner to spring, summer, autumn, winter, as well as images connected to those seasons. However, it also offers a variety of listening points for those individual compositions, so one can more readily explore the music. If the composer labels it with a seasonal connection, what perspectives on that seasons might one expect, and how does the music express it?

Sometimes, the inspiration is clear. Antonio Vivaldi (1678 – 1741) provided poetic additions that clarify the scenes behind the music in his *Four Seasons*. Claude Debussy (1862 – 1918) and Ottorino Respighi (1879 – 1936) both had in mind a particular painting of nymphs dancing in the springtime; they give it different levels of intensity, but one can seek out that dancing spirit while listening to the music. For Charles Ives (1874 – 1954), autumn meant Thanksgiving, though the former church organist was less concerned with roast turkey than with the hymns he played in worship services.

Others take a more abstract view. By its title, the *Concierto de estio* by Joaquin Rodrigo (1901 – 1999) is a summer concerto, though in fact, it is more a reaction to Vivaldi than to the steamy summer weather of Rodrigo's native Spain. For Mozart father and son, hunters galloping after their prey demanded skipping rhythms and, ideally, bold horns to evoke the hunters themselves; that sort of hunting is mostly an autumn endeavor, so one can suppose that, for them, such musical colors were part of an autumn experience.

Admittedly, words may make those connections even more vivid, though music still plays a role. In his *Le Bonne chanson (The Good Song)*, Gabriel Fauré (1845 – 1924) takes a text of blissful lovers reveling under summer skies and provides a piano accompaniment that flutters like gentle breezes. As for *Carmina Burana* by Carl Orff (1895 – 1982), here one finds little gentleness, but plenty of bold expression. "Behold, spring," it seems, must be declaimed in a forthright manner. Vocal works appear in Chapter Seven.

In this survey, we'll consider what happens in the music to reinforce a specific seasonal idea. However, some works having apparent seasonal references in their titles actually have other inspiration. Any Soviet composer using the word October was almost certainly referring to the nation's 1917 Revolution. The rest of the world would have said that event began November 7, but Tsarist Russia still used the old Julian calendar, by which resource the date was October 25. One way or the other, the inspiration is national pride and politics with nothing relating to fall foliage.

Similar caution is required when considering American composers working after September 11, 2001, and using the word September in the title of a work. Such compositions are often important and sometimes compelling, but they are not <u>about</u> September itself.

One Soviet composer, Sergei Prokofiev (1891 – 1953) wrote some vividly wintery music that is less seasonal than historic in inspiration. His score for the 1938 film *Alexander Nevsky* tells of a 13th century Russian prince who scored a magnificent victory when the opposing forces fell through the surface of a frozen lake, while the more lightly mounted Russians survived. Prokofiev scores it splendidly, but the imagery is of warriors in close combat, not the season per se. His opera *War and Peace* finds itself in the same situation. One could hardly tell of Napoleon's armies approaching Moscow and ultimately failing in their assault without evoking wintery weather. Snow is crucial to Tolstoy's novel, so it must appear in the opera, but nevertheless, it is not an opera about winter.

Another case is May Day. On one level, it's a spring celebration, pagan in origin, with flowers and dancing around a ribbon-festooned May Pole. On another, it's a day honoring the working classes, one commemorated in many nations. The coincidence of events is due to an American working class strike of massive proportion held on May 1, 1886; authorities in Chicago over-reacted, leading to the deaths of protesters. From this view, May Day has nothing to do with pretty young ladies with flowers in their hair. It is workers' rights and dignity, a cause that relates in no way to the subject of this survey. So when it comes to May Day, it is scenes from a thoroughly non-violent and not protest-related ballet by Sir Arthur Sullivan (1842 – 1900) that appears in Chapter Three.

A similar situation arises with two Shakespeare plays: *A Midsummer Night's Dream* and *A Winter's Tale*. Both have seasonal words in their titles, and especially the former is widely famed and much favored for musical expression. Few classical concert promoters and even fewer classical radio announcers could resist including selections from *A Midsummer Night's Dream* of Felix Mendelssohn (1809 – 1847) in a summer program. However, neither of those plays can properly be said to be specifically <u>about</u> those seasons. Nonetheless, given the treasured reputation of Mendelssohn's work and of the opera of the same name composed by Benjamin Britten (1913 – 1976), both deserve mention, as do two respected musical reactions to *A Winter's Tale*. Thus, Chapter Eight offers some *Shakespearean Diversions* en route to the closing pages of this collection.

Certain other grand theatrical works make reference to seasons without necessarily being <u>about</u> those seasons. In the opera *Vanessa* by Samuel Barber (1910 – 1980), the title character sings an aria that begins with the text, "Must the winter come so soon?" The opera's scenes do take place in winter, but in context, she is reflecting less upon the weather than on the fact that she is beginning to feel the advancing years. Then there's *La Bohème*. Its composer, Giacomo Puccini (1858 – 1924), set all four acts in winter, two of them at Christmas. However, the settings serve largely to make the harsh life of the Bohemians that much clearer. Love is the only bright spot in their lives, a fact made all the more vivid by the snowy backdrop.

How would one reflect any of these ideas in a musical composition? Imagine a theoretical composer writing music to suggest a splendid summer afternoon at the park. To one side, children frolic in a playground, calling to one another as they zip down slides, fly on swings, and clamber over the jungle gym. On nearby benches sit a few adults, ostensibly keeping an eye on the kids, though also chatting with one another. Beyond the playground, a group of teens plays volleyball, and well away from the crowds picnicking couples lounge with bottles of wine. Juxtapose lively music for the kids, even more energetic music for the teens, gently romantic melodies for the couples, and occasional sharp remarks for the adults near the playground; use restless high woodwinds for the kids, assertive brass for the teens, flowing strings for the couples, and percussion for the adults' calls of caution. A summer afternoon is given musical life.

Seasonal Music Insights:
Vivaldi and Much More

Whatever this season or that one might mean to a specific listener, some composer has likely had a similar reaction that led him or her to give it musical expression. Even works by composers whose reactions have been quite different from one's own can yet be diverting to explore. Each of the following articles includes suggestions as to what one might find that would surprise and delight. Consider it a musical scavenger hunt, the suggestions serving as the list of things to seek and find. Surely that facilitates a far more directed – and, perhaps, more rewarding – process than just random listening.

This survey includes nearly all the usual suspects in the realm of seasonal music, along with a variety of less familiar choices. Each chapter covers over 200 years of music, some rather more, and each chapter includes somewhat recent music, six of them with articles concerning current composers. Vivaldi is delightful, but there is so much more to consider.

The selection of works to be included began with a list of the required choices: those works without which one could not pretend to be commenting upon seasonally inspired compositions. Then alternative options were added, some by well-known composers, other ranging further into corners of the repertoire. An attempt was made to cover many generations and also many genres, so it is not simply a selection of orchestral pieces or a contrasting list of piano music: some of both are here, as well as other options. In boiling that list down to the final top choices, some preference was given to more ambitious scores, though in some cases, even short ones make an appearance.

An additional factor in musical selection was whether recordings were available. It seemed unfair to generate curiosity in readers about this work or that one, only for the readers then to discover that the item they wanted to hear wasn't available for listening. The vast majority of works featured in this survey can be found in CD form, and also online on the voluminous Naxos Music Library; a very few are new enough that one may still need i-Tunes to find them. However, barring sudden and unavoidable changes in digital sources, the music is there for hearing and acquisition.

How does a season sound? That varies depending on where one lives: Different flowers grow in different spring gardens, summer need not necessarily have thunderstorms, leaves don't always turn colors in autumn, and, in many places, winter isn't about snow. However, the fact is that most prominent composers – let alone great ones – have tended to live in temperate climates where those conditions might occur. Yet there is no right or wrong about seasonal imagery in music: there are just possibilities. Debussy once observed of his career field that music theory was relatively unimportant, adding "You merely have to listen." Here are guide points to help direct that listening in a seasonal direction.

Seasonal Music Insights: | 9
Vivaldi and Much More

Chapter Two: Full Cycles

♪♪♪♪♪

Countless composers have set about capturing the entire year in music. Antonio Vivaldi (1678 – 1741) may be the most famed example, and thanks to chronology, he'll be the star of our first featured article in another two pages. However, as his music served to head Chapter One, the honor of appearing at the head of Chapter Two goes to another man. Alexander Glazunov (1865 – 1936) was composing a ballet, not a violin concerto. Dancers would be needed for full expression, though, as we'll find, the music of his *The Seasons* stands quite well on its own.

The music at the head of this chapter, leaping upward to brilliant high notes, is the theme with which Glazunov captures the explosive excitement of an autumn bacchanal. That's exactly the word used by the composer in the subtitle, a fact suggesting that either Glazunov was immensely fond of drink (a notion supported by facts from his life) or that he simply thought an exuberant harvest festival, with much sampling of new wine, would be a splendid way to celebrate the season. Certainly, his *Autumn* music is the most ebullient portion of his ballet *The Seasons*.

Like Glazunov's and Vivaldi's seasonal compositions, the works featured in this chapter all offer perspectives on the entire year. Each composer gives to each season a different character, and they don't always agree as to what mood that season might exhibit. One composer even declined to give specific seasonal labels to the individual movements, having found that he and his soloist disagreed as to which season was which. Cheerful or grim, relaxed or weary, playful or nervous, lively or frantic: any pair of adjectives might describe one season or another, depending on the personality and background of the composer – or the listener.

Nationality also matters. American composer Charles Ives (1874 – 1954) chose to represent summer with the Fourth of July. French composers, on the other hand, might opt for Bastille Day instead, though Frenchman Albert Roussel (1869 – 1937) apparently preferred lounging in the moonlight to cheering at patriotic celebrations. Then there's Argentine composer Astor Piazzolla (1921 – 1992), for whom summer came at Christmas-time, a point he set aside in favor of sultry tango rhythms.

One could draw similar contrasts in each of the other seasons, that one composer viewed it quite differently from another. They also might agree about one season, though not about others, and two of our chosen composers go one step further, dividing the year not by four, but by twelve, so as to have musical pictures of each individual month. Whatever the approach might be, there is plenty of room for varied expression.

♪♪♪♪

Vivaldi: *The Four Seasons* –

> Concerto no. 1 in E major, opus 8, no. 1, *Spring*
> Concerto no. 2 in g minor, opus 8, no. 2, *Summer*
> Concerto no. 3 in F major, opus 8, no. 3, *Autumn*
> Concerto no. 4 in f minor, opus 8, no. 4, *Winter*

Violinist, composer, teacher, almost incidentally priest, charismatic personification of the Italian Baroque: Antonio Vivaldi (1678 – 1741) was all of those. Here was a man who, in addition to priestly and academic duties, found time to write dozens of operas and over four hundred concerti, while continuing to tour as a violin soloist. When Vivaldi came to town, it was headline news, and few would miss the opportunity to see exactly how much excitement could come from an ensemble of strings and harpsichord with solo violin.

The great majority of those hundreds of concerti were for his own concerts, allowing us to still sense what must have been features of his performing style. Rushes of rapid passagework and lines of lyrical beauty appear in almost equal measure, the violin's voice alternating with that of the orchestra, generally simpler music for the ensemble while the attention-getting material goes to the soloist. Certainly, that's what most composers of Vivaldi's generation would have been likely to do, but it also allows a modern audience to imagine those long-ago performances, attention shifting rapidly from one area of the stage to another.

So his compositions sum up late Baroque Era trends, while also branching out. When, in 1725, he published a set of twelve violin concerti collectively known as *The Contest Between Harmony and Invention* and given the misleadingly low opus number of 8, Vivaldi also used the first four of those concerti as a musical canvas to suggest scenes suitable for each season. To ensure that no one would miss the point, he included with each of those four concerti a sonnet describing what he had in mind, the music vividly evoking those specific visions. A century onward, the idea of instrumental music having plot content would be widely popular and would come to be known as "program music"; in Vivaldi's own time, it was almost unknown.

Listen, in the first movement of *Spring*, as three violins entwine in birdsong, then are sent to cover by a raging thunderstorm. In its second movement, the soloist's restful phrases suggest a shepherd's valiant attempt to nap, despite his barking dog, represented by a repeated bow-wow effect in the violas. For the finale, drawn-out undertones convey the drone of a bagpipe underlying danceable lines for the soloist and higher strings.

Marvel, in *Summer*, as the turtledove sings to the rhythm of her name (in Italian, "tortorella") in the first movement. Vivaldi writes it so that the four-syllable word has its longest note on the third syllable, and then falls in pitch, exactly as one would speak the word. In the second movement, rumbles of low strings provide the buzzing of flies and in the last, strident themes of a summer hailstorm flatten the farmer's fields.

Observe, in *Autumn*, high spirits of the first movement's opening lines, orchestra and soloist calling out to one another in turn. Quieter passages, and then short, swaying phrases suggest the unsteady footsteps of a drunken reveler at a harvest celebration, before a brief recollection of music from the *Summer* concerto implies that someone is sorry to see summer go. In the second movement, very long lines for the soloist and a gentle pulsing from the ensemble give the drinkers time to sleep it off. The last movement brings bouncy dotted rhythms as mounted hunters set off in pursuit of their crafty prey, which falls just before the ebullient closing restatement of the movement's opening phrases.

Shiver with Vivaldi as a snowstorm blows in during the first movement of *Winter*. The orchestra pulses along while the soloist's intricate passagework suggests chattering teeth. In the second movement, a weary traveler lingers by the fire, perhaps singing gently, while orchestral pizzicato notes imply the popping of the wood as it burns. With the third movement, that respite has ended and Vivaldi takes us out again into the storm. First, the action seems cautious, though rapid downward flowing phrases, for orchestra and soloist alike, suggest a few slips and falls on the ice.

In not using this music for either *Fantasia* film, the folks at Disney missed an opportunity, though perhaps they wanted less specific guidelines than those Vivaldi provided. An attentive listener's imagination can make much of Vivaldi's music, and the poems themselves provide perfect guidance. You'll find them – with translations – in Appendix One (pages 274-277).

Often, additional data is appended to the titles of Vivaldi's works: numbers following the abbreviation RV. The letters stand for Ryom Verzeichnis, a catalog of the composer's works compiled in the 1970s by Danish musicologist Peter Ryom. The project was undertaken to bring some order to the composer's vast catalog, since much of it had not come to print in organized form. Fortunately, the *Four Seasons* do have opus numbers. However, for those who would also like to know the RV numbers, they are *Spring*, RV 269; *Summer* RV 315; *Autumn*, RV 293; *Winter*, RV 297.

♪♪♪♪

Haydn: *The Seasons* – oratorio

When it comes to oratorios, it is *Messiah* (1742) that leaps most readily to mind: that glorious work by George Frideric Handel (1685 – 1759) blending chorus, soloists, and orchestra in praise of their Lord. Yet Joseph Haydn (1732 – 1809), too, composed oratorios, and not without his predecessor's influence.

In the 1790s, the Austrian-born Haydn made two extended visits to London where he heard *Messiah* performed at St. Margaret's Chapel. Back home in Vienna, he decided to write oratorios himself. Two would arise in the next half dozen years, both based on German translations of English lyric poetry. The second of these was *Die Jahreszeiten* (*The Seasons*). Derived from a text by British poet James Thomson (1700 – 1748), it debuted April 24, 1801, its music rife with humble village scenes and nature sound effects, ranging from roosters to frogs to lightning.

However, *Die Jahreszeiten* is not just a tapestry of natural beauty. It also reflects on human interactions with nature, and how that nature influences man's activities and feelings. Joyous villagers celebrate a fine harvest with wine; a wary traveler fears he will lose his way in the snow. Such varied feelings are abundantly conveyed by Haydn's delightfully varied score.

Four separate cantatas, one for each season and each spanning roughly half an hour, come together to make up the full oratorio. Nowhere is there a specific plot; rather, it is scene setting, using music and words to suggest vignettes suitable to each season. Each cantata has a handful of movements, including choruses, arias, ensembles, and occasional narrative recitatives to introduce the next scene. Spotlighting a few movements in each season should pique a listener's interest, as well as provide glimpses into how Haydn applies his artistry.

In *Frühling* (*Spring*), one finds the chorus "Komm, holder Lenz" (Come, fair spring) flowing as peacefully as a brook through a meadow. Distinct contrast arrives with the baritone's jolly Ackermann (Plowman) aria, in which the farmer's moods are bolstered by burbling bassoon (a brook beside his fields?), the fuller orchestra occasionally diverging into jaunty phrases borrowed from the composer's own Symphony no. 94 in G major, "Surprise," which had premiered in London March 23, 1792. Perhaps that premiere date left it connected in Haydn's mind with spring.

Sommer offers, amongst other delights, the soprano aria "Welche Labung für die Sinne" (Such a balm for the senses). In the blend of gently smiling vocal lines and frequent oboe spotlights of restful demeanor, a blissful, pastoral atmosphere is beautifully captured. The lady depicted in the music might be lingering beneath a shade tree, with a lovely view before her. Later, a thunderstorm develops, inspiring suitably anxious music, though the subsequent chorus "Die duster Wolken trennen sich" (The dark clouds split away) then celebrates the passing of that storm in rather hymn-like fashion. Amidst the choral passages, Haydn makes room for his three vocal soloists (soprano, tenor, and baritone); they have character names – Hanne, Lukas, and Simon – but no defined roles, other than what the music suggests. The varied forces allow new colors with each change of phrase, whether phrases of music or phrases of text.

Herbst (*Autumn*) begins in leisurely mood, though that relaxed aura does not continue uninterrupted. The baritone aria "Breiten Weisen" (Wide Meadows) has impressively contrasted moods, vocal lines musing thoughtfully upon the view even as the orchestra is given more restless phrases. Well before Haydn is finished with autumn, he has had enough of lounging in the sun. The final chorus "Der Wein ist da!" (There is the wine!) is a boisterous drinking chorus interspersed with shouts of delight. In the center of that chorus, the composer shifts to a folk-dance spirit, with bagpipe effects in the strings beneath graceful phrases for women's voices. In all, the scene ensures that no listener is likely to overlook the village spirit.

As for *Winter*, Haydn sets his tenor soloist recounting an anxious traveler in the snow in the aria "Hier steht der Wand'rer" (Here stands the wanderer). At first, both vocal lines and instrumental ones are tinged with caution, though the aria closes with cheerful thoughts of Freude (Joy). Before long, one finds the Spinning Chorus for soprano soloist and ladies of the chorus. Their music has such determined drive that one might suppose spinning to be quite a serious endeavor. Eventually, in the last movement "Dann bricht der grosse Morgen an" (Then the great morning dawns), one finds true splendor, complete with trumpet fanfares, an impressive double fugue with eight layers of music juxtaposed directly against one another, and a rapturous finale complete with Amens. So brilliantly shaded is this closing movement that one cannot doubt this is the most splendid of sunrises.

Haydn's *Die Jahreszeiten* is far from the only vocal expression of seasonal moods. However, it is one of the grandest in scope, both in number of performers and in the detail with which it explores all four seasons. Thus, it earns a place in this chapter of full seasonal cycles, rather than in Chapter Seven, where other, more humbly proportioned songs and choral works have their place. Besides, the great majority of the sixteen composers featured there would have been familiar with Haydn's grand and spirited oratorio, and may have actively wondered if they might perhaps try something of like nature.

Selected texts/translations in Appendix Two.
(pages 282 – 287)

♪♪♪♪♪

Spohr: Symphony no. 9 in b minor, op. 143,
        Die Jahreszeiten (*The Seasons*)

Having a lifespan encompassing all of Mendelssohn's and most of Beethoven's, German-born composer Louis Spohr (1784 – 1859) has long lain in the shadow of those great masters. However, in his own time, he was an important figure. At age fifteen, Spohr was not just composing, but also filling his first professional position, as a chamber musician for Duke Karl Wilhelm Ferdinand of Brunswick. By the age of twenty, Spohr had earned significant acclaim on the concert circuit.

Soon, Spohr's abilities as a conductor, one of the first to use a baton, rather than a violin bow, added to his growing reputation. His own compositions brought further notice, as did his authoring of an influential violin teaching method reflective of his own virtuoso abilities. One may hear little of him today, but that fact is not due to any lack of success in his own time.

In comparison to his more famous contemporaries, Spohr's style tends to be somewhat more dramatic than Mendelssohn's though rather more orderly than Beethoven's. A fine example of this balance is found in his Symphony no. 9, *Die Jahreszeiten* (*The Seasons*) (1850), which sets out to capture the spirit of all four seasons: one in each movement. Spohr spent much of his career in north central Germany, so his personal experience with those seasons would have been flavored by that particular, generally moderate climate.

Spohr's *Seasons Symphony* opens with winter, as do many seasonal surveys by composers dwelling in the Northern Hemisphere. Spohr paints winter as stately and a touch melancholy, with march-like and dance-like passages appearing in turn. Nothing suggests fearsome blizzards; often, Spohr sets woodwinds and strings in dialog, repeating and commenting upon each other's phrases, like friends chatting beside the fire.

Spring, by contrast, is of gentle demeanor, its flowing string textures flavored at times by woodwinds, especially trills from the flute, as if Spohr were thinking of birdsong. Summer, it seems, is a time for wilting in the heat; in addition to leisurely tempos, one finds melancholy moods, again focusing upon strings, though also having richer contrasting colors provided by clarinet and horn.

All the joviality of Spohr's seasonal symphony is reserved for the last movement's evocation of autumn. Opening horn calls suggest the signals of distant hunters, and the prancing triple meter energy that follows implies that these hunters are now riding out after their prey. It is wholly cheerful music: outdoorsy in the forthright manner that elegant drawing room music would never be, ever eager, and often sparkling with brilliant brass. If this closing movement is taken as evidence, Spohr, it seems, was a great fan of autumn and its spirited activities. Certainly, it is an optimistic way to close an excursion through the calendar.

♪♪♪♪

Fanny Mendelssohn Hensel: *Das Jahr (The Year)*

In early 19th century Germany, most cultured young ladies learned music, likely piano, perhaps singing. It was considered an important social skill to be able to divert oneself, one's family and friends, with elegant, if not necessarily virtuosic, playing. Fanny Mendelssohn Hensel (1805 – 1847) was of exactly that social set, and her parents, devout patrons of the arts, encouraged her to take more than usual interest in music. A career, however, was not in her future; that happy fate would fall to her younger brother Felix (1809 – 1847), who we shall consider later.

Fanny remained devoted to music throughout her life. Not only did she play the piano with professional, if not thunderous, skill, she also helped her brother when he needed a spare pair of hands at rehearsals and even composed her own music. Her catalog contains many songs and solo piano pieces, as well as a few larger scale works. Some were published at the time, though generally under Felix's name, as it was thought unseemly for a lady's name to appear in print.

One of Fanny's most ambitious works – not in number of performers, but certainly in length and variety of musical ideas – is the solo piano suite *Das Jahr (The Year)*, completed in 1841 as a Christmas gift for her husband, court painter Wilhelm Hensel (1794 – 1861). It is a set of thirteen solo piano pieces, one for each month, then one more as a postlude. Each bears a heading alluding to the intended scene; the resulting music is remarkably reflective of those scenes.

Seasonal Music Insights: Vivaldi and Much More

January begins with solemn, falling phrases, perhaps suggesting snow, though the heading makes clear that the poet dreams of the "soft, sweet songs of spring." That reference places the gently flowing theme of the central pages in different context. February is a spirited scherzo intended to evoke the holiday known in most European lands as Carnival, though elsewhere as Mardi Gras. March has less to do with spring than with bells ringing at Easter-time. Central pages quote the hymn *Christ ist entstanden* (*Christ is Risen*). By contrast, April is a meditation upon how the sun might give way suddenly to storms. The music does exactly that, exchanging serenity for high drama.

May is sunny and song-like with a heading that speaks of spring blooming in the valley. Subtitled *Serenade*, June offers a flowing, song-like theme over wave-like accompaniment; perhaps this serenade is being sung from a gondola. July's verses speak of languishing in the heat, and the music is strongly suggestive of that: lazy energy with occasional hints of – or wishes for – storms. August recognizes the colors of the harvest with playful, folksy rhythms and a flamboyant close.

As for September, it offers sweetly regretful moods with intricate ornamentations on a graceful theme; the poet is watching a river flow past, finding in it his happiness. Spirits brighten again for October, a lively hunting scene with nimble dotted rhythms. November, its verses reflecting upon winter arriving in the forest, is largely melancholy, though with splashes of quick passagework and occasional higher drama: apparently, it is a month of unpredictable weather.

December is a Christmas vision: a brilliant scherzo of eager energy, though with tender, starlit moods in the central pages. There, Fanny quotes another hymn, *Dem Himmel hoch* (*From Heaven Above*). The brief Postlude also makes use of a hymn melody, in this case, *Das alte Jahr vergangen ist* (*The Old Year has Passed*). Given the reflective and reserved nature of Fanny's treatment of the theme, perhaps she felt some regret at the passage of time. This Postlude brings the suite to a thoughtful conclusion, though there have been plenty of high spirits and even higher drama in earlier pages. Fanny had been dissuaded from pursuing a professional career, but in *Das Jahr*, one finds a fully professional level of craftsmanship.

♪♪♪♪♪

Verdi: *Four Seasons* ballet music from
 Les vêspres siciliennes (*Sicilian Vespers*)

Giuseppe Verdi (1813 – 1901) was Italian-born, and the great majority of his 28 operas premiered in his native land. So he usually composed according to Italian expectations. However, occasionally it was worthwhile to explore other markets, and the mid-1850s found Verdi in Paris. There, he faced a demand virtually unknown in the Italian theaters: the esteemed Paris Opéra possessed a skilled corps de ballet, and refused to stage any operas not making use of that resource. So *Les vêspres siciliennes* (*Sicilian Vespers*), written specifically for the Paris Opéra, where it premiered June 13, 1855, includes ballet music.

Later productions at Italian theaters under the Italian title *I Vespri siciliani* sometimes deleted those scenes as superfluous to the story-telling. Besides, if there were no singers, Italians were not much interested. However, the music is a rare example of an operatic genius in purely instrumental mode. Orchestras wishing to explore Verdi's music should take note.

In the context of their original setting, the ballet scenes occur in the third of *I Vespri siciliani*'s five acts as entertainment for a social gathering at an aristocratic palace. The palace is that of the opera's principal villain, and the dance scenes are almost the only ebullient music in what is otherwise a dark and tempestuous drama. Spanning nearly half an hour, the ballet is imagined as depicting the moods of the seasons, and in Verdi's vision, those moods are highly varied, not merely from one season to the next, but even within a single season.

Spring opens with string tremolo and gentle flute phrases, as if of birdsong at dawn, before allowing clarinet to present a heart-felt, song-like melody that Verdi might just as easily have handed to his leading tenor. Sudden outbursts occur from time to time, and pages late in the scene suggest cheerful villagers celebrating springtime. *Summer*, too, is changeable, with rumbling suggestions of a storm on the horizon, as well as a melancholy oboe theme. A folksy demeanor appears for the central pages, though the scene concludes with a reprise of the oboe theme and a surge to a dramatic close.

Longest of the four scenes is *Autumn*, which, like the others, contrasts folk-moods with suggestions of serene natural beauty. Here, the song-like central theme is for cello, and seems designed to inspire choreography for a romantic *pas de deux*, before folksy exuberance resumes. As for *Winter*, it begins in almost martial mood: cheerful soldiers, but, nonetheless, ones on the march. A wary transition leads to anxious music rife with short repeated phrases that further increase the tension. More cheerful themes follow, even suggestions of a waltz; ultimately, the scene concludes with high – and ominous – drama. In the context of the opera itself, assassins are approaching, though taking the *Four Seasons* scenes purely as dance music, one might well imagine it is a climatological storm on the horizon.

♪♪♪♪♪

Raff: seasonal symphonies, op. 205, 208, 213, and 214

Joachim Raff (1822 – 1882) was born in Switzerland where his German father had moved to avoid the repeated wars of the German/French border region. Though first a schoolteacher, young Raff was composing by his early twenties and was not yet twenty-five when he walked from Zurich to Basel to hear a piano recital by Franz Liszt (1811 – 1886). The elder master took the young man under his wing, helping him to obtain musical employment in Germany. Later, Raff returned to Liszt's fold in Weimar to serve as the master's orchestration assistant, but also continued to compose his own music.

During the 1870s and 80s, Raff taught at Frankfurt's music conservatory, connecting his earlier Romantic Era generation to its late 19th century successors. His music, including chamber works, much solo piano music, and nearly a dozen symphonies, rewards listeners with a rich lyricism and masterful handling of the orchestra that will remind some of Raff's younger contemporary, Johannes Brahms (1833 – 1897).

Each of Raff's last four symphonies (no. 8-11) is named for a season of the year. All but one of the individual movements (four per symphony) have descriptive subheadings telling listeners what aspect of that season the composer had in mind. Other than the nature inspirations, which were not without precedent at the time, the symphonies follow most of expectations of the era, with contrasting tempos and structures for variety, and a virtuosic use of orchestral color. However, the slow movement of each symphony comes third of the four movements, rather than second, which would have been more customary.

Symphony no. 8 in A major, *Frühlingsklänge* (*Sounds of Springtime*) has a first movement in which spring is exuberantly welcomed – *Frühlings Rückkehr* (*The Return of Spring*) – and a second movement depicting restless gatherings of witches the night of April 30 in Germany's Harz Mountains: *In der Walpurgisnacht* (*Of Walpurgisnacht*). The third movement *Mit dem ersten Blumenstrauß* (*With the First Bouquet*) is the most tender of romances, whereas excitement returns with the jaunty, occasionally brass-driven fourth movement *Wanderlust* (*Urge to Travel*).

The summer views of Raff's Symphony no. 9 in e minor, *Im Sommer*, begin with *Ein heißer Tag* (*A Hot Day*), the shimmering energy of its first lines being varied with folk-song-like passages and even a late thunderstorm. The second movement *Die Jagd der Elfen* (*The Hunt of the Elves*) contrasts scampering woodwind lines with a lyrical cello solo and, in other places, an exuberant, forthright spirit. In the third movement *Ekloge* (*Pastorale Scene*), a winsome oboe theme is soon shared with strings, as well as other woodwinds, all suggestive of a shepherd calming his flock with song. With the fourth movement *Zum Erntekranz* (*The Harvest Wreath*), an almost reverential sense comes first, gradually growing in intensity and excitement. Quiet interludes occur, but the dominant idea is one of celebration.

Eindrücke und Empfindungen (*Impressions and Feelings*) is the heading for the first movement of the Symphony no. 10 in f minor, *Zur Herbstzeit* (*In Autumn Time*). Gentle at first, those feelings become ever more brilliant, flowing along on broad, lush phrases. The second movement *Gespenster-Reigen* (*Ghostly Dances*) is reminiscent in mood of the Walpurgisnacht scene of the *Spring* symphony, though here, Raff imagines All Soul's Eve (October 31), rather than Walpurgisnacht. His third movement *Elegie* has tenderly regretful colors, perhaps bidding farewell to summer. For the final movement, Raff offers *Die Jagd der Menschen* (*Men at the Hunt*) with dotted rhythms to evoke galloping horses and prominent French horns for hunting calls. Brief anxieties are quickly and favorably resolved.

Growing up in Switzerland may have left Raff with an appreciative view of winter, despite the minor key on which his *Winter* symphony is based. His Symphony no. 11 in a minor, *Der Winter*, casts its first movement *Der erste Schnee* (*The First Snow*) in mostly bright and playful tones – once he's moved beyond a slow introduction. The second movement bears no subtitle, though its danceable energy suggests an evening gathering, the French horn perhaps welcoming the guests and then bidding them farewell. The third movement *Am Kamin* (*By the Hearth*) finds the bassoon lingering calmly by the fireside, then sharing its gentle theme throughout the orchestra. The last movement *Karneval* finds us at Mardi Gras with timpani rolls, splendid brass, and rapid action for all. It is a celebratory close to Raff's survey of the seasons.

♪♪♪♪

Tchaikovsky: *The Seasons, op. 37a*

Late in 1875, Peter Tchaikovsky (1840 – 1893) had completed three symphonies, but was still awaiting true success on the international stage. Not yet having enough demand for his works to keep him busy, Tchaikovsky was willing to listen when the editor of a monthly music magazine requested some piano pieces that could be published in the magazine.

The plan was that one piece would appear each month, each of those pieces appropriate to the month in which it would be published. Tchaikovsky agreed, but had little fondness for the task, often needing reminders of looming deadlines. On those occasions, he would quickly dash off the next month's offering in a few hours, then forget the assignment again until the next reminder. The twelve short pieces appeared in the magazine from December 1875 through November 1876. Eventually, all came to print together under the collective title *Les Saisons* (*The Seasons*). During Tchaikovsky's time, educated Russians tended to use French, rather than Russian, in their daily dealings.

Helpfully, each of the pieces appeared with a subtitle making clear what specific idea the composer had in mind – or at least what came to the magazine editor's mind when he received each installment. However, each individual piece has more than one mood. In each case, Tchaikovsky opened with one melodic idea, proceeded onward to another of contrasting character, then closed by returning to the first idea, now somewhat altered, bringing each short piece full circle.

January places one *By the Fireside*, apparently relaxing there, not fretting about whatever weather might be happening outside the window. More flowing, song-like material occupies the central pages. February is *Carnival*-time, which Tchaikovsky evokes with spirited energy for the opening and closing pages, though more relaxed moods in the center. March brings *The Song of the Lark*, that lark apparently singing against a sober backdrop, perhaps of cloudy skies. The short melodic fragments with which Tchaikovsky suggests his lark are allowed to evolve and grow in detail, much as a bird might make subtle variations in his own song.

April is *Snowdrop*: not frozen precipitation, but rather a small, early-blooming flower. It is one of the shortest of the dozen pieces, and quite tender of mood, though with more playful touches; perhaps a child has spotted the new blossom. *Starlit Night* is the subtitle for May, generally calm and delicate in its opening pages, as if suggestive of stars, though the central pages are quite a bit livelier in mood. Tchaikovsky labels June as a *Barcarolle*, that is, a boating song. Here, too, the piece begins and ends in sweet demeanor, with most of the energy reserved for the central pages.

Countryside activities are the focus for summer. July brings *The Song of the Reaper,* with exuberant farm workers who become even livelier in the central pages. August is *Song of the Harvest*, its outer pages a spirited scherzo, though with restfully paced central ones suggestive of a midday respite. September's *The Hunt* brings bold energy and fanfare-like effects, middle pages of restless energy, and the heroic opening moods returning to bring September to a close.

October is *Autumn Song*, in this case, a melancholy song, as if, being a Russian, Tchaikovsky was all too aware that soon, months of cold and grayness would be upon him. Here, the two contrasting melodic ideas are both rather sober, though shaded somewhat differently for the sake of contrast.

In November, one finds little sobriety, as the image is of the *Troika*: a very fast little Russian sleigh. Tchaikovsky allows the would-be passengers to gather in seemly fashion before the middle pages, vibrant with all the spirited energy of a brisk and joyous journey through the snow; the piece closes with a reminiscence of its opening. Not only has the composer brought the music full circle; he's also brought those passengers safely to their destination.

Just one piece remains, one Tchaikovsky has dubbed *Christmas*. It begins in peaceful demeanor, though soon becomes waltz-like with much nimbler energy. Although Tchaikovsky's Christmas ballet, *The Nutcracker*, is yet fifteen years in the future, here he already proves that Christmas and waltzing are congenial companions.

One often encounters orchestrations and arrangements of Tchaikovsky's *The Seasons*, at least of individual movements, expanding beyond the initial keyboard form for the sake of even more vibrant colors. Whether or not these alternate versions are by the composer himself, they yet serve to bring Tchaikovsky's seasonal tour to wider audiences. Still, the original piano settings are to be valued as a rare glimpse of Tchaikovsky working with a single instrument to impressive effect.

♪♪♪♪♪

Albéniz: *The Seasons*, op. 201

Spanish-born Isaac Albéniz (1860 – 1909) was a child prodigy pianist who, tiring of his parents forcing him to perform and then living off his earnings, ran decisively away from home at the age of twelve, stowing away on a steamship to South America. By the time he returned to his native land at age fifteen, he was an intercontinental star.

To that point, young Albéniz had focused on piano performance. Once he returned to Europe, serious composition studies followed, sometimes resulting in solo piano pieces, but also in grander dramatic scores, including an opera on legends of the Arthurian wizard Merlin. Nonetheless, the majority of Albéniz' catalog is comprised of solo instrumental works, often in several short movements. Frequently, one hears them in guitar transcriptions; consider his beloved *Asturias*. However, piano was the original intended medium.

Amongst those piano suites is a suite of four pieces attempting to capture the moods of the seasons as Albéniz saw them. One might give them the collective title *The Seasons*, or *Les Saisons*, under which title they were published in Paris. However, the set first came to print in London in 1892 as *Album of Miniatures*, with only the titles to the individual pieces admitting to the seasonal connections.

Spring is expressed in generally light and nimble fashion, though with a few more outspoken moments. More ebullience occurs in *Summer*, with torrents of rapid sixteenth notes offset by contrasting central lines. *Autumn* Albéniz casts with tenderness and melancholy, as if regretful that those high spirits of summer have passed. By contrast, *Winter* is launched on tiptoe, perhaps cautiously stepping through the snow. Broader phrases dominate the central pages, before the opening theme reappears, very low pitched, slow and somber. Thus Albéniz closes out his calendar year – spanned in scarcely ten minutes in all, but nonetheless imaginatively crafted.

German: *The Seasons*

First, consider the composer's name. Englishman Edward German (1862 – 1936) was born in Shropshire as German Edward Jones, the first name pronounced "GAIR-mahn" and being of Welsh derivation. Neither he nor his name had any connection to the homeland of Beethoven and Brahms. During studies at the Royal College of Music, the youth who had always been known as Edward Jones altered his name to Edward German, the better to distinguish himself from another Edward Jones on campus. So it is under the name Edward German that this gentleman's music reached the public. Much of it was written to accompany dramatic stage productions, as he was music director for London's Globe Theatre. However, German also composed large-scale symphonic works, and often lamented that his lighter stage works attracted more attention and success. His ghost would no doubt be pleased that it is one of the symphonic scores, rather than the stage music, that concerns us here.

German's *The Seasons* (1899) was composed for the Norwich Festival. One could call it a symphonic suite, a genre it shares with Rimsky-Korsakov's famed *Scheherazade*: a multi-movement orchestral work of pictorial content, one that might not conform to the expectations of what a formal symphony generally does, but that nevertheless uses orchestral resources to impressively vivid extent.

As is often the case in seasonal suites, German begins with spring and proceeds through the year to winter. His *Spring* opens delicately before building to exuberant expression, driven along on a tide of lively dotted rhythms. One imagines that the tender buds of the opening lines have burst into full bloom. A contrasting theme suggestive of wistful moonlit romance appears. These two ideas – the first buoyant, the second more thoughtful – alternate throughout the remainder of the movement.

Summer begins in playful mood, becoming grander of spirit as more of the orchestra – particularly the brass – joins the action. *Autumn* is more languorous, with first woodwinds, then strings in the spotlight. Passages of high drama appear, though the season closes in serenely pastoral demeanor with a tender, song-like solo for English horn, the alto cousin of the oboe.

German's *Winter* is the only one of the four movements to open with high drama: bold brass and percussion joined by turbulent strings and woodwinds suggestive of a tremendous storm. This tempestuous atmosphere is contrasted by passages of reflection, perhaps upon the passing year, though an undercurrent of restless energy begins to appear. Higher spirits, with woodwinds and even tambourine, seem to suggest winter revels. However, the storm returns, and it is with swirling musical winds that German closes his survey of the seasons.

♪♪♪♪

Glazunov: *The Seasons*, op. 67

The stars seemed bright for Alexander Glazunov (1865 – 1936). Born to wealthy and musically inclined parents, he first studied composition with Nicolai Rimsky-Korsakov (1844 – 1908). He was only sixteen when he completed his first symphony and saw it performed to a public openly skeptical that a youth could write such a fine composition. Surely, they asserted, the Glazunovs had paid Rimsky to write it for him; but, no, it was Alexander's own work.

Before his 20th birthday, he would attract the favorable attention of piano master Franz Liszt (1811 – 1886), hear his music performed in Germany, and make his conducting debut in Paris. In 1899, Glazunov joined the faculty of the St. Petersburg Conservatory, later serving as director; his students would include such prominent members of the next generation as Sergei Rachmaninoff (1873 – 1943), Sergei Prokofiev (1891 – 1953), and Dmitri Shostakovich (1906 – 1975). As the 20th century began, no one stood more in the center of Russian music than Glazunov.

Yet Glazunov's music remains less well known that that of his mentors and students. Why? Many of his colleagues remarked upon his heavy drinking; unless all were exaggerating, the situation surely affected his work ethic. Moreover, he was generally conservative, clinging to old Romantic stylistic traditions even as a new world was dawning. Some thought he was simply behind the times; however, admirers of grand orchestral statements in the manner of the late 19th century find much satisfaction in Glazunov's works.

His 1899 ballet *The Seasons* offers a wealth of melodic invention along with imaginative seasonal portrayals. The piece was written at the request of choreographer Marius Petipa (1818 – 1910), who in earlier years had worked with Tchaikovsky on *Sleeping Beauty* and *The Nutcracker*. Glazunov's ballet is shorter than any Tchaikovsky ballet and also lacks a specific plot. Rather than telling a story through exposition, development, and finale, *The Seasons* is a set of mythological scenes appropriate to the work's title. He may have been stylistically conservative, but Glazunov understood that a shorter ballet was ideal for an evening of several different works, as long as it has enough variety of its own to offer choreographic opportunities and to hold the audience's attention.

He begins with *Winter*, cast in magical colors before suggestions of swirling wind develop. He proceeds to a set of four variations, as they are known in the ballet world: short spotlights for individual dancers. These are Frost, Ice, Hail, and Snow, with delicate staccato passages, then tenderly flowing lines, then sprightly energy, then smooth textures evocative of a landscape blanketed with snow.

By contrast, *Spring* is much shorter: perhaps in Russia, spring comes and goes quickly. The music is often playful and waltz-like, though with more languid passages for the sake of contrast. *Summer*, too, sets nimble energy against flowing phrases. Here, however, Glazunov indulges at times in grander, more vibrant moods, and his Waltz of Cornflowers and Poppies has the spirited bounce of a country dance.

Autumn is where Glazunov reaches for revelry, even labelling it a Bacchanale and driving the celebration along with tambourine. Briefly, the party is interrupted by recollections of the previous seasons, bringing back passages from the *Winter* introduction, a leisurely *Spring* interlude, and *Summer*'s flower waltz, though *Autumn*'s exuberance intrudes on the memories before those *Summer* flowers can fade. The subsequent serene Adagio was surely intended for a sweet *pas de deux* for two principal dancers, before the Bacchanale resumes once more. At last, the cold winds of *Winter* make a last appearance, brushing away the falling leaves and suggesting clear, starry skies. *The Seasons* is vivid, evocative, and memorable: Glazunov was quite the master of orchestral effect.

♪♪♪♪♪

Roussel: Symphony no. 1, "Le poeme de la forêt"

Industry or politics? Those were the careers that one might have expected of Frenchman Albert Roussel (1869 – 1937), the former being his father's profession and the latter his grandfather's. Yet both gentlemen died before the boy reached his teens, leaving him in the care of an aunt and uncle. Under their guidance, young Roussel studied music, though not devotedly. In 1887, still in his teens, he entered the French naval college, eventually becoming a commissioned officer. His naval service would take him to distant ports, even to the Far East, but long cruises meant a certain amount of time on his hands.

Given free time, some sailors might turn to drink; Roussel chose music, toying with composition and finding it sufficiently pleasurable that when he was 25, he resigned his commission in favor of music. His compositions were earning public performances before he turned 40. Other than a brief return to military service during World War I, Roussel would devote the rest of his life to composition; his music strikes a sensitive balance between Impressionistic melodic flow and clean Neoclassical structures.

Roussel's Symphony no. 1 was his first large-scale work; three more symphonies would follow, along with a generous quantity of chamber music, stage works, and songs. The first of those symphonies was the only one to carry a subtitle, *Poem of the Forest*; that the individual movements also have subtitles clarifies what this grand poem has to say about the forest, and also that the composer imagines a full year in sylvan surroundings. He begins in winter, proceeds to the renewal that comes with spring, before imagining a summer evening, and lastly the cavorting of mythological characters in what one must now suppose is a harvest celebration. Roussel's Symphony no. 1 premiered in Brussels March 22, 1908.

The first movement *Forêt d'hiver* (*Forest in Winter*) opens with long, floating lines; contrasting phrases of shimmering color appear at times, and often the oboe takes the spotlight. Midway, a late winter storm seems to have arisen, with tempestuous activity and many brass outbursts, though the movement ends calmly in the care of the French horn.

The second movement isn't headed "Spring," but what else can the composer intend by *Renouveau (Revival)*, especially coming immediately on the tail of winter? Woodwinds offer phrases suggestive of birdsong, while string tremolo might be the flutter of new leaves. Fuller colors develop, as spring advances, and a few outspoken outbursts appear. These, however, do not bring a storm, only exuberance, and the movement ends in brilliant sunshine.

Having titled the third movement *Soir d'été (Summer Evening)*, Roussel gave himself many options for inspiration: a summer evening might be spent romancing in the moonlight, or, conversely, dancing at a festival. The music itself makes clear that Roussel is imagining something more like the former, with long, sustained tones from the strings, a gentle French horn solo, and woodwind phrases perhaps suggestive of nightingales. More rapturous moods make a brief appearance midway, but calm and serenity are the dominant idea.

In the final movement *Faunes et dryads (Fauns and Dryads)*, the mood shifts to one of vibrant activity. Dancing rhythms, especially for woodwinds, acquire even more energy when the tambourine joins in, and though the scene is never frenzied, it is reliably nimble of spirit. More robust passages appear for contrast, yet all will ultimately drift to a gentle close. Perhaps throughout their revelry, those forest spirits have been indulging in wine, and now have fallen into a doze. Certainly, it serves as a serene ending for Roussel's tour of the seasons.

♪♪♪♪

Hadley: Symphony no. 2 in g minor, op. 30,
    Four Seasons

One often hears that Leonard Bernstein (1918 – 1990) was the first superstar American conductor. That may be true, if one emphasizes the first half of the word "superstar;" after all, Bernstein had the advantage of television and airplanes at his disposal. However, long before Bernstein's arrival on the scene, there was an American-born composer/conductor who attracted highly favorable notice, both at home and abroad, and that was Henry Hadley (1871 – 1937).

Growing up in suburban Boston, young Hadley had ready access to the city's abundant musical resources. Moreover, his father taught music, his mother played piano, and his brother was a Boston Symphony cellist, so a music career may have been inevitable. Hadley was not yet twenty when his compositions were being performed in public, so successfully that within a few years, he set off on the almost-obligatory studies in Europe – in his case, mostly in Vienna.

Hadley developed passions for both composition and conducting, even guest conducting in Berlin; that the American was welcomed to the podium in a city accustomed to top European talent proves that his skills were not inconsequential. Back in the US, Hadley would become, in 1911, the first conductor of the newborn San Francisco Symphony. He would also serve as associate conductor of the New York Philharmonic; his last years, he founded the orchestra's

Berkshire Music Festival. Throughout his career, Hadley sought to bring top-level interpretations of the finest music to audiences, proving that one didn't need to be European-born to direct an orchestra.

In his own works, Hadley revealed a close knowledge of how varied timbres of different orchestral instruments can be manipulated for greatest effect. His Symphony no. 2 showcases that familiarity with an orchestra that includes piccolo, English horn, glockenspiel, and an array of varied percussion, in addition to the usual suspects. Hadley's craftsmanship was such that the work triumphed at two composition competitions in 1901, one sponsored by Polish pianist/composer/statesman Ignacy Paderewski (1860 – 1941), the other by the New England Conservatory of Music. Equally impressive is the fact that the Philharmonic Society of New York included it with music of Bach, Beethoven, and Richard Strauss, violinist Fritz Kreisler as headline soloist, in a program given December 20 and 21, 1901, at Carnegie Hall.

Hadley subtitled the symphony *Four Seasons*, and identified each of the four movements by its season; the work proceeds in calendar order, beginning with winter and concluding with autumn. On the occasion of the New York premiere, the program annotator provided various poetic references to accompany the moods and scenes of each movement. However, as that author then admits the ideas are his own, sanctioned by Hadley, though not necessarily exactly Hadley's own vision, these are not repeated here. The music seems vivid enough to stand without literary additions.

The opening movement *Winter* begins with majestic drama yielding to a thoughtful theme for cello and woodwinds, before a crash of percussion signals a change to a rapid tempo. Here, anguished phrases pass between strings and winds, often in intricate layers of counterpoint, as if of a fearsome storm with winds swirling from all directions. The passing of that storm is suggested by the movement's close: a wistful solo flute supported by gentle closing chords.

Altogether more cheerful is the second movement *Spring*, its opening and closing pages replete with nimbly playful spotlights for woodwinds, suggestive of bird song in the woods. If, indeed, one supposes those are birds, then during the restful central pages of the movement, those birds may be napping in the midday sun. Even more leisurely moods arrive with the third movement *Summer*, with flowing phrases that tend to drift downward in pitch. Richer, more romantic ideas appear at times, but these fade away. Perhaps on this particular summer day, it is, for the moment, simply too hot to pursue passions.

Hadley has saved *Autumn* for last, with danceable phrases and peaceable moods appearing in turn. At the tempo change from rather slow to quite fast, the brass take on renewed prominence with what might be a hunting scene. Cymbals and timpani suggest an approaching storm, but that drama passes quickly, leading to a restatement of the movement's sunny opening lines. The hunting music will also recur. At last, however, all fades and slows to a restful close as Hadley ends his musical year with what seems to be a serene sunset.

♪♪♪♪

Ives: *New England Holidays*

The four orchestral pieces of *New England Holidays* by Connecticut-born Charles Ives (1874 – 1954) might be imagined as a Yankee *Four Seasons*. Not only do the four holidays in question lie in four different seasons, but also when the set was published, each movement had a season appended to its own descriptive name.

The individual movements had been long on Ives' desk. *Thanksgiving* was written in 1904, *Washington's Birthday* in 1909, *Decoration Day* in 1912, and *The Fourth of July* in 1913. Published as a set in 1936, they would not be performed together until a concert in Minneapolis on April 9, 1954, only weeks before Ives' passing. Before that American premiere, three of the four (not *Thanksgiving*) had been given in Europe, where Ives' progressive ideas about complex rhythms, bursts of dissonance, and complex layers of disparate themes raised fewer eyebrows. Ives may have been American in his inspirations, but American audiences were slow to grasp his musical vision.

Presenting the four pieces not in order of composition but rather in order of the calendar places *Washington's Birthday* first. Here, Ives attested that he had in mind a dreary New England winter night in which the old folks cluster around the hearth while the younger generation partakes in a barn dance. As often happens in Ives' music, fragments of popular songs appear to give the flavor of the time.

Seasonal Music Insights: | 43
Vivaldi and Much More

For *Decoration Day*, now known as Memorial Day, the scene begins on the village green before proceeding to the cemetery. Solemn moods suggest town authorities; spirited ones may imply a throng of small boys at play. In Ives' own New England childhood, Decoration Day looked back to Gettysburg. Echoes of *Taps* serve as recollections of Ives' father, who played cornet in a Union Army band and later led the town band in Danbury, Connecticut. The appearance of *Nearer My God to Thee* further underscores the memorial mood.

For *The Fourth of July*, Ives' music suggests fife and drums and musical fireworks; he even adds the old American patriotic song *Columbia, the Gem of the Ocean*, suitable to the occasion he had in mind. This movement was dedicated to Ives' long-time business partner, Julian Myrick. Myrick worked in insurance, not music. Knowing that his unique approach to music was unlikely to earn much financial support, Ives maintained a parallel career as an insurance executive to pay the bills.

The set concludes with *Thanksgiving*. One might imagine family feasts of turkey and pumpkin pie, especially as the movement is dedicated to the composer's brother-in-law Edward Twichell. However, as a young man, Ives had been a church organist in New Haven, and here he borrows themes from organ preludes and postludes he had composed for worship services. One also finds the hymn tunes *Duke Street* and *Shining Shore*, as well as *God, Beneath Thy Guiding Hand*. This hymn of the Puritans first making their way to a new world appears near the close of the work, at which point Ives adds a chorus to the orchestra – simply scored in octaves, as if for an untrained congregation to sing. Fading dissonant bell tones lead into the final measures; thus Ives closes his Yankee year.

♪♪♪♪♪

Malipiero: Sinfonia no. 1, "in quattro tempi,
　　　come le quattro stagioni"
　　(In four tempos, like the four seasons)

One need not necessarily be Italian to compose instrumental music influenced by Vivaldi's *The Four Seasons*. However, if one is Italian and is based in Vivaldi's home town of Venice, the odds may improve. Moreover, if, as a scholar of earlier Italian music, one will soon be supervising new publications of Vivaldi's instrumental works, it may be inevitable. Such is the background against which Gian Francesco Malipiero (1882 – 1973) composed his Sinfonia no. 1, *in quattro tempi, come le quattro stagioni* in 1933.

Admittedly, it is a symphony, not a set of four violin concerti. Nonetheless, the inspiration was there. Perhaps there is no violin soloist because Malipiero wanted a broader canvas, with more variety of solo possibilities. The work is generously scored for full orchestra with a quantity of percussion, including timpani, chimes, celesta, and snare drum. Such tools prove distinctly useful for giving the movements – even individual passages within those movements – decidely different flavors. Wind instruments are similarly used, with horns, muted trumpets, oboes, clarinets, and their colleagues enjoying frequent opportunity to shine. As for the strings, they, too, have spotlights, often restating in new form a phrase that had previously given to a wind instrument. Other Italians of his generation might have studied closely what could be made of the singing voice, but here Malipiero indulges his love of vibrant orchestral voices.

Although movement headings do not name the seasons, the composer himself declared that he had started with spring and worked his way through to winter. The first movement captures a gentle spring morning, with frequent song-like, cantabile lines for woodwinds, suggestive of bird songs. Even as strings, brass, and percussion speak up, the moods remains serene, with only brief passages of higher drama. By contrast, the second movement gives to summer a boisterous, even unpredictable, energy that dances or marches as the spirit dictates. Summer, it seems, is a time for action.

In the third movement, one finds a quiet autumn afternoon: restful without falling into melancholy. Malipiero continually switches his focus from one section of the orchestra to another, so that the music takes on kaleidoscopic colors. By contrast, the final movement suggests a winter carnival, with dancing, marching, and chorale singing all occurring in short order. Energy builds toward the end, with brilliant grandeur for the final lines. For Malipiero, the year seems to close with fireworks and cheers.

♪♪♪♪♪

Piazzolla: *Cuatro estaciones porteñas*
  (Four Seasons of Buenos Aires)

Born in that heartland of the tango, Argentina, Astor Piazzolla (1921 – 1992) mostly grew up in New York City where his family had emigrated when he was a small child. By his early teens, he discovered Harlem's jazz clubs. This all-American music, as sassy in its own way as tango, though with very different rhythms and harmonies, soon captured his affections. However, young Piazzolla did not completely forget his heritage, for he played the accordion-like bandoneon so central to the tango sound. When Argentine tango legend Carlos Gardel (1890 – 1935) came to New York in the 1930s to make movies, he was told about the young musician. Upon hearing him play, Gardel immediately hired Piazzolla to join his band. It was 1937, and the teenager was on his way to the tango clubs of Argentina.

Piazzolla quickly became a well-regarded tango artist. Expanding interests led him begin composition studies, first with noted Argentine composer Alberto Ginastera (1916 – 1983), then in Paris with Nadia Boulanger (1887 – 1979), who had mightily influenced Aaron Copland (1900 – 1990), amongst so many others. Back in Argentina, Piazzolla created a musical amalgam that blended the tangos of Buenos Aires with the jazz of New York, seasoned with a dash of the compositional finesse he had picked up in Paris. This new style, energetic and rhythmic, so very international in origin, was uniquely Piazzolla's own; it is thanks to his efforts that *nuevo tango* (new tango), was born.

In its earliest form, *Cuatro estaciones porteñas (Four Seasons of Buenos Aires)* (1970) was intended for Piazzolla's *nuevo tango* ensemble, with the composer himself taking the solo role on bandoneon. However, after the composer's death, several arrangements were made for classical ensembles, including one for string orchestra with solo violin by a Ukrainian composer with the most un-tangoish name of Leonid Desyatnikov (b. 1955). In this incarnation, the work has earned most of its performances, in large part because of its kinship with Vivaldi's *The Four Seasons*. This is not to say that Piazzolla had written a Baroque style piece; rather, his *Four Seasons* are liberally tango flavored, in a manner that would have utterly bewildered the Italian master. However, Desyatnikov incorporated quotes from the Vivaldi set that an observant listener will perceive, even as the playing techniques remain exotic.

Working from a Southern Hemisphere perspective, the cycle begins with *Autumn* (*Otoño Porteño*), which opens in highly dramatic fashion before proceeding to quick-fingered playing for the soloist and percussive effects for the supporting ensemble. A secondary solo role emerges with principal cello, given luscious and lyrical lines that blend with those of the violin soloist. Changeable tempos and exciting harmonic double-stop effects are everywhere. Next comes *Winter* (*Invierno Porteño*), beginning with the string ensemble in a mellow mood gradually dispelled by the increasing drive of the soloist, who ranges into fiendishly high-pitched pyrotechnic displays. Vivaldi's winter storm music appears briefly, yet most of the movement has a sultry, melancholy mood, with some of the world-weary sensuality of the tango.

For *Spring* (*Primavera Porteño)*, the music opens in the string ensemble, with much percussive effects from the basses, joined by the soloist for some wistful themes. Despite frequent tempo changes, the general sense is of power and drive, the music charging into its final pages. Yet just when one imagines the tango will rule to the last moment, a theme from Vivaldi's *Spring* appears briefly. Last of all comes *Summer* (*Verano Porteño*), here alternately fiery and sultry, with percussive details from the string ensemble. Echoes of Vivaldi's *Summer* hailstorm intrude, and the soloist has demanding slides up and down the strings, intensifying the sense of drama at this close of the cycle.

♫♫♫♫

Ashmore: *The Four Seasons* –
    suite on English folk songs

English composer Lawrence Ashmore (1928 – 2013) spent most of his career in British television and film. Nevertheless, his *Four Seasons* suite (1989) is a concert work. Ashmore drew upon British folk song melodies related specifically to each of the seasons; other composers have done so, though generally in choral works. By contrast, Ashmore imagined a concerto-like piece for string ensemble with light percussion and solo clarinet.

The intended soloist was gifted American clarinetist Richard Stoltzman. Knowing of Stoltzman's wide ranging skills, which include familiarity with jazz idioms, Ashmore indicated places in the score where the soloist might improvise upon the provided material, adding greater personal expression. Thus, the results may vary in detail from one performance to the next, though always exhibiting deft juxtaposition of contrasting themes and variety of coloration, as well as melodic material that will likely be, at least in part, familiar to some portion of the audience.

In Ashmore's hands, *Spring* slips gently in the door on whispered strings and peaceful clarinet, moods slowly building to richer expression of the ballad-like folk song *The Springtime of the Year*. The melody is ornamented and varied, not only by the soloist, but by the ensemble as well. Ultimately, more eager activity develops with a new tune, *It was a Lover and His Lass*. Strictly speaking, it isn't a folk song, as it is a setting by Thomas Morley (c. 1557 – 1602) of lines from Shakespeare's *As You Like It*; it shall recur in Chapter Seven. Nonetheless, any melody that's been around for four centuries may be considered part of a nation's heritage, and Ashmore puts it to good use, sending the clarinet into the highest extremes of its range.

Summer he imagines as a scherzo, a compositional pattern known even to Beethoven and calling upon a bouncy, 6/8 meter and the use of one theme for the opening and closing pages, and another of different character for the central portion. The initial theme is the livelier of the two, the Medieval song *Summer is A' comin' In*, cheerful of spirit, though becoming even more ebullient as the soloist provides more and more detailed ornamentation. The more wistful central theme is *Scarborough Fair*: not as Simon and Garfunkel had it, but a vastly earlier alternate version of that folk song. Diligent scholars of folk music have noted that a single basic song may take on different personality from one region to the next, and here one finds a perfect example of that process.

Autumn uses only a single folk theme, *Cherry Ripe*. The song itself might be sung in effervescent fashion, or more thoughtfully: Ashmore opts for the latter interpretation. He develops the theme, allowing it to become richer as it proceeds, but remaining reliably calm, both in the care of the clarinet soloist and in the string ensemble. The thoughtful moods one finds throughout the movement are an ideal background for the contrast of timbres of the single woodwind set against the textures of strings.

English folk music is rich with *Winter* themes, though apparently Ashmore was most moved by those demonstrating the Christmas spirit. The two featured melodies are *On Christmas Night, All Christians Sing* and *In Dulci Jubilo*. He begins with shimmery string phrases and delicate touches of wind chimes, perhaps suggestive of starlight. The clarinet adds the *Christmas Night* theme in lullaby-like demeanor and all continues in serene fashion, even as *In dulci jubilo* appears. That serenity is not uninterrupted: for a short time, Ashmore transforms *Jubilo* into a playful waltz, before the calm of the evening returns. Ultimately, he closes his *Four Seasons* with a reminiscence of the subtle moods with which *Spring* had begun, bringing his survey of the year full circle.

♪♪♪♪♪

Schickele: *A Year in the Catskills*

Most frequently encountered through his satirical alter ego PDQ Bach, American composer Peter Schickele (b. 1935) also crafts his own music well removed from the realm of satire, and is often the composer of choice for those seeking something that balances new ideas and old traditions. When the resident wind quintet of Vanderbilt University's Blair School of Music was offered funding to have a current composer write something especially for them, they immediately requested Schickele's services. Not only were they confident he could combine sobriety and humor, they also knew that Schickele, himself a bassoonist, is also familiar with the demands of working with the combination of flute/oboe/clarinet/bassoon/horn that makes up a standard wind quintet. The result, his *A Year in the Catskills*, premiered in 2009.

The quintet is in five movements: one for each season, beginning with Spring, then an exciting finale to bring the year to a close. In Schickele's care, *Spring* is a mostly gentle dream-scene, though one with room for jauntier statements and solo spotlights that pass from one player to another. *Summer* offers short, intertwined phrases built into a sequence of so-called "canons:" a compositional technique in which overlapping layers of music are based upon a single melody, each of its different statements offset in time from the others, so that the melody is essentially co-existing with itself. Pachelbel's *Canon* is, by far, the most famed example of the approach, but here Schickele offers a 21st century version.

Fall also draws upon the canon technique, though here, Schickele tells us that he has borrowed the basic melody from the supporting bass line from JS Bach's esteemed *Goldberg Variations* (1742). One might not think of the revered Bach as a particularly playful guy, but here Schickele takes a stately melodic line and gives it much eager activity. Most of the restfulness one finds in *A Year in the Catskills* is reserved for the *Winter* movement, subtitled *Lament*. Perhaps the lamentation is in reflection upon the passing of warmer days; certainly, the music is of generally sorrowful demeanor. The first sighs go to the oboe, though the other players also have their turn, and no member of the ensemble is left lingering in a supporting role for long. Schickele understands that, in chamber music, all participants share an equally prominent role.

Subtitled *Fast Driving*, *A Year in the Catskills*'s fifth movement finale seems to imagine a spirited exit from the region en route to other places. The action begins with jaunty horn lines which lead to much swirling energy from the rest of the ensemble. Before long, one is reminded that this set of five players actually includes six instruments, as the flutist briefly brings out the higher pitched piccolo to add just the right sparkle to the textures. Here and there, one might sense a bit of jazzy energy, suggesting that this person leaving the Catskills may be heading off to an urban jazz club. Wherever the driver is going, it is certainly an exciting trip, or at least there is much eagerness to reach the destination.

♪♪♪♪♪

Glass: Second Violin Concerto
    American Four Seasons

Born in Baltimore, Philip Glass (b. 1937) first studied mathematics and philosophy at the University of Chicago before beginning composition studies, initially at the Juilliard School, and later in Paris. It was during this Paris sojourn that Glass was engaged to transcribe sitar music of Ravi Shankar (1920 – 2012) into Western notation. The assignment triggered within the young composer a lasting fascination for things Asian. Before long, he would reject the strict modernism of the time in favor of a new style drawn from ancient roots. It would be the beginnings of minimalism, with its hypnotic flowing lines and steadily pulsing beats.

However, his Second Violin Concerto (he chose not to call it Violin Concerto no. 2) is of a very different style. It was written for American violin Robert McDuffie, who suggested the new work might make a companion to Vivaldi's famed *Four Seasons* cycle. Glass agreed, and the concerto premiered December 9, 2009, with the Toronto Symphony Orchestra and McDuffie. An American premiere followed at Colorado's Aspen Music Festival July 22, 2010, again with McDuffie as soloist.

Both the Vivaldi set and that of Glass have an orchestra of strings and keyboard. Vivaldi wanted a harpsichord; Glass, working nearly three centuries later, wants a synthesizer. Of the vast array of sounds that a synthesizer can produce, Glass specifies a harpsichord-like timbre; using the synthesizer rather than an actual harpsichord allows not only for amplification but also for a grittier edge to its voice. Often, the synthesizer is drawn into duet passages with the violin soloist, in which the varied timbres of the two instruments make for a deft contrast.

Glass does not title the concerto's four movements as to which season is which. It might begin in spring, or might not, and it does not necessarily proceed in calendar order. In fact, he and McDuffie found that they differed as to which movement made them imagine which season; thus, audience members might have their own ideas on the subject. Additionally, Glass prefaced each movement with a solo cadenza, imagining that the cadenzas might be extracted to make up a solo suite without orchestra.

Whatever season one might imagine it depicts, Glass' first movement is intense and demanding, instantly seizing the attention of listeners and performers alike. The second brings contrast with slow, lyrical moods. Then, the concerto accelerates again, increasing verve propelling it through the last two movements.

Glass' *American Four Seasons* reveals little patience for clamoring dissonance, and throughout, the music is characterized by beautiful sounds distributed over several movements of different tempi. Mozart or Beethoven would have done much the same thing, though without the synthesizer. Admittedly one finds Glass' trademark of rising and falling arpeggios, though also richer textures and more varied tone colors than would be usual for this composer. New ideas and old traditions come together in a single work.

♪♪♪♪♪

Pēteris Vasks: *Gadalaiki (The Seasons)*

Latvian composer Pēteris Vasks (b. 1946) spent much of his twenties as a bassist in orchestras in the Baltic states. He had also studied composition, but with Latvia under Soviet control, a composer's works were unlikely to reach the public if their creator did not embrace Soviet ideology. This Vasks was unwilling to do, so it was not until the 1990s that his music at last began to attract world attention. Finally, audiences could discover the loosely tonal atmospheric moods of Vasks' music: inventive in character, though stopping short of intimidating modernism. His music manages be new without being frightening.

Vasks' *Gadalaiki (*the Latvian word is pronounced "GUH-duh-lie-kih"*)* is a portrayal of the seasons. Its component pieces were not originally intended as a four-movement suite. Vasks wrote them one at a time over a period of nearly thirty years, finally deciding he needed "to complete the cycle." Taken together, they offer a range of distinctly contrasting moods, reflective not only of the seasons, but also of Vasks' enduring fondness for nature, which he calls his "main source of inspiration."

Earliest of the four is *White Scenery (Balta ainava)*, a winter meditation dating from 1980. Its widely spaced notes seem suggestive of open, snowy vistas. Of the silences, Vasks says, "Silence is very important," adding that the world could use more of it today.

The following year (1981), Vasks turned his attention to autumnal scenes, with *Autumn Music* (*Rudens muzika*). This season the composer chose to capture with tentative repeating phrases that lead to sweeping glissandos and generally falling lines. Occasional dissonance suggests a certain degree of tension in this season of variable weather, though *Autumn Music* ends much as it had begun, with cautious motion, as nature, in Vasks' words, "surrenders its splendor."

Spring Music (*Pavasara muzika*) came next, in 1995. Here, very high pitched musical fragments are often off-set by very low ones, with occasional startling silence bringing into even sharper relief the statements that precede and follow them.

With the last of the four pieces, *Green Scenery* (*Zala ainava*) of 2008, summer has at last arrived, a season that, for Vasks, represents an "intense feeling of joy." Rushing passagework and brilliant colors infuse the glimpse of summer with almost uninterrupted sparkling vitality, a wisp of a Latvian folk song appearing at the close. In Latvia, it seems, summer is a time for celebration.

As the individual pieces of *Gadalaiki* were composed separately, one might begin in any season and then proceed forward. However, since winter-themed *White Scenery* was the first to be composed, and as winter must seem predominant at Latvia's latitude, there is logic in starting with winter. Wherever one might launch the sequence, the fact remains that it is music more of feeling than action, but those feelings rise from the heart.

♪♪♪♪

O'Connor: *The American Seasons –*
Seasons of an American Life

Imagine an adolescent musical genius besting his elders in violin competitions, matching the adults at every turn. Centuries ago, it was Wolfgang Amadeus Mozart (1756 – 1791); here, it's Mark O'Connor (b. 1961 in Seattle), who, as a young teen, was triumphing at bluegrass fiddle contests against competitors three and four times his age. A career in bluegrass and country music followed. However, by the time O'Connor was in his 30s, he began to conceive of bigger musical ideas requiring broader canvases than folk music offered. So, like some of the great names of music before him – Gershwin and Ellington come to mind – he decided to branch out from the circles in which he had begun.

O'Connor began investigating the world of so-called "classical music." Since then, he has composed a half dozen concertos for violin (some labelled "fiddle concerto"), a symphony on American themes, and a variety of smaller scale works that have even come into the repertoire of such noted classical artists as cellist Yo-Yo Ma and violinist Nadja Salerno-Sonnenberg.

O'Connor admits that his *American Seasons* is, in part, a reaction to Vivaldi's famed seasonal cycle; as a violinist/composer, he could hardly be immune to that influence. Nonetheless, it is Vivaldi refracted through O'Connor's own American folk-flavored voice.

O'Connor's *American Seasons* also has an additional influence, reflected in its subtitle *Seasons of an American Life*, and one reaching back even before Vivaldi to Shakespeare. In Act II, Scene VII of *As You Like It* (c. 1599) one find the soliloquy beginning with the famed lines "All the world's a stage, and all the men and women merely players." Melancholy Jaques then goes on to reflect upon the seasons of a man's life, of which he enumerates seven, from infancy to oblivion. O'Connor's idea was to write a concerto that would not only express seasons of the calendar, but also seasons of life. So the concept is admittedly not just about flowers, sunshine, falling leaves, and drifting snow but also about those same aspects of human existence. However, with a violin leading the charge, O'Connor's *American Seasons* is a reimagining of Vivaldi, as much as Shakespeare.

Labelled for the seasons of the calendar and proceeding from spring through winter, the four movements draw upon idioms of American folk music styles, with plenty of skipping dotted rhythms and splashes of syncopation, as well as much sliding from one pitch to the next. O'Connor has remarked that, for a bluegrass fiddler, this last technique is second nature, though for the orchestral parts of strings and harp, he needed to be very specific in notation. Orchestral players generally prefer knowing exactly what they are expected to do, and even after *American Seasons* first began to reach the public, he went back to those parts to add greater specificity.

The *Spring* movement opens with the soloist quite alone, eagerly leaping into this new experience. The string ensemble joins the action, and at times, gets the spotlight quite to itself. Most of the flash is for the soloist; such is the nature of concertos. Nonetheless, a wise composer saves some of the fun for the larger ensemble, not only to keep them motivated, but also to link solo effects to those of the orchestra.

Summer begins in languorous fashion, as if the heat of a summer day has driven everyone into the shade. Both soloist and ensemble have lines of rather woozy, bluesy coloring as they elaborate on short phrases borrowed from the first movement. Midway through, a greater sense of energy and forward propulsion develops; perhaps the setting sun has brought cooler temperatures and a greater willingness for motion.

The subsequent *Autumn* movement is dreamily nocturnal in spirit, especially in the soloist's lines, as the string ensemble provides long, sustained tones of support. In the central pages, attention shifts rather more to the string ensemble, though the soloist is never long silent. At times, the long, sustained tones pass to the soloist's care, while the ensemble has more overtly thematic material. Vivaldi sometimes did much the same thing in his slow movements.

O'Connor's *Winter* finale opens with determined drive and development of earlier material, ensuring that all four movements connect with one another. Midway through the quarter-hour movement (longest of the four), one finds a quick shift to more thoughtful, less demonstrative, lines for the soloist. For pages at a time, the soloist is quite alone, reflecting, it seems, upon the past year – or, in the Shakespearean sense, the progress of life. Finally, following a perpetual motion series of rapid figurations for the soloist, the string ensemble rejoins in celebratory mood. Together, they prance into the final chord, as O'Connor brings his *American Seasons* to a close.

♪♪♪♪♪

The twenty works selected to stand prominently in this chapter are far from the only options for full-year seasonal expressions. They are, generally speaking, the most famous ones, but others, both great and small, also deserve attention. Here are six additional choices:

- Henry Purcell (1659 – 1695): A Shakespearean-flavored dramatic stage work for voices and instruments, *The Fairy Queen* includes in its Act Four the Masque: a sequence of short scenes that muse upon the four seasons. Spring is playful, summer jaunty, autumn weary and winter regretful. Woodwinds and strings are joined by solo singers to set the mood.

- Frederic Delius (1862 – 1934): In 1890, the English composer published *Three Small Tone Poems*, these being *Summer Evening*, *Winter Night: Sleigh Ride*, and *Spring Morning*. One might lament the absence of autumn, or one could simply borrow the third movement of his String Quartet, subtitled *Late Swallows*. His colleague Eric Fenby (1906 – 1997) arranged it for orchestra.

- Selim Palmgren (1878 – 1951): A Finnish member of the late Romantic school, Palmgren's works include the orchestral suite *The Seasons* (*Vuodenajat*). Here, spring has the sparkle of new growth, summer the fervor of folk dance, autumn the graceful action of falling leaves, and winter the charging energy of a sleigh ride.

- Nathanael Berg (1879 – 1957): A founding member of Sweden's composers association, Berg subtitled his Symphony no. 2 *Årstiderna* (*Seasons*). In his hands, spring dances, summer is resplendent, autumn frets, and winter shivers, though with a delicate dusting of snowflakes.

- Sergei Prokofiev (1891 – 1953): The Russian master's ballet *Cinderella* tells a familiar tale that would normally have no overt seasonal links. However, late in Act One, he has the fairy godmother bring along four lesser fairies, each representative of a season. Here, too, autumn is the only troubled season, though in these four very short scenes intended as solo spotlights, those troubles pass quickly indeed.

- Joaquin Rodrigo (1901 – 1999): The Spanish master's *Musica para una jardin* (*Music for a Garden*) is a delicately shaded orchestral score. A short prelude is followed by four lullabies, each for a specific season. He begins in autumn and finishes with summer, with most of the eagerness reserved for the two central seasons.

♪♪♪♪♪

One could also craft a Four Seasons symphony or string quartet by applying visual imagery to many Classical or Romantic Era instrumental works. In those days, it was customary to write a four-movement piece in which the first movement was dramatic (cheerful or fearful, as its creator chose). The second movement would then bring tender thoughts, the third eager energy, and the last further drama (bright or dark, according to the composer's tastes). Surely, one could set that first movement amidst late winter blizzards, the second gazing upon the buds of spring, and the third with busy activity of a summer day. As to the fourth, that might be autumn storms or autumn festivals, depending on how the composer had chosen to slant that closing movement.

Consider, for example, how ideally Beethoven's famed Symphony no. 5 would serve that vision: a generally dark first movement for those blizzards, then relaxation, flavored with excitement for spring, then a boisterous summer day, and lastly a gloriously excited fall festival. Beethoven himself specified no such scenario, but the music could still bring vividly seasonal imagery to its listeners, if those listeners keep their minds open to such possibilities.

Seasonal Music Insights: Vivaldi and Much More | 63

Chapter Three: Spring

Here is the opening phrase of the opening melody of the opening movement of Beethoven so-called "Spring" Sonata for violin and piano. It happens that these notes are from the violin part, though within moments, the pianist will play them in reply. The rapid passagework – flowing, though not overly hurried – has reminded many a listener of rapturous bird-song in the springtime, hence the sonata's nickname. Perhaps two lovebirds call to one another on a spring morning? It's music that was referenced in Tom Gauld's cover for *The New Yorker* magazine (April 16, 2018), along Vivaldi, Stravinsky, and the calls of robins.

No season is more beloved by composers than spring. Apparently birds, flowers, and soft breezes were an irresistible stimulus to the musically minded. Of course, spring brings different things in different climates, and different ideas to different imaginations. In his *Spring Concerto,* Antonio Vivaldi (1678 – 1741) included a thunderstorm, leading to wet, frightened birds, but the sunny side of the season has proven more generally inspirational, and most of the music featured in this chapter is of ebullient spirit.

Along with plenty of birds, this Spring-themed chapter also offers new growth, the raptures of young love, and high-spirited dances, often folk-like in flavor. Nearly always – as long as it isn't by Igor Stravinsky (1882 – 1971) – there's even a happy ending in view, and here and there, visions of paintings inspired by the season. In springtime, it seems, storms are ever brief and the sun is never long absent from the sky – unless the moon is there to take its place. Relatively few composers wished to think dark thoughts when imagining nature's rebirth.

♫♫♫♫

Beethoven: Violin Sonata no. 5 in F major, op. 24, "Spring"

It was not the composer himself who dubbed this chamber work "Spring:" the word appears nowhere in his surviving manuscript, which, moreover, describes it as a sonata for piano and violin, not one for violin and piano. Ludwig van Beethoven (1770 – 1827) played both instruments, and viola, too, though his strong preference was for the more highly dramatic piano. The nickname does not even appear in early published editions, and its exact origin is uncertain. However, for generations, it has been known as the "Spring" sonata, and given the largely buoyant spirits of the work, the label is not inappropriate; certainly, long usage has given it some authority. Ask any violinist about the "Spring" sonata, even without naming a composer, and this is the one that will be the focus of any ensuing discussion.

Dating from 1801, before the composer became fully aware of encroaching deafness and dedicated to his supporter, the Court Moritz von Fries, the "Spring" Sonata is fifth of Beethoven's ten sonatas for this pairing of instruments. It is also the first of his violin sonatas to have four movements, rather than only three. Three movements (first fast, then slow, then fast of tempo) had been the old expectation, a left-over from Mozart's time, but Beethoven's generation was beginning to expand the envelope of musical expression. So this sonata is structured in approximately symphonic terms, having a spacious first movement with contrasting themes and development of those themes, a gentle second movement, a spirited third movement in a 6/8 triple meter, and a lively closing movement juxtaposing themes of markedly dramatic variety. All of this Beethoven packs into this sonata for just two instruments, while also conveying a spirit of such sunny demeanor that, rather against his will, if not against that of the music's character, his Violin Sonata no. 5 has come to be known universally as "Spring."

The first movement *Allegro* opens in blissfully serene manner with flowing melodic lines for the violin and gentle support from the piano, a parceling of parts that is reversed as soon as this opening theme is allowed to repeat. Beethoven would be the last to leave the pianist long out of the spotlight. For contrast and variety, more active ideas follow, though the central pages, in which thematic fragments are further developed, rely mostly upon portions of the initial theme, often with bird-song-like bits echoing from one player to the other.

The second movement *Adagio molto espressivo* is, as advertised, relaxed and quite expressive. Here one finds a romance-in-the-moonlight atmosphere, with melodic phrases shared between the two players, one taking the spotlight first, then yielding to the other. When phrases reappear, they are often ornamented in different fashion than when they were last heard, ensuring that, though thematic material is largely based upon a central idea, that material is ever taking on new colors.

The third movement *Scherzo* is, for Beethoven, unusually short, almost serving as an introduction to the actual final movement. However, in scarcely a minute, Beethoven yet manages to juxtapose two ideas against one another: the first playful, the second more forward-driving. The playful idea returns long enough to bring the movement swiftly to a close.

For the fourth movement *Rondo*, Beethoven choses to begin with piano quite alone, then bringing in the violin to share in the action. Various ideas are set against one another: some sweet, others mildly fretful, with occasional diversion into something approaching anxiety. However, much of the mood is of gracefully song-like character.

Beethoven might not have wished the sonata to be called "Spring." However, his Violin Sonata no. 5 certainly does a delightful job of capturing the character of an ideal spring day: changeable, but ultimately filled with optimism and delight.

♪♪♪♪♪

Schumann: Symphony no. 1 in B-flat major, op. 38, "Spring"

Few artistic partnerships are more endearing than that of Robert and Clara Schumann. The beginning, at least, of their relationship, might have been imagined by a novelist, and indeed, once inspired the 1947 film *Song of Love* starring Katharine Hepburn as Clara.

Robert (1810 – 1856) was a composer and influential music journalist. Clara (1819 – 1896) was a renowned pianist who, since childhood, had been famed across the continent. He composed for her; she played for him. Out of this ideally symbiotic relationship arose great masterpieces of the piano and chamber repertoires. Although their later years were darkened by tragedy with Robert's declining emotional health, the optimism of their early marriage is preserved in Robert's life-affirming works of the 1840s.

After years of opposition from Clara's father, this musical couple married September 12, 1840, one day before the bride's 21st birthday. The inspiration provided by having Clara in his daily life sent Schumann into a torrent of productivity, resulting in dozen of songs and piano pieces, the beginnings of a piano concerto, and this symphony, which courses with the joy of a blissful bridegroom. It would premiere March 31, 1841, with the Leipzig Gewandhaus Orchestra conducted by the Schumanns' friend, Felix Mendelssohn (1809 – 1847). The piece was published later that same year.

Despite the winter months in which it was composed – or perhaps because of them – this buoyant symphony carries the subtitle "Spring," and was inspired by a poem by Adolf Böttger (1815- 1870), the last line of which reads, "In the valley, spring is bursting out all over!" As Böttger was himself of Leipzig, Schumann probably relied upon his audience recognizing the reference. Incidentally, Böttger was an active translator of the English Romantic poets into German, especially Byron, and even delved further into crafting German retellings of Shakespeare; though little remembered now outside of Germany, his reputation at the time was strong.

For Schumann, it seems, spring "bursts" with a majestic brass fanfare (the composer wrote the musical term *Maestoso*) that broadens into a magnificent orchestral theme as stately as something Beethoven might have written two decades earlier. Winsome passages arrive, as well as upward-dashing phrases, dancing rhythms, and occasional firm chords for punctuation. Of the second, brisker portion of this first movement, Schumann has requested the tempo *Allegro molto vivace*: fast and very lively. Although the brass sections speak the most brilliantly, the other orchestral sections also have their moments of attention.

The second movement *Larghetto* is, at first, a tender romance suggestive of a young lady amongst the flowers. It is, after all, supposedly spring. Woodwind phrases provide further sweetness, and greater drama gradually develops, though the movement ultimately subsides back into languor.

The comparatively brief third movement *Scherzo* sets two ideas, both using a propulsive 6/8 triple meter, against one another. It opens with bold determination, cut through with playful interludes. Central pages recall some of the more eager, leaping rhythms of the first movement, serving to link the symphony together as an organic whole.

The final movement practically prances in the spring sunshine. Assertive outbursts ensure that attention will not waver, though the overall mood is one of resolute good cheer. Schumann has labelled it *Allegro animato e grazioso*: quick, animated, and graceful. It is surely that. Although the composer's disgruntled father-in-law dismissed it as the "Symphony of Contradictions," a less biased listener can only conclude that here is a work suffused with happiness. For Schumann, newly married and in the springtime of his career, the season conveys a mood of optimism rarely surpassed in his later compositions.

♪♪♪♪

Paine: Symphony no. 2 in A major, op. 34,
    "In the Spring"

Until the late 1800s, fine music was not a home-grown American product. American composers were known for parlor songs, piano pieces, and sacred hymns. However, more ambitious music remained a European creation. Americans were happy to listen, and even to perform, but reluctant, it seems, to create.

These facts make the career of John Knowles Paine (1839 – 1906) all the more notable. Born in Portland, Maine, he had the advantage of music loving parents who noticed and supported his musical interests. The youth studied piano and organ, and also composition before, in 1858, heading off to Germany for advanced training. There, he received much favorable notice, especially for his organ playing. That instrument would ultimately bring him back to the US to teach organ at Harvard beginning in 1861. Four years later, he became the first chairman of Harvard's new Department of Music; remaining in that position until 1905, Paine upgraded the curriculum, so that it was no longer a practical necessity for would-be American composers to cross the ocean for their studies. To this day, the main recital hall at the Harvard Department of Music is named Paine Hall.

One of Paine's most ambitious compositions – in fact, one of the most grandiloquent of all American musical works to that point in history – is his Symphony no. 2, which premiered in Boston March 10, 1880. Little less than an hour in length, it is nearly as grand in conception as Beethoven's magisterial *Eroica* Symphony (1805), despite having less precedent. Beethoven, after all, had built upon a thriving tradition of Viennese symphonic creations, whereas Paine's predecessors had scarcely begun to imagine anything beyond a few minutes of musical diversion. Clearly, Paine had come home from Europe with a clear vision of what could be done with symphonic forces, and here gave that vision tangible form.

Paine's wide-ranging symphonic tone painting bears the subtitle "In the Spring," almost begging for further descriptive details so as to paint the scene as the music proceeds. Furthermore, individual movements have their own descriptive subtitles, though these were added at a later date and were not necessarily Paine's initial ideas. Nonetheless, the changing tempos and moods of the different movements, as well as the composer's skilled use of instrumental colors, perfectly suit these visions. So when he later decided that the first movement was *Departure of Winter – Awakening of Nature*, the second *May Night Fantasy*, the third *A Romance of Springtime*, and the last *The Glory of Nature*, one can hardly quibble with their accuracy.

Much as a Viennese master would likely have done, Paine structured his Symphony no. 2 in four spacious movements. The first is mostly brisk of tempo, though also includes a somber, reflective introduction that opens the door for its more spirited first theme. From that point onward, peaceful woodwinds, scurrying strings, and brilliant brass all have their time in the spotlight. As for percussion, this is limited to timpani, and most often in a supporting role, though it adds valuable fullness to the most expressive passages.

The second movement is an eager scherzo with danceable, triple meter rhythms, contrasted by more gently romantic central pages. Paine's subtitle tells us this is a fantasy of an evening in May; the music itself suggests this evening might combine the opportunity for frolic with the occasional romantic liaison.

The third movement is one of poignant longing. Never does it become so poignant that one suspects the loved one to be lost for all time; he or she is just temporarily absent. Passages of greater or lesser yearning appear, as passions rise and fall, but never entirely abate.

In the final movement, Paine paints with a broad brush, using brilliant colors, eagerly scampering lines, and occasional bold outbursts. Reverent chorale-like lines appear from time to time, but these are soon interrupted by pages of ebullience. Phrases pass from one player to another, for Paine, having well learned the inherent contrasts to be found within the timbres of different instruments, here places that knowledge on impressive display. Given the brassy splendor of this closing movement's last pages, one can easily imagine that it is, as promised, a scene of natural glory, one fully the equal of its European predecessors, and far superior to anything else an American composer had tried to that time.

♫♫♫♫♫

Sullivan: *Victoria and Merrie England* – ballet

Sir Arthur Sullivan (1842 – 1900) dearly wanted to be taken seriously as a composer. Having trained in Leipzig as the first winner of the Mendelssohn Scholarship, the Englishman dreamed of writing glorious works, and several such items are found in his catalog. In such context, to be type-cast as a composer of high-spirited operettas, even including *The Pirates of Penzance* (1879), grated on his nerves.

One hopes that earning a knighthood in 1883 was some consolation to Sullivan, particularly as his business partner William Gilbert (1836 – 1911) would have to wait another quarter century before being so honored. However, it was reliably to Sullivan that attention turned when music was needed for some occasion in the royal family, and surely the composer must have admitted that this was an honor.

In 1897, London's Alhambra Theatre decided to commemorate Queen Victoria's 60th year on the throne with a Diamond Jubilee ballet, bringing to the stage not only imagery of Victoria's own reign, but also thoat of earlier times. These included the Restoration in the late-17th century, the glory days of Elizabeth I, as well as traditional folk tales. The work premiered May 25, 1897. At the time, British ballets had little to do with the grand story ballets of the Franco-Russian tradition; rather, they tended to feature short, varied episodes, more scenic than plot-driven. This was the lighter side of dance, but, nonetheless, very popular: Sullivan's resulting work, *Victoria and Merrie England*, spent months on the Alhambra stage, attended again and again by enthusiastic audiences, as well as various members of the royal family.

If the work is little known today, that is due in large part to the original score having long ago vanished. However, individual excerpts survived, and the Sullivan Society recently set a team of dance historians on the task of filling in the gaps. Crucial to the reconstruction process was the survival of detailed correspondence between Sullivan and his secretary, as well as contemporary press accounts of the ballet. If, in places, Sullivan mavens swear they hear reference to one or another of his operettas, the correspondence makes clear that, indeed, some of this recycling occurred.

Victoria and Merrie England has eight scenes. Scene I is Ancient Britain, including the Druids. Scenes II and III are largely Elizabethan, specifically imagining May Day celebrations of the Tudor Era, though also diverting into tales of Robin Hood. Scenes IV and V step into Windsor Forest for legends of Herne the Hunter. Scene VI offers Christmas revels in the time of Charles II, who reigned from 1660 to 1685. Scene VII brings Victoria's coronation, which had occurred June 28, 1838, and was now being commemorated throughout the realm. Here, Sullivan provides an Imperial March in tribute to an event that had occurred before his own birth. Last is Scene VIII, *Britain's Glory*, in which soldiers and sailors paraded; the Albert Memorial is remembered, all culminating in a grand statement of *God Save the Queen*.

If one wished to craft from *Victoria and Merrie England* a short ballet on seasonal themes, one could do so from either the Elizabethan May Day themes or the Restoration Christmas revels. For spring, consider beginning with *Festivities on the Village Green*, largely vibrant and cheerful of mood, more than a bit suggestive of those hearty sailors of *HMS Pinafore*, though with restful central pages that might suggest the lads thinking of their girls back home.

One might present next the *Procession of Mummers and Revelers*, in which a bagpipe-like drone underlies eager rhythms, stately interludes appearing at times. The *Morris Dance* recalls an old village dance, often performed with bells and waved sticks; Sullivan imagines these Morris dancers to be a very graceful lot.

Follow that with the brief solo scene for the *May Queen*, tender and delicate of spirit, before concluding with the cheerful *Maypole Dance*. There, Sullivan revealed faith in the dancers, or at least in the orchestra, as he crafted intricately layered fugue-like passages for the central pages. Those five scenes together, lasting about a quarter hour, make for an imaginatively varied musical tapestry of spring, bright of spirit and light of heart.

♪♪♪♪♪

Rimsky-Korsakov: *May Night* Overture

In the century that has passed since his death, Nicolai Rimsky-Korsakov (1844 – 1908) has come to be known for his orchestral scores, particularly the admittedly marvelous *Scheherazade* and *Capriccio espagnole*, both from 1887-1888. However, he was also a busy man of the stage, with twelve completed operas to his name, and much of his orchestral catalog comprises suites from those operas. They are now rarely staged outside of Russia, due in part to the difficulties of assembling casts adept in Russian. Yet their music is well worth exploration, even in orchestral excerpts.

May Night stood early in Rimsky's output, being only his second opera. The tale of sweethearts kept apart by the young man's father but finally united by the magical influence of the Queen of the Water Nymphs was drawn from a short story by Nicolai Gogol (1809 – 1852). Rimsky drafted his own libretto and in his autobiography, said of the work that it expressed "my enthusiasm for the poetry of pagan worship." The opera premiered in St. Petersburg at the Mariinsky Theater January 21, 1880, by the old style calendar then in use in Tsarist Russia; the nation did not come to use the modern Gregorian calendar until after the Russian Revolution.

The *May Night* Overture is a colorful summation of the work's most prominent musical moments, with themes borrowed from arias and duets for the principal characters and from some of the composer's favorite scenes – or at least ones he thought would still communicate well even devoid of voices. It opens with the delights of a dawn scene, complete with bird-like woodwind trills and distant French horns, suggestive of an outdoorsy atmosphere. Broader phrases and fuller colors develop, interspersed with both mellow interludes and tenderly romantic ones. Turbulence arrives with assertive brass, though the overture closes with vibrantly festive coloring borrowed from the opera's last scene. Lacking a staged performance of *May Night,* one finds here much of its aural glories. Rimsky-Korsakov, after all, wrote a textbook on orchestra that is still widely read, so even without the singers, his *May Night* still has much to offer.

♪♪♪♪♪

Fibich: *Spring (Vesna)*, op. 13

Bedřich Smetana (1824 – 1884), Antonín Dvořák (1841 – 1904), and Zdeněk Fibich (1850 – 1900): the last and youngest of these three may be the least immediately familiar, but he, too, arose from Bohemian roots which would flavor his music. Son of a forestry official and raised in the countryside, Fibich yet was exposed to fine culture, thanks to his Viennese mother. General education both in Vienna and in Prague was followed by musical studies in Leipzig with Ignaz Moscheles (1794 – 1870), who as a young man had been part of Beethoven's professional circle. So Fibich's training was top-drawer, and his music is well worthy of discovery: perhaps a bit more German in flavor than that of his more famed countrymen, but still revealing an inspired touch for tonal variety and melodic development.

Fibich's gifts are particularly well displayed in his orchestral music, especially in the numerous tone poems: single-movement instrumental works of scenic or dramatic inspiration. Some of those symphonic poems derive from Czech folk lore, others from stage dramas, yet others from Fibich's own ideas, as is the case with *Spring*. The work has no specific plot, but much variety of musical color suggestive of activities and emotions he imagined to be appropriate to the season. As it premiered in Prague March 25, 1881, one supposes the listeners should have had no difficulty relating to the notion of what spring might bring, especially to their own neighborhoods.

The work begins with solo clarinet, utterly alone with serenely flowing phrases. This theme will recur again and again, frequently taking on new form, and not always in the care of the clarinet: as it becomes the main theme of the nearly quarter-hour-long piece, one might imagine that it is a theme for spring itself. Gradually, other instruments join in peaceful mien, as of a pre-dawn scene. Before long, however, all builds to brilliant outbursts of musical excitement. Suggestions of spirited folk dancing appear, evidence that Dvořák was far from the only Bohemian who wished to capture the musical voices of the common people. Brighter and brighter the scene becomes, ultimately leading to a stately expansion upon that spring theme. However, Fibich has no intention of ending the piece in august fashion; ultimately, his *Spring* will close much as it had begun, with gentle and peaceable woodwinds. Spring has its brilliance, but is, perhaps, essentially a time of soft coloring and tender new growth.

♪♪♪♪♪

Foerster: *Springtime and Desire*, op. 93

Here's another gifted Czech composer overrun in history by his genius colleague/countryman Dvořák: Josef Bohuslav Foerster (1859 – 1951). Foerster spent the bulk of his career abroad, specifically in Hamburg and Vienna, before returning to his native city after World War I to teach at the Prague Conservatory. By that time, Dvořák had breathed his last, and though one cannot say that Foerster had the entire field to himself, he had at least come to be known and respected for his own musical voice.

That voice – less overtly Czech than Dvořák's, and somewhat more Western European than Eastern – is on clear display in Foerster's orchestral tone poem *Springtime and Desire* (1912). The composition is more of a mood piece than an attempt to paint a specific sequence of scenes. Foerster never clarified where this spring experience is occurring, nor who desires what. Is it springtime in the Czech countryside and desire for that pretty young lady who lives up the road? Conversely, might it be the springtime of a person's life, as that person matures toward adulthood and come to desire a purpose in life? Either idea, or almost any other, would have been well in line with the artistic/musical Symbolism movement of the decade. Perhaps the title means whatever the listener thinks it means; like most great art, it still has a purpose.

However one might interpret the title, the music itself is a tapestry of varied mood painting. The work begins in relaxed and thoughtful mood, the sense of forward motion gradually increasing. Occasionally, brilliant chords punctuate the action, more and more of these as what might be a sunrise scene – or, conversely, a growing insight into one's life's purpose – develops. Foerster's orchestral writing becomes increasingly luxuriant, with melodic fragments reappearing throughout the ensemble. At times, solo violin takes the lead, first languidly, then with greater urgency. Its flowing theme, which one might suppose represents the "desire" of the title, broadens, becoming ever more spirited as it moves throughout the orchestra. It seems this desire is no passing wish, but an all-consuming passion.

Gentler passages appear for contrast, though Foerster has no intention of fading to a sweet conclusion. Again and again, cymbal crashes and formidable brass break in on the action, and the final few lines are thoroughly heroic in spirit. Whatever had been the object of all that desire apparently is gained at last.

♪♪♪♪♪

Ippolitov-Ivanov: *Spring Overture*, op. 1 (*Yar'khmel*)

Russians, Czechs, and Hungarians were not the only Eastern Europeans making significant contributions to fine music. Consider, too, Mikhail Ippolitov-Ivanov (1859 – 1935), of Georgian/Caucasian roots. When his career began, his homeland was on the fringes of Imperial Russia; by the end of his time, it had been swallowed up into Stalin's Soviet Union. Those facts are testimony not only to Ippolitov-Ivanov's time in history, but also to his ability to gain approval for himself and his music from a wide variety of observers. Particularly in his orchestral scores, one finds brilliant color and energy, often driven by folk and peasant rhythms, a character that helped Ippolitov-Ivanov and his music to survive the changing times.

Composed in 1881 and standing at the very beginning of Ippolitov-Ivanov's catalog of published works is his *Spring Overture* – or, to give its Armenian title, *Yar'khmel*. The musical colors he crafts suggest that spring in Armenia is a time for anything from peace to storms to celebration.

The placid atmosphere at the opening might be first light, with woodwind birdsong set against a string tapestry of sunrise. This calm morning scene is interrupted by stern brass and tumultuous strings, though a playful oboe, suggestive of folk dance, soon eases the tension. That oboe melody becomes the main theme of the overture's central pages, passed from one section of the orchestra to the next. Crashing cymbals lead to exuberance lasting nearly to the overture's close: nearly, but not quite. Ippolitov-Ivanov's village dancers seem to have worn themselves out, and the overture ends as gently as it had begun. It was for his later *Caucasian Sketches* that Ippolitov-Ivanov would win his reputation, but even here, at the launch of his career, he already proved his finesse with orchestral flavors.

♪♪♪♪♪

Debussy: *Printemps (Spring)*

Customarily, Claude Debussy (1862 – 1918) is described as an Impressionist composer, implying a link between his music and the soft, gentle paintings of Monet and Renoir. Certainly, there is sometimes a resemblance between the work of the three men, particularly in their shared fondness for soft lines and subtle shading. Nonetheless, when it came to art, Debussy himself expressed a preference for the stark colors and shapes of American painter James Whistler (think of *Whistler*'s *Mother*, aka "Arrangement in Grey and Black") to those of his countrymen, and Whistler's music has little to do with water lilies and boating parties.

Other artistic styles also influenced Debussy's music, sometimes leading to his most vibrantly shaded works. Pre-dating his more famed *Prelude to the Afternoon of a Faun* by most of a decade, *Printemps* (French for "Spring") was composed in 1887 and inspired by *Primavera* (Italian for "Spring") of Sandro Botticelli (1445 – 1510). The painting depicts lithe, diaphanously draped nymphs dancing gracefully in a forest clearing; the only sober note in the scene is a dark spirit, often interpreted as the west wind, attempting (apparently unsuccessfully) to make off with one of the nymphs.

Debussy's original conception for the composition would have given voices to the nymphs, for the piece was intended to be performed by chorus and orchestra. Yet that original score, apparently never performed, was lost in a fire; the only remaining version was a reduction for two pianos and voices. In 1913, another composer, Paul-Henri Büsser (1872 – 1973: indeed, surviving nearly to his 102nd birthday), asked Debussy for permission to re-orchestrate the piece. Debussy agreed, and *Printemps* took on new life. The vocal parts fell entirely by the wayside: as it exists today, *Printemps* is solely an instrumental work. Its specific scoring is by Büsser, though the instrumental choices are ones often favored by Debussy himself, and certainly, the phrasing, harmonies and development of materials is largely as the elder master would have had them.

Debussy's *Printemps* begins sweetly with flowing lines from strings and short phrases exchanged amongst the wind instruments. Gradually, this opening portion (with the tempo marking *Tres modere* – very moderate) builds to richer textures and colors, without entirely setting aside its opening mood of grace. Tender phrases build and evolve, growing into more dramatic statements, though these, too, gradually subside. A slight tempo change – from *Tres modere* to *Modere* – leads to passages of greater motion and, gradually, greater splendor. Here, one finds the most heroic brass and percussion that one is likely to encounter in any Debussy score; it may be as much Büsser's idea as Debussy's, but the effect is surely splendid. Spring, it seems, has truly arrived. Exuberant moods, dancing energy, and finally glorious festive colors serve to bring Debussy's *Printemps* to a brilliant close.

Incidentally, Debussy's catalog also includes another instrumental work alluding to spring in its title. The last of three movements of his orchestral suite *Images* (1910) is *Rondes de Printemps* (*Springtime Dances*). Despite the similarity of names, *Printemps* and *Rondes de Printemps* are distinct from one another, having little in common other than stylistic touches that are largely hallmarks of Debussy's personal style.

The Botticelli painting that inspired Debussy also spoke to Ottorino Respighi (1879 – 1936). That gentleman's *Primavera*, appearing later in this chapter, makes a striking contrast to that of the Frenchman. Perhaps, being himself Italian, Respighi had strolled over to the Uffizi Gallery to sit in front of the painting itself as he worked. Debussy would have had to proceed from memory – or from a good textbook on art.

♪♪♪♪♪

Sibelius: *Spring Song (Varsang)*, op. 16

When one encounters the name of Finnish master Jean Sibelius (1865 – 1957), it is usually through his patriotic tone poem *Finlandia*, op. 26 (1899). However, Sibelius had been composing long before then, and his fine touch with orchestral resources was already well-honed before he reached the age of thirty. It was just before that momentous birthday that Sibelius wrote the orchestral tone poem *Spring Song*. It is not spring as Vivaldi made it, with bird song and village dances. However, Sibelius was Scandinavian: to a Finn, spring is apparently something that sidles subtly in the door and only gradually wins one's heart.

Premiering in 1894, then, in revised form, having a second premiere the following year, Sibelius' *Spring Song* opens with peaceful strings and winds, textures gradually building like the dawn. This initial theme is stated again and again, ever more lushly, as spring settles decisively into Sibelius' northern climate. Gradually, the music takes on even more vibrant moods with heroic brass. Even chimes join the action to ensure brilliant coloring for this ebullient spring song. After a suspenseful pause, the tenderly peaceable moods return, and after a last surge of orchestral color, all drifts to a serene close. In all, it is an impressive musical tapestry that builds, sings rapturously, then slips away. Perhaps that is the nature of springtime in Finland.

♪♪♪♪♪

Roussel: *Pour une fete de printemps*, op. 22
   (*For a Spring Festival*)

In the late 19th century, some French composers tended toward what came to be known as the Impressionist style, with soft corners and gentle attitudes reflective of Impressionist art. Others preferred to continue with standard Romanticism. Albert Roussel (1869 – 1937) was the odd man out. He did not take up music professionally until the age of twenty-five, and even then never settled fully into either stylistic camp. He had no objection to the smooth flow of melodies that Debussy was advocating, but preferred to attach such ideas to the tidy blueprint of rediscovered Classical ideals. Artistic elegance united with vintage structures: such is Roussel's vision.

His tone poem *Pour une fete de printemps (For a Spring Festival)* premiered in Paris October 29, 1921. At the time, his nation, freshly emerged from war was, perhaps, in desperate need of a reminder of life's splendor. Here, Roussel obliges, with languorous woodwinds and brilliant brass exchanging places in the spotlight. A dance-like energy develops, as if, with the coming of spring, one can hardly remain still. Sparkling piccolo, harp, and tambourine prove to be the ideal final touches to Roussel's rich orchestration, just the thing for those fervent celebrations, though the focus tends to lie elsewhere for the calm serenity with which the tone poem begins and ends. Roussel, it seems, was a master of orchestral possibilities.

♪♪♪♪♪

Suk: *Jaro (Spring)*, op. 22a

At the Prague Conservatory, Antonín Dvořák (1841 – 1904) taught composition to countless musically minded students. However, strong evidence suggests that his favorite was Josef Suk (1874 – 1935), who in 1898 would marry his mentor's eldest daughter, Otilka. Three years later, they had a son also named Josef, and their grandson, yet another Josef, would carry the family's musical traditions into the 21st century. The elder Suk was a gifted violinist who gave thousands of concerts with the highly acclaimed Czech Quartet. Additionally, from 1922, he taught composition at the Prague Conservatory, ultimately becoming its director. He was also a talented composer in his own right, with a catalog of works that includes orchestral scores, chamber works, and solo piano pieces. The excellence of those creations proves that Suk's place in music history is not solely due to family connections.

In 1902, a few months after the birth of his namesake, Suk found himself reflecting upon the musical nature of seasonal experiences. He captured those ideas in a pair of solo piano suites, one devoted to spring, the other to summer; alas, he never got around to finishing out the year. Together spanning rather less than half an hour, the two suites were published in 1902 with linked opus numbers: 22a and 22b. By writing them for solo piano, rather than piano and violin, thus including also his own instrument, Suk may have hoped to increase marketability.

Jaro (Spring), op. 22a, has five short movements, all but one bearing descriptive subtitles hinting at the imagery Suk had in mind. The first movement, also labelled *Jaro (Spring)*, opens with alternating passages of exuberant energy and serene beauty: plausibly two sides of the season. Frequently, those themes are ornamented with the extra sparkle of rapid trills and runs. The second movement *Vanek (Breeze)* is light and playful, more nimble than driven, and closing with a long, high-pitched trill. It is altogether more delicate than the movement that precedes it.

With the third movement *V ocekavani (Awaiting)*, it seems to be the return of loved ones that is awaited, tender poignancy and brief good cheer appearing in turn, central pages characterized by a gentle rocking motion. The fourth movement has no subtitle, though its musical spirit implies tears and sorrow, more tender than demonstrative in spirit. Fortunately for those who prefer happy endings, the final movement *V roztouzeni (Longing)* opens gently but builds in eagerness, ultimately leading to rapturous delight. The loved one, it seems, has returned safely, and brightness returns to this spring day.

♪♪♪♪♪

Respighi: *Three Botticelli Pictures* – I. Primavera

In a nation of composers largely devoted to opera and church music, Ottorino Respighi (1879 – 1936) was a markedly atypical Italian. He produced exactly one sacred work and completed only eight thoroughly insignificant operas, including one for a marionette theater. The two fields that absorbed so much of his countrymen's attention simply held little interest for Respighi, who had studied in St. Petersburg, Russia, with Nicolai Rimsky-Korsakov (1844 – 1908). Already internationally revered for the orchestral raptures of *Scheherazade* – and much else – Rimsky encouraged his student's interest in colorful, vibrant scoring. In the process, the young Italian developed a musical language more typical of Russian styles. Still, the Italian sun shone strongly enough to outweigh Slavic melancholy and a Respighi orchestra is one that often shines brilliantly.

Respighi's *Three Botticelli Pictures* (1927) might be considered a response to *Pictures at an Exhibition* (1874) by Rimsky's colleague Modest Mussorgsky (1839 – 1881). One difference is that Mussorgsky had personally known the painter whose works he was expressing in music, whereas Respighi had missed Botticelli by fully four centuries. However, Florence's Uffuzi Gallery displayed many of the Renaissance painter's works, and Respighi chose several canvases to which he would give musical expression.

The first of the suite's three movements is inspired by Botticelli's *Primavera* (*Springtime*), in which a gathering of revealingly dressed forest nymphs dance around the goddess of springtime in a forest glade. A single darker spirit that some interpret as the North Wind intrudes from the right, frightening one of the gathered dancers. However, Respighi having no patience for darkness, concerns himself with springtime frolics.

The movement opens with shimmering tremolo in the strings and boisterously leaping horn motifs – the exact phrases that one finds at the head of this chapter. The addition of trumpets brings further brightness, and exuberant, danceable lines soon develop. Strings and woodwinds prance; brass provide punctuation. Gentler moods appear in the middle pages, with particular attention granted to woodwinds, before that leaping horn phrase reappears, though at first with the oboe before horns take custody once more. The celebratory spirit continues to the close.

The other movements of *Three Botticelli Pictures* evoke *The Adoration of the Magi* and *The Birth of Venus*. The work as a whole was dedicated to American arts patron Elizabeth Sprague Coolidge (1864 – 1953), founder of the Berkshire Festival of Chamber Music in Massachusetts in 1918. Respighi's score is far from a chamber composition, requiring not only an orchestra, but one given further sparkle by the presence of harp, piano, and celeste. However, Mrs. Coolidge's musical tastes were not limited to small groups of players, and Respighi was wise enough to respect her role as a patron of the arts.

Botticelli's *Primavera* also inspired another, somewhat older composer, Claude Debussy (1862 – 1918), whose *Printemps* is featured earlier in this chapter. Both composers agree that Botticelli's canvas is imbued with the bright and vibrant side of spring. The difference lies in how they set about capturing that spirit.

♪♪♪♪♪

Bridge: *Enter Spring*, op. 22

For many observers, spring might be a gentle season of flower buds and baby birds; certainly, some of that quaint imagery is here. However, the phrasing of the title chosen by English composer Frank Bridge (1879 – 1941) suggests not just spring in general, but specifically the arrival of spring, perhaps long-awaited after a particularly cold, northern winter. Surely, that would be an occasion to celebrate, and indeed, Bridge's tone poem *Enter Spring* (1927) tends toward exultation, often quite lush and demonstrative. This vision of spring offers splendor and mystery in turn, further livened with passages of playful spirit. Evoking neither the crystalline spring of Vivaldi nor the playful spring of Botticelli, Bridge has chosen the hearty spring of the English countryside.

Part of the work's glory lies with its orchestral forces. To the usual suspects of woodwinds and brass in pairs, strings, and timpani, Bridge added piccolo, English horn, bass clarinet, contrabassoon, additional French horns, trumpets, and trombones, two harps, celesta, bells and glockenspiel. It is a varied assortment, not only in pitch – from the very highest possibilities to the very lowest – but also in timbre.

For example, tuba and contrabassoon occupy rather similar ranges, though the shading they give to those pitches is markedly different, the tuba generally brighter and the contrabassoon somewhat earthier in flavor. Similarly, though the English horn and the oboe are cousins overlapping in range, the English horn is richer and mellower of voice. In giving prominent solo passages to the English horn, rather than the oboe, Bridge was making a conscious choice. The same selection process lay behind his use of harps, celesta, bells, and glockenspiel: each could play most of the others' music, but none sounds quite the same. Bridge well understood the art of orchestration, and in *Enter Spring*, the listener gets to enjoy the fruits of that craftsmanship.

♫♫♫♫♫

Stravinsky: *The Rite of Spring*

Flower buds and baby birds: not in *The Rite of Spring*. Not even the passions of young lovers. Rather, in what may still, over a century onward, be the most scandalous ballet ever brought before the public, Igor Stravinsky (1882 – 1971) imagined an ancient tribal culture honoring the return of spring with pagan dances and ritual, culminating in human sacrifice. His vision of that scene is rarely pretty, but it is usually compelling.

The Rite of Spring premiered May 29, 1913, at the Théâtre des Champs-Elysées in Paris, being greeted with both boos and cheers, each side equally strident in its views, such that the police were called in to break up the riot. The furor was not solely over Stravinsky's music, which admittedly was sometimes dissonant with savagely erratic rhythms. However, the choreography by Vaclav Nijinsky (1889 – 1950) was often abruptly angular and little akin to classic ballet technique.

The controversy over whether this work was fit for public viewing lasted for weeks and months, newspapers fueling the fire. One Parisian paper, reporting on the riot that had occurred five days earlier, judged this radical score to be "the most dissonant and the most discordant composition yet written. Never was the system and the cult of the wrong note practiced with so much industry, zeal and fury." Later that summer, a London newspaper, after noting that *Rite* "baffles verbal description," valiantly insisted on describing it anyway, finally settling on the word "hideous."

So the conservatives were unimpressed, even as the radicals, as well as those not radical per se, but at least open-minded, were fascinated by what they had seen and heard. *The Rite of Spring* is scarcely a springtime vision like any other, but it is definitively one possible view of spring, because the composer tells us it is. These tribal peoples, he declares, wishing to ensure the fertility of the earth now that spring has returned, dance in celebration of the re-born season, exactly as their traditions dictate.

Act One of *The Rite of Spring* opens with utterly solo bassoon, so lonely as to establish an unsettling mood further amplified by subsequent restless melodic fragments given to other woodwinds. The effect is of a blend of impromptu sounds overlapping with one another, as if each is calling out over the others. The subsequent *Augurs of Spring* section is wildly and dramatically different; the tribal people leap into action, suggested by a pounding pulsation on a single pitch that drives on relentlessly, accents ever shifting to new and unexpected places.

Calm will not be restored until the *Springtime Rounds* scene, in which the village women process gracefully onto the stage, accompanied by long trills and flowing phrases from the woodwinds. Their gliding motion gives way abruptly to a new set of irregularly pounding phrases. Indeed, if one needed to sum up *The Rite of Spring* in a single adjective, "irregular" might be the perfect choice. The act powers to a close with the tribal people in a frenzy of action as the village elder enters to bless the earth with a kiss.

In Act Two, to ensure fertility of the earth, one of the tribe's young women will be singled out for sacrifice, an event to which Stravinsky builds over the course of a quarter hour or so. The act opens with gently pulsing woodwinds, one instrument rising in pitch while the other falls. This same technique is used again as the spotlight shifts to violas.

Once one of the young women is selected, the music explodes into action once more, with pounding rhythms and brilliant splashes of high pitches. A bold horn fanfare suggests the entrance of authority figures to preside over the sacrifice, as the Chosen One dances herself to death. Stravinsky has opted for ever-changing meters, with a new number of beats occurring in nearly every measure. In his autobiography, Stravinsky recalled that, during the rehearsal process, the dancers literally went on strike, declaring that it was impossible for dancing. Orchestral musicians might not call a work stoppage, but certainly the most diligent attention to the conductor is vital to keep it all together.

Short falling phrases and erratically appearing accents drive the music toward its final chord, in fact two of them. A short upward surge for piccolo, flute, violin and viola earns an immediate and emphatic reply from brass, cellos, basses, and percussion. One can imagine that the first of those chords is the victim's final leap, and the second brings her crashing to the ground. *The Rite of Spring* ends with the most definitive of bangs.

♫♫♫♫

Bax: *Spring Fire*

From a composer's point of view, there was perhaps something inherently spring-like about 1913. On May 29 of that year, Stravinsky's *The Rite of Spring* was given its literally riotous premiere in Paris. A few months later, English composer Arnold Bax (1883 – 1953) – not yet having earned his knighthood – completed his own *Spring Fire*.

An orchestral score, in contrast to Stravinsky's ballet, Bax's work was similarly inspired by a vision of pagan celebrations of spring. *Spring Fire* triggered no riots, in part because of unusually bad luck for the composer. Its premiere the following year was cancelled due to the outbreak of war; two subsequent intended premieres fell by the wayside when conductors judged there was insufficient rehearsal time for such a challenging score. *Spring Fire* would not reach the public until after the composer's death. The long delay is especially tragic as Bax's skillful touch with orchestral timbres is never better in evidence than in this vividly shaded score.

Spring Fire is structured in five interconnected movements, intended to be played without pause. For the pre-dawn-flavored opening lines, Bax balances winds and strings with focus shifting from one section to the other in a manner than might suggest the subtle shades of sunrise. Daybreak arrives, and the birdsong-like voices of oboe and flute slowly yield to the splendor of brass, harp, and cymbals. With midday, one finds both exuberance and relaxation, often in close order, with numerous tempo changes, as if the gathered crowds are torn between dancing and dozing.

Bax reserves the most extended passages of languor for a romantic scene, in which a dialog between violin and flute suggests a pair of lovers. If so, these lovers may be closely observed by woodland songbirds, as brief spotlights for various woodwinds are heard. This love scene is gently placid, which cannot be said for the final movement, in which a bevy of wild Grecian spirits explodes into action. Sparkling brilliance becomes the dominant mood with plenty of attention for brass. Bax's *Spring Fire* will not be settling down to embers any time soon.

♫♫♫♫

Milhaud: *Concertino de printemps*, op. 135

Imagine a concerto for soloist and orchestra in which the work in question bears the title of a season of the year: most music lovers will immediately conjure up Vivaldi's *The Four Seasons*, and particularly the one named for spring. Indeed, the *Concertino de printemps* is a violin concerto with spring-like imagery.

However, rather than being the work of Italian Baroque composer Antonio Vivaldi (1678 – 1741), it's by 20th century Frenchman Darius Milhaud (1892 – 1974), and that makes a substantial difference.

Like his Italian predecessor, Milhaud composed four separate concerti, each named for a different season. Unlike those of Vivaldi, Milhaud's do not have accompanying poetry specifying the scenes in question; moreover, his were not published as a set, nor do they use the same solo instrument in each season. He began in 1934 with the *Concertino de printemps* (*Spring Concertino*) for violin and chamber orchestra. Seasons would not return to his compositional imagination until 1950, when *Concertino d'automne* (*Autumn*) for two pianos with octet appeared; the *Concertino d'été* (*Summer*) followed later that same year, scored for solo viola and chamber orchestra. Milhaud's seasonal series came to completion in 1953 with *Concertino d'hiver* (*Winter*), for solo trombone with string ensemble.

One might speculate as to whether Milhaud found something particularly apropos about pairing those selected solo instruments and their chosen seasons; certainly, having begun with spring, and its musical connections to Vivaldi's widely beloved *Spring*, the choice of solo violin seems logical. As for the accompanying chamber orchestra, it includes one flute, one oboe, one clarinet, one bassoon, one horn, one trumpet, strings, timpani, and other lighter percussion. It's quite a different mix than that chosen by Vivaldi, but seems ideal for the so-called Neoclassical styles that enjoyed much popularity in the 1930s when Milhaud was at work.

A single movement work scarcely ten minutes in length, the *Concertino de printemps* begins with chirpily bird-like woodwind phrases. Supporting textures of smooth strings are added, and then the solo violin joins with dance-like, dotted rhythmic features. The mood is generally playful, with only brief passages of tension. Brass and percussion contributions remain subtle, and the trumpet is made to play muted so as to limit the brightness of its voice. The last page of the soloist's music is all perpetual motion, zipping to its conclusion in the highest of spirits. In all, Milhaud's work has many a smile to be shared.

♪♪♪♪

Lili Boulanger: *D'un matin de printemps*
(Of a Morning in Spring)

The name Boulanger is prominent in great music. One finds it amongst the composition professors who taught Aaron Copland (1900 – 1990) and influenced Leonard Bernstein (1918 – 1990), as well as many others of their generations and the next. However, that Boulanger was Nadia (1887 – 1979) for whom teaching music became a passion. The Boulanger who concerns us here is younger sister Lili (1893 – 1918). Even before reaching formal school age, Lili was tagging along with Nadia for classes at the Paris Conservatoire. By the time she reached her teens, Lili had focused her attention upon composition studies and at 19 became the first woman to win the prestigious Prix de Rome composition contest. Alas that, never of robust health, she was already living on borrowed time.

That somber fact is quite absent from her short tone poem *D'un matin de printemps (Of a Morning in Spring)*. Written in her last year, the work shows Lili Boulanger's decline only in the tentative handwriting on the page, not in the level of professional craft that went into the shakily sketched notes. It deftly balances light and effervescent moods with less eager ones that together perfectly capture the intended scene. Her ensemble principally draws upon the colors of strings, woodwinds, and horns, with occasional dashes of more vivid shading from muted trumpets and percussion. In all, it is a work that sparkles with sunlight and shimmers with the chromatic harmonies then so popular with French composers. One can readily lament that Lili would have too little time remaining to pursue a full career.

♪♪♪♪♪

Copland: *Appalachian Spring*

Copland himself imagined it as "Ballet for Martha," and began it at the request of American arts patron Elizabeth Sprague Coolidge, who wanted something for dancer/choreographer Martha Graham (1894 – 1991). The more familiar title by came from Graham, who borrowed it from Hart Crane's poem *The Bridge*. In the stanza of that poem Crane called "The Dance," one finds:

> O Appalachian Spring! I gained the ledge;
> Steep, inaccessible smile that eastward bends
> And northward reaches in that violet wedge
> Of Adirondacks!—

So Copland had nothing to do with the title, nor did Crane; it was all Graham's idea. In later years, the composer was often amused to find fans declaring to him how much his music sounded to them like the Appalachians in spring, when that was never his specific original intention.

According to the scenario that Graham had provided to Copland, a pioneer celebration is underway in a Pennsylvania farmhouse as a young couple is due to be married by a revivalist preacher before a small gathering of friends at the home the couple will soon share. Dawn is ushered in gently with strings and winds. Friends gather, and folk-flavored dancing ensues for the entire group as well as for the couple. As the day concludes and the guests drift away, Copland evokes the regional setting by quoting the old Shaker hymn *Simple Gifts*, widely known in the area and even more widely beloved since Copland brought it to wider attention. That theme is stated in the clarinet, then restated throughout the orchestra in ever varied character. *Appalachian Spring* closes not only in the same quiet mood as that with which it had begun, but also with the same delicate chords, so that sunset and sunrise mirror one another.

Appalachian Spring premiered at the Library of Congress in Washington DC on October 30, 1944. That facility's performance area was more often used for chamber music, and was too small to accommodate an entire orchestra together with dancers. Being aware of this in advance, Copland had scored the piece for double string quartet, along with individual players on bass, flute, clarinet, bassoon, and piano.

Not quite a year later, on October 4, 1945, an orchestral suite of selections from the ballet would be presented in concert by the New York Philharmonic: full orchestra, but no dancers. It is in this form, rather than as a choreographed ballet, that *Appalachian Spring* is most frequently encountered. However, either version serves as a beloved tapestry of moods: thoughtful, eager, restless, grand, and relaxed, as the scenario required. The composer attested he was not thinking of spring itself, but surely the fresh vitality of the new season inhabits every page; perhaps that fact says something about Copland's own personality.

♪♪♪♪♪

Kabalevsky: *Spring (Vesna)*, op. 65

Dmitri Kabalevsky (1904 – 1987) belonged to an awkwardly placed generation of Russian-born composers: too young at the time of the 1917 Revolution to easily escape the new Soviet regime, but unable or unwilling to find a path to the West in later years. So he remained in his homeland, managing to avoid negative attention from authorities, and building a successful career that was largely hidden from Western audiences. Even the most attentive devotee of fine music would be unlikely to have heard much of Kabalevsky's catalog, other than the once ubiquitous *Colas Breugnon* overture or perhaps excerpts from his children's theater piece *The Comedians*. However, both of those compositions date from 1938, at which point Kabalevsky's career was far from over. Many musical delights are to be found in his works of later years.

Kabalevsky's symphonic poem *Spring* dates from 1960. It is, like all symphonic poems, an orchestral response to a not-specifically-musical idea, in this case, to visions of a season that one must imagine would be especially welcome in as northerly a land as Russia; the composer himself had been born in St. Petersburg. It is also, in all but name, a spring waltz built much as Johann Strauss Jr. and the other Viennese masters would have done: a gentle introduction opening the door to subsequent waltz themes.

In Kabalevsky's case, one finds fewer individual waltz themes than the Viennese would have used, but rather continued development and evolution of a central theme, so change is still there, along with a degree of compositional finesse in showing how much can be made of a single melody. Here and there, he sets up winsome dialogs between instruments, especially the woodwinds; at others, he builds to splendid brass-driven passages, as if one has stepped out the door to feel the sunshine full on one's face. All along the way, the strings are present, complete with harp and piano, as well as a bit of percussion, to provide support or rise to prominence, as the moment requires.

Kabalevsky ensures that spring comes to his listeners' ears in all the variety and glory that its character deserves. A fair proportion of fine music from the 1960s is of radically progressive character, breaking abruptly from established traditions: not Kabalevsky's delightful celebration of spring.

♪♪♪♪♪

What other musical options might serve for a seasonal celebration of spring? Given the almost unchallenged popularity of the season, the list would be expansive. Simply amongst the English Pastoralists, one finds:

- Frederick Delius (1862 – 1934): Delius was English, but his *On Hearing the First Cuckoo in Spring* features a main theme borrowed from Norwegian folk music; he and Norwegian master Edvard Grieg were close friends.

- Sir Arnold Bax (1883 – 1953): Bax composed his graceful *Maytime in Sussex* (*Morning Song*) in 1947 for the 21st birthday of she who was then still Princess Elizabeth. Its gently sunny spirit is exactly what one would likely expect of music for the birthday of a young member of the royal family.

- Eric Coates (1886 – 1957): *Springtime Suite* – Specializing in light music suited for pops concerts, Coates wrote his *Springtime Suite* in 1937, attempting to capture morning, noon, and night of a spring day in England.

Looking elsewhere in Europe:

- Edvard Grieg (1842 – 1908): *Last Spring* (*Våren*), the second of his *Elegiac Pieces*, opus 34, is a wistful recollection of past delights.

- Gustav Mahler (1860 – 1911): His serene *Blumine* was originally intended to be part of his Symphony no. 1, then extracted from that work; Mahler himself suggested that it was meant to represent flowers.

For a more exotic approach to the season:

- Guanren Gu (b. 1942): *Spring Suite* – Scored for Chinese folk orchestra, though having the breadth and variety of a Western orchestral suite, *Spring Suite* is, by turns, spirited, restful, and often quite beautiful.

Chapter Four: Summer

Song-like or dance-like? One way or the other, the notes above are those of the oboe in cheerful demeanor early in the third movement of Beethoven's Symphony no. 6. The composer himself declared it to be evocative of a collection of happy villagers and the spirit of the music surely implies some boisterous souls gathered at the village tavern, a few (or more than a few) bottles being passed around, songs soon to follow.

Beethoven labelled the symphony "Pastoral," meaning a countryside scene. He never said it was specifically summer; however, the descriptive headings of the movements, combined with the fact that he'd written it largely while on summer holiday in a village outside Vienna, suggests that summer scenes were uppermost in his mind.

The other works featured here are all determinedly summery in inspiration, though representing many different types of summers. The Mediterranean coast, the English countryside, Irish folk songs, Swedish lakes, New England seascapes, the American Midwest, even elegant summer soirées all have their place, thanks to vibrant music intended to bring it home to listeners and performers alike.

♪♪♪♪

Beethoven: Symphony no. 6 in F, op. 68, "Pastoral"

For a man who grew up in a city of moderate size and spent the bulk of his career in one of Europe's largest, Ludwig van Beethoven (1770 – 1827) was not, at heart, a man of urban tastes. Friends and neighbors alike recalled him stalking down streets lost in his own thoughts, ignoring everyone around him, at his ease only at the piano or in the countryside, where he could take long, solitary walks. Even once his hearing failed when he was in his mid-30s, depriving him of the sounds of nature, Beethoven still reveled in the experience of being immersed in the countryside. Those moods are abundantly displayed in his Symphony no. 6.

Early sketches for this symphony date from 1802, though work largely occurred in the summers of 1807 and 1808, which Beethoven spent in the village of Heiligenstadt. It was a rural retreat, a green escape from city heat, and Beethoven would likely be dismayed to know that now, the place has been swallowed up by Vienna. In Heiligenstadt, his mind was at rest, and he was able to complete not only this work, but also the Symphony no. 5 in c minor and three chamber works. So many new compositions came from his desk at this time that he was uncertain which symphony was finished first. Initially, Beethoven cataloged the *Pastoral Symphony* as number five and the c-minor Symphony as number six. The numbering was only reversed at publication.

Both symphonies premiered December 22, 1808, on a massive, four-hour concert of Beethoven premieres. For some audiences, hearing the Symphony no. 6 will always bring to mind the adventures of centaurs and other mythological creatures, as that was what Disney's animators imagined for the first *Fantasia* film. As for Beethoven's own vision, he helpfully provided descriptive subtitles for each movement.

The first, *Awakening of Cheerful Feelings on Arriving in the Country (Erwachen heiterer Empfindungen bei der Ankunft auf dem Lande)*, sets an idyllic mood. Dotted rhythms with a sort of skipping rhythm occur throughout this movement, suggestive of children at play. The second movement is *Scene by the Brook (Szene am Bach)*, in this case, a gentle brook frequented by quails, cuckoos, and nightingales, whose voices are evoked by the woodwinds: oboe, clarinet, and flute respectively. In the original score, Beethoven noted each bird's name beside the specific phrases meant to represent them. Both of those movements give prominence to woodwinds and strings, with brass and percussion largely subdued.

By contrast, the third movement has human inspiration, with a *Merry Gathering of the Country Folk (Lustiges Zusammensein der Landleute)*. Strings swirl and the oboe warbles, its opening phrase standing at the head of this chapter; the clarinet laughs, and the horns sing out exuberantly. The music progresses in an ebullient, if somewhat wandering, fashion, as if portraying a band of barely able, or barely sober, village musicians. Phrases are often interrupted and sudden declarations break into the melodic flow.

Like all merry-making, this party, too, comes to an end, in this case, with a change in the weather, as the fourth movement, *Thunderstorm* (*Gewitter*), arrives with no pause to separate the two movements. The storm rages away throughout the orchestra, though especially with full brass and percussion, which finally come out of the shadows. The action gradually subsides with a seamless transition into the beginning of the fifth movement, *Shepherd's Song* (*Hirtengesang*) – *Happy, Thankful Feelings after the Storm* (*Frohe und dankbare Gefühle nach dem Sturm*). Here, Beethoven gives first to the clarinet, and then the horn, his *Shepherd's Song*, which gradually grows to become a serene and rapturous melody, the one that he wishes to leave in his listeners' ears as the symphony ends.

So after much activity and a substantial amount of drama, Beethoven's Symphony no. 6 ends on a tranquil note. Perhaps dusk has fallen on Heiligenstadt, and the composer, relaxing on a summer evening far from the heat of the city, is resting from his labors.

♪♪♪♪

Glinka: Spanish Overture no. 2 –
  Summer Night in Madrid

Predating Tchaikovsky by nearly forty years, Mikhail Glinka (1804 – 1857) was the first important Russian composer to attempt to give his music a Russian flavor, quoting his nation's folk music. So whence a "Spanish Overture"? Glinka's sensitivity to his own culture's musical roots left him open to discoveries relating to other cultures, and no European folk culture was more deeply fascinating to other nations than that of Spain.

Remember that *Carmen*'s bullfighter was imagined by a Frenchman. Dozens of other cases of non-Spaniards finding musical inspiration in Spain might be cited, and one of these is Glinka's Spanish Overture no. 2 (1851)

The subtitle *Summer Night in Madrid* informs us that, in addition to a Spanish flavor, one will also find a nocturnal mood. Admittedly, night-time in Spain can be many things, from mysterious to alluring to vibrant. As the overture begins, Glinka seems to imagine a tenderly moonlit serenade, with woodwinds taking turns in the spotlight over supporting textures of strings. Before long, however, a greater sense of dance-like motion begins, complete with castanets – which one might suppose were hard to come by in Russia in 1851. Various musical images appear, some brilliant with brass and crashing cymbals, others more thoughtful in character. In all, *Summer Night in Madrid* is replete with vibrant color and varied energy, vividly evoking a Spanish mood, though it was first put onto paper a thousand miles from Madrid.

♪♪♪♪♪

Mendelssohn: *Fantasia on The Last Rose of Summer*, op. 15

In the view of Romantic composers of the 19th century, a "fantasia" was a musical flight of fancy in which the composer followed personal expressive ideas without too much attention to formal structure. When Felix Mendelssohn (1809 – 1847) composed this particular solo piano fantasia in 1827, he was only eighteen, but already well experienced in the craft of composition.

He'd been taking private lessons in the field since boyhood, and was also a gifted pianist well able to imagine what would work on the keyboard. Had he wished, he could have taken this same melody and made of it a complicated fugue; however, he apparently judged that the theme would be best served by a less constraining structure.

The melody itself is an old Irish folk song to which, in 1805, the Irish poet Thomas Moore (1779 – 1852) gave new words, making of it a heartfelt ode to a fading season. Mendelssohn was German, not Irish, but Moore's song was widely published and internationally beloved, long before German composer Friedrich von Flotow (1812 – 1883) further popularized it in his opera *Martha* (1847). For young Mendelssohn, *The Last Rose of Summer* was a perfect trigger for his musical imagination.

Mendelssohn begins with a brief and winsome introduction before stating the theme itself in straight-forward fashion. What follows is, in general terms, a set of variations upon the theme, though with more side roads and less strict organization than variations usually involved. Sometimes, the theme is sweet, at others tearful, and often restless diversions break up the musical action in an almost Beethovenian fashion. As the closing pages approach, Mendelssohn restates the theme slowly and elegantly, though with altered rhythms, and at last allows his fantasia to drift to its final chords. This "last rose," it seems, is quietly fading at the close of the season

♪♪♪♪♪

Ernst: Etude no. 6 in G from 6 Polyphonic Studies –
   Die letzte Rose (*The Last Rose*)

Why should pianists have all the fun with solo showpieces on hit tunes? Such seems to have been the view of Moravian violinist/composer Heinrich Wilhelm Ernst (1814 – 1865). Considered in his time to be nearly the equal of Nicolò Paganini (1782 – 1840), Ernst learned by ear a few of the Italian virtuoso's unpublished works; then, Ernst wrote some of his own, including works for solo violin and orchestra, chamber pieces for violin and piano, and a great many utterly solo pieces. Ernst convincingly proved that a violinist can command attention even when alone on the stage.

The last of Ernst's 6 Polyphonic Studies follows a popular trend of the time to craft variations upon familiar opera arias or folk songs. In this case, the central theme is both, *The Last Rose of Summer* having transcended its folk roots to appear prominently in the opera *Martha*. Using a recognizable melody as basis for a set of variations allowed listeners to readily follow the theme even as it undergoes musical evolution.

Ernst begins with a gentle introduction liberally decorated with trills leading into the theme itself. The first variation is a sweet lament, as if consciously recalling that there will be no more roses this year. Subsequent variations exhibit quicker and quicker passagework, at times further ornamented with pizzicato passages, double-stops, and formidable leaps from one note to the next.

The complexity is astonishing, though, after all, this etude is one or Ernst's "Polyphonic Studies," so one should expect a high degree of intricacy. That's what the term "polyphonic" suggests: several melodic lines juxtaposed against each other simultaneously. Etudes are often intended as practice pieces, but here, it would have to be for players of the very highest order.

♪♪♪♪

Waldteufel: *Soirée d'eté*, op. 188 – concert waltz

Despite his Germanic family name, Emil Waldteufel (1837 – 1915) was thoroughly French, born in Strasbourg, in that border region near the Rhine over which the two nations have so frequently quarreled. His father, professor of music at that city's conservatory, recognized the boy's interests and gave him early encouragement, even moving the whole family to Paris when Emil was eleven for studies at the more prestigious Paris Conservatoire.

Financial difficulties caused young Waldteufel to leave the Conservatoire before graduation. However, he'd already learned enough to launch a career as piano teacher and accompanist, and to find work testing new pianos at the factory, even earning an appointment as court pianist for French Empress Eugenie. Favor for Waldteufel's compositions would follow, particularly in ballroom settings, for which he composed about 250 works, largely though not exclusively waltzes. He would be Paris' answer to Vienna's Johann Strauss Jr. (1825 – 1899).

Les Patineurs, op. 183 (*The Skater's Waltz*) of 1882 is handily the most famed of the many hundreds of items in Waldteufel's catalog; as one likely presumes those skaters to be taking to the ice, not the roller rink, it shall appear with other wintery selections in Chapter Eight. However, *Soirée d'ete*, op. 188 (*Summer Soirée*), dating from the following year, shares many of the same delightful features and deserves its time in center stage.

Waldteufel begins with a peaceful introduction, not yet in waltz-time. Had anyone in the ballroom not managed to notice that the music had begun and dancing would soon follow, that person would not long remain inattentive, especially as Waldteufel closes the introduction closes with an outspoken burst of brass and a crash of cymbals and snare drum.

A brilliant, fanfare-like transition leads into the waltz themes themselves. That's "themes" plural: Waldteufel offers several in turn, some graceful, some buoyant, some boldly expressive. Strauss' concert waltzes do the same thing, so perhaps Waldteufel imagined his audience would expect it, too. Just as likely, he would have realized that having several different waltz themes of contrasting character allows for more variety of effect, as well as more opportunity for the composer to showcase his creative imagination. These were, after all, not just for the ballroom, but also intricate enough to be worthy of the concert hall.

♪♪♪♪♪

Humperdinck: *Moorish Rhapsody* –
   Tarifa: Elegy at Summer

Long before an English pop singer purloined his name, the original Engelbert Humperdinck (1854 – 1921) was an influential figure in fine music. The German composer was only 25 when Richard Wagner (1813 – 1883) brought the young man to serve as his assistant in Bayreuth. Humperdinck was kept busy copying out Wagner's opera manuscripts to prepare them for performance and publication: one can scarcely imagine a more thorough introduction to Wagnerian style composition practices. In later years, Wagner's widow Cosima engaged Humperdinck to teach composition to her son Siegfried Wagner (1869 – 1930). When his Wagnerian employment was over, Humperdinck would train Kurt Weill (1900 – 1950).

Humperdinck also pursued his own composing career, producing stage works (most famously *Hansel und Gretel* of 1893), choral pieces, and songs, though also chamber music and orchestral pieces. Amongst this last category is his *Moorish Rhapsody*, composed in 1898 and published the following year. Morocco and Moorish Spain might seem an unlikely choice of inspiration for a composer grounded in Wagnerian-style German nationalism. However, Humperdinck had visited the region after his time of Wagnerian service ended, and apparently the region's moods remained in his heart. Moreover, by the late 19th century, many composers began to reflect their personal travels in musical terms.

Like Rimsky-Korsakov's famed *Scheherazade*, *Moorish Rhapsody* is a symphonic suite of several movements giving musical expression to perceptions of a Middle Eastern culture. Humperdinck sets the first of three movements in the Moorish-influenced far south of Spain, just across from Morocco in Tarifa for what he tells his listeners will be an "elegy at summer." This is not an elegy <u>for</u> summer; he is not lamenting the season's passing, but simply having rather somber reflections during the time of summer. Humperdinck's *Tarifa* is a largely restful recollection of the scene there not far from Gibraltar.

Humperdinck begins with smooth string textures to which he adds an exotically-flavored oboe and violin dialog. Smoothly, textures swell and subside before livelier woodwind phrases appear in juxtaposition to more reserved string lines. Humperdinck mixes and varies these ideas, though he'll close largely as he had begun: with oboe and violin in peaceable mood.

It seems that summer at Tarifa is a time to indulge in languor. Livelier moods are withheld until the following two not-specifically summery movements: *Tanger: A Night in a Moorish Coffee House* and *Tetuan: A Night in the Desert*. In all, Humperdinck's *Moorish Rhapsody* is a colorful immersion in a vibrant culture quite different from the composer's own. His *Hansel und Gretel* may be more deeply rooted in Humperdinck's own homeland, but with the *Moorish Rhapsody*, his imagination had room to roam.

♪♪♪♪♪

Delius: *Summer Night on the River*

Frederick Delius (1862 – 1934) was a man of divergent interests. How else could an English composer of German descent have produced pieces titled *Florida, Hiawatha, Hassan,* and *Paris,* as well as an assortment of songs to Norwegian texts? Musical inspiration came to Delius not only in travel, but also in great literature, leading to settings of verses by Tennyson, Nietzsche, Ibsen, and Whitman. He wrote ballets and operas, concertos, quartets and sonatas, dozens of songs, and, though no symphonies, many short orchestral works. With such a prodigious output, it is unfortunate that Delius' career has come to be represented by only a few compositions, often of rather Impressionistic demeanor.

In October of 1913, Delius published two short pieces for small orchestra, each with its own individual title. *On Hearing the First Cuckoo in Spring* and *Summer Night on the River* are the epitome of English watercolors in music. Here, rather than sudden contrasts, one finds a sensuous blend of sonic colors, like a reminiscence of the English countryside before the intrusion of harsh reality with World War I. *Summer Night* is gently shaded in grays and lilacs: this river is, apparently, not London's mighty Thames, but rather by a quiet stream beside which one might lounge with a picnic and a book. Woodwinds pulse softly, horns provide further color, and strings – particularly viola – rise to prominence when a greater motion is required. Always, it remains music of a mild-mannered sojourn with nothing urgent on the agenda. Sit back and enjoy the evening!

♪♪♪♪♪

Peterson-Berger: *Frösöblomster* (*Blossoms of Frösö*)

In terms of late 19th century Scandinavian composers, one most frequently hears of Norway's Edvard Grieg (1843 – 1907), Finland's Jan Sibelius (1865 – 1957), or perhaps Denmark's Carl Nielsen (1865 – 1931). Sweden, standing prominently in the center of the region, comes less readily to mind. Consider, then, Wilhelm Peterson-Berger (1867 – 1942). Like his better-known colleagues, Peterson-Berger wrote in a style that steps slightly beyond trends of the early 19th century while not yet testing the progressive waters of the early 20th century. His works remind one that Mendelssohn is long gone without yet threatening one with suggestions of Schoenberg.

Peterson-Berger was born in a community midway along Sweden's extensive coast. His mother was a good amateur pianist, a fact that may have influenced Peterson-Berger to devote the bulk of his time for composition (he was also music reviewer for Sweden's leading newspaper) to producing short, solo piano pieces. They're the sort of thing that Grieg was then calling "lyric pieces;" the Germans, by contrast, favored the term "character pieces," each individual piece setting out to capture a different mood or character.

Peterson-Berger's three collections of *Frösöblomster* (*Blossoms of Frösö*) take their name from an island in Lake Storsjön in Sweden's central mountains. It is a lovely pastoral place where he maintained a vacation home which would gradually become his permanent residence. If one judges by the music, Frösö is a locale of which the composer had only good feelings, and anyone wishing to imagine spending a summer amidst beautiful scenery can capture much of that vision in these little pieces.

Five of the eight pieces in Book One of *Frösöblomster* provide a delightful summer excursion in music. The first, *Rentrée (Return)*, juxtaposes the effusive joy of returning to a beloved place with gentler passages that may suggest anticipation of a quiet evening on the terrace. *Sommarsäng (Summer Song)*, the second piece is, by contrast, more generally serene, though with fuller expression in places, as if the singer is becoming more and more involved in the song.

Third comes *Lawn Tennis*, with many scampering sixteenth notes and rarely a break in the action. Add the fourth piece, *Til Rosorna (For the Roses)*, and one will have moods of sweet tenderness, with only brief effusive passages: perhaps the person viewing the roses has just discovered a new bud worthy of excitement. The last of the eight Book One pieces, *Fäsning (Greeting)* at first suggests regret, one supposes at leaving someone or something behind. Increasingly, however, there is excitement, perhaps at the notion of impending return, and then a gentle close as one relaxes into the moment. One could scarcely imagine a more positive course of events for a summer excursion, and one hopes that, for Peterson-Berger, it was drawn from life.

♫♫♫♫♫

Alfvén: *Midsommarvaka*, op. 19 (*Midsummer Vigil*)

He was not really a one-hit wonder, but modern audiences may well be under the impression that Swedish composer Hugo Alfvén (1872 – 1960) wrote just a single composition, for only one remains in the active repertoire. Yet Alfvén was a busy and prolific man of music. Born in Stockholm, Alfvén was attending that city's conservatory by his mid-teens, studying violin, composition, and even painting. His first professional employment was as a violinist in the city's opera orchestra, but by 1904 he had taken up conducting, particularly choruses, with which he would be occupied until nearly the end of his life.

Alfvén's catalog includes much choral music and songs, chamber music, five full symphonies, several ballets, sets of incidental music for plays, film scores, and an assortment of short orchestral tone poems. Often, he drew inspiration from the history and culture of Sweden, and though language difficulties may make the vocal pieces seem remote to Western audiences, that perceived handicap has not impacted the instrumental works. Even so, of all those works, only the ebullient and beloved *Midsommarvaka* (*Midsummer Vigil*) has maintained an international audience.

Midsommarvaka (1903) is a tone poem, that is, a single movement work having a story to tell or a scene to paint purely with instruments: no singers, no dancers, no narrators. One also hears the term "program music," though program music might also have several movements.

Alfvén gave *Midsommarvaka* the subtitle Swedish Rhapsody no. 1; he would later compose the Swedish Rhapsodies no. 2, *Uppsala*, op. 24, and no. 3, *Dalarhapsodie*, op. 27. In addition to being a vision of Nordic summer, *Midsommarvaka* also contains fragments of folk music suggestive of a country wedding, adding hints of plot content, all shaded in rich and colorful fashion with deft use of instrumental timbres for varied effect. That Alfvén's orchestra includes piccolo, English horn, E-flat clarinet, bass clarinet, both tenor and bass trombones, and two harps, along with more usual choices, gives the composer much material with which to work.

Midsommarvaka begins with light, dance-like rhythms launched by clarinet which soon shares that idea around the ensemble. Given the sense of increasing energy, one might suppose wedding guests are beginning to gather for festivities. The music has all the exuberance of a village celebration, and though the focus is often upon woodwinds and strings, as would be common in folk music, Alfvén does not neglect the brass and percussion.

A gentle, nocturne-like passage appears midway, perhaps suggesting that a couple has slipped away from the throng for a quiet interlude. Here, an English horn solo is accompanied by pizzicato string reminders of fragments from the opening clarinet theme. Alfvén builds up to a lush, romantic mood before the ebullience returns. After much shifting of focus from strings to brass to woodwinds, Alfvén settles again into a boisterous mood that gallops into the final bars.

Suk: *A Summer's Tale, op. 29 (Pohádka Téka)*

Czech composer Josef Suk (1874 – 1935) is sometimes remembered as more as student and son-in-law of his nation's greatest musical voice, Antonín Dvořák (1841 – 1904) than as a creative artist with his own voice. However, Suk was also a world-class violinist, teacher, and representative of a new generation. In Suk's care, Czech music stepped into the 20th century, adopting somewhat more progressive musical coloring. Far from a wild modernist, he was someone who thought it was time to begin experimenting with a wider palette of tonal shades. That tendency is especially vividly clear in Suk's grand orchestral works, such as *A Summer's Tale*.

Premiering in Prague early in 1909, *A Summer's Tale* is an ambitious orchestral tone poem of the sort that Bavarian-born Richard Strauss (1864 – 1949) was writing. Using only instruments – if rather a lot of them – let a story be told or scene painted by orchestral means. In the case of Suk's work, this orchestra would have its brass section expanded to include six French horns, along with trumpets, trombones, and tuba, and its woodwind section also welcoming piccolo, English horn, bass clarinet, and contrabassoon, as well as the usual pairs of flutes, oboes, clarinets, and bassoons. Suk also requires two harps, celesta, triangle, crash cymbals, and tam-tam, so there is quite a bit more here than his mentor Dvořák would have required. A new generation required new tools, and Suk had come to realize exactly what could be achieved with those tools, especially when one had an ambitious idea to cast in orchestral form.

The movement headings found in *A Summer's Tale* (five movements in all) suggest a kind of inner quest for an unnamed protagonist, perhaps seeking solace in the Bohemian countryside amidst the goodness of nature and the common people. Certainly, the expansive first movement *Voices of Life and Consolation* opens soberly, its sustained string lines and peaceful woodwind shading then abruptly riven by fearsome brass and percussion. Sweet, reflective spotlights for woodwinds reappear, though the high drama of the brass statements are never long absent. About the time that hope starts to become more enduring, an exquisite violin solo appears. These peaceable ideas are long uninterrupted, but calm will eventually win through to lead the movement to its close.

This relaxed demeanor also serves to open the second movement *Midday*. Suk uses tender woodwinds and long French horn tones set against strings to paint a restfully sunlit scene. Fullness increases with brief and determined outbursts, though the noon-time mood is generally one of lounging in the sun – or just out of the heat in the shade.

The third movement *Intermezzo: Blind Musicians* offers folksy string rhythms and a pair of English horns engaged in a plaintive sort of dialog, representing those imagined folk musicians, perhaps visiting over a stein of beer in the village pub. After several minutes, this conversation is handed to violin and viola, though the double reeds will soon be back in the center of activity. Peaceable sounds from the larger string ensemble will bring the movement to its close.

With the fourth movement, there are no chats over drinks, but plenty of demonic energy, as Suk tells us he is imagining a scene *In the Power of Phantoms*. Haunting string tremolos and wispy phrases from woodwinds set a dimly lit scene before a bass clarinet spotlight (rare in any repertoire) leads to restless danceable rhythms. These phantoms are not drifting eerily in the moonlight, but zipping here and there, not necessarily on good-hearted missions. Outbursts of brass and percussion underscore the anxious mood, and, despite brief passages of quiet, the movement is largely characterized by almost frenzied action.

The fifth movement of *A Summer's Tale*, bearing the simple subtitle *Night*, brings woodwinds back into a gentle spotlight. Some anxious passages develop, as if our protagonist fears this evening scene is not all he might wish. However, richer, fuller pages begin to emerge from the anxiety, eventually leading to gentle romance with various woodwinds and string taking briefly to the spotlight. Suk restates themes from the previous movements, as if summing up this personal journey by reminding his listeners where the adventure has taken us. *A Summer's Tale* gradually ends in a restful settling into its final chords. The sun seems to have set, and if our protagonist had, indeed, been seeking solace, the music suggests he found it. Perhaps it is Suk himself, whose wife had died all too young of a heart condition. Suk himself, his music, his memories of her, and his nurturing of their young son, endured.

♪♪♪♪♪

Kodály: *Summer Evening (Nyari este)*

Culturally speaking, Zoltán Kodály (1882 – 1967) was Hungarian, though he was past thirty before that became political reality. Hungary had long ago been swallowed up by the mighty Austrian Empire, a forced marriage that continued until the end of World War I. Yet Kodály was already devoted to an appreciation of Hungarian culture. While in graduate school, he and his classmate Béla Bartók (1881 – 1945) travelled throughout Hungarian regions with an Edison recording machine, collecting folk songs and dances that they analyzed to define its rhythms and harmonies so as to reflect that spirit in their own works.

Summer Evening (Nyari este) arose from that research. Kodály's orchestra of strings, woodwinds, and French horns, the usual forces supplemented by English horn, is more inclined to subtle tone colors than to high drama. Perhaps he thought the timbre of the English horn was particularly folk-like, since he begins with its mellow voice and often returns to it. At times, those English horn spotlights pass to elsewhere in the orchestra, as if a folk singer's song were being echoed back to him by others across a meadow.

Summer Evening is a tone poem containing elements of folk dance. At times, the dance-like energy absents itself in favor of a more generalized outdoorsy mood, providing a tidy opportunity for performers and listeners alike to revel in the varied colors that a fine craftsman can draw forth from an orchestra of only moderate size.

Summer Evening (Nyári este) was Kodály's graduation project from the Liszt Academy, where it premiered October 22, 1906, exactly 95 years after the birth of Franz Liszt (1811 – 1886), the most renowned of all Hungarian-born composers. A quarter century later, Kodály revised it for a performance in New York City on April 3, 1930. In the second version, details are refined and smoothed, but the essential spirit remains as it was: dancing and relaxing, playfulness and passion in fairly equal portions. What more could one ask of a summer evening?

♪♪♪♪♪

Webern: *Im Sommerwind*

Anton Webern (1883 – 1945) was one of the stars of early 20th century modernism, using all the cutting edge techniques of the day and even inventing more of his own. All of that is absent from *Im Sommerwind* (*In the Summer Wind*), a rapturous orchestral tone poem completed in 1904. Here, young Webern takes as role model not radical modernists, but rather the only slightly progressive Richard Strauss (1864 – 1949): testing new waters without stirring up tempests.

At the time, Webern had not yet begun studying with Arnold Schoenberg (1874 – 1951), from whom Webern learned many of his radical ideas. *Im Sommerwind* is more an attempt to master existing styles than to step out on his own. As such, it allows one to explore Webern's music without needing a grasp of pointillism or dodecaphonic techniques, both of which dominate his later music but neither idea plays a role here.

Its title deriving from the work of German writer Bruno Wille, *Im Sommerwind*, was composed on a summer holiday at Webern's family's vacation home amidst the lakes, forests, and hills of Austria's Carinthia. The music is marvelously evocative of such a setting, its serene lines and languid moods ideal for lingering in a pretty place with a nice view. Although strings are dominant, there are also woodwinds, brass, and percussion, adding up to the largest orchestra that Webern ever used in a composition. Rich, rapturous passages arise from time to time, but the most frequent mood is one of a restful idyll. Musically, it is more of a summer breeze than a summer wind.

About a quarter hour in length, *Im Sommerwind* is yet the longest single movement Webern ever composed. He would eventually develop a reputation as a miniaturist: saying a great deal in very short fragments of music. *Im Sommerwind* was sufficiently different from the direction in which Webern's style developed that he never published it; the work only came to print in the 1960s, well after its composer's death.

♫♫♫♫♫

Clarke: *Midsummer Moon*

Born in England to an American father and a German mother, Rebecca Clarke (1886 – 1979) was a composer and violist at a time when women were scarcely welcomed on stage, except as singers or pianists. Her gender ought not have been an issue, but in her generation, the fact that she had studied at the Royal

Conservatory of Music carried very little weight outside her native land. When her Viola Sonata won second prize in a composition competition at the Berkshire Festival of Chamber Music in Massachusetts in 1919, no one was more surprised by the composer's gender than those judges who had voted for the piece without knowing who'd written it.

Clarke wrote more chamber music than orchestral scores, though not from lack of ambition or lack of familiarity with larger forms. Her first professional position in music was as a member of the Queen's Hall Orchestra. Rather, a chamber work written for friends was more likely to obtain an immediate audience than a score requiring a full orchestra. Moreover, as Clarke had an active performing career as a violist, she had plenty of foreknowledge of upcoming recitals by friends who might need something extra for their programs. Thus, the genesis of her *Midsummer Moon*, a short work for violin and piano. She wrote it for her colleague, violinist Adila Fachiri, who premiered it May 12, 1924 in London.

Almost impressionistic in its first pages, *Midsummer Moon* begins with fluttery lines for both players, as if this moonlight were beaming upon a nightingale. The music rises and falls with flowing arpeggios before a sequence of more dramatic melodies begins to appear. Strength and sweetness are both explored, making *Midsummer Moon* more varied in character than some of Clarke's contemporaries would have expected of a showpiece by an Englishwoman not yet forty years of age. It is not just drawing room music: it is music of vivid imagination.

♪♪♪♪

Prokofiev: *Summer Day*, op. 65b

From the earliest years of his career, Sergei Prokofiev (1891 – 1953) knew how to make a splash. A double-major in composition and piano performance, for his graduation exercise, he played his own Concerto no. 1; his classmates played concerti by Beethoven and Company. Some of the judges were shocked, but all admitted that here was a young man with a future.

Certainly, that kind of self-confidence might lead a composer to grandiloquent musical statements and Prokofiev is, after all, the man who composed an opera on Tolstoy's epic novel *War and Peace*. However, Prokofiev could also think on more intimate scales, particularly when younger ears were the target. In 1936, that resulted in *Peter and the Wolf*, composed for a Moscow children's theater, having his own two young sons in mind. In 1935, it was *Music for Children,* op. 65, a twelve movement suite for solo piano. The pieces were simple enough that a good young pianist might learn them, and even a non-pianist could enjoy hearing them.

In 1941, Prokofiev returned to that score. War was in progress and the German army was at Russia's door. With full orchestra performances becoming difficult to arrange, Prokofiev thought he'd rework some of the movements of his *Music for Children* in a version for chamber orchestra. Selecting seven of the original twelve, and setting them in a new order, he crafted orchestrations that provide even greater color and definition to the original thematic material. By this time, Prokofiev's opus numbers were approaching 100, a momentous number that, in 1944, would go to his Symphony no. 5. Yet rather than giving this new score a current opus number, he reused the original, adding a letter to indicate that the new creation was somewhat different from the other.

Giving the new suite the title *Summer Day*, Prokofiev gave each movement a descriptive title, guiding listeners in what may be happening in the summer day of this young protagonist. Waking, games, a waltz, regret for some small offence, and lastly the quiet of the evening follow in turn. For the last of these, according to Prokofiev's sub-title, the moon sails over the meadows. Most familiar of all the movements stands sixth of seven, a jaunty march with which the child recovers from his repentance. In all, it is a charming little score, and may have seemed a fine tonic to the composer, given the dark days of 1941 when he composed it.

♫♫♫♫♫

Honegger: *Pastorale d'ete (Summer Pastorale)*

Whether he was Swiss or French is something a matter of interpretation, but officially, Arthur Honegger (1892 – 1955) was Swiss, a fact he never troubled himself to alter. His parents were Swiss, and he studied music at the Zurich Conservatory; however, he'd been born in Le Havre, France, where his father's business had brought the family; the elder Honegger worked in the coffee trade. Advanced studies at the Paris Conservatoire followed, and it was in that city that Honegger spent much of his career. Nonetheless, Switzerland never forgot that Honegger had been one of their own, and for a time, his image appeared on the Swiss twenty franc bank note.

Honegger still believed in using old ideas, but giving them new colors of expression, something that one can sense in hearing his music. Honegger's major works include five symphonies, short orchestra pieces, often of programmatic content, many operas and ballets, mostly for the Paris stage, chamber music and songs, and dozens of film scores, most prominently the 1927 epic *Napoleon*. He was the first prominent orchestral composer to bother much with music for the screen, a field that fascinated him for the first thirty years of grand cinema's existence. Long before Aaron Copland (1900 – 1990) delved into film music, let alone John Williams (b. 1932), Honegger proved that a serious composer can be equally serious in other venues.

One of Honegger's most lyrical scores is the 1920 tone poem *Pastorale d'ete (Summer Pastorale)*. It is less a sequence of specific summer events than a general sense of an occasion. Honegger's chosen title indicates the setting, and the music adds the further thought that it might be morning, a sort of dawn awakening with gentle low strings soon joined by relaxed French horn. The music quite ignores the notion of summer storms or even oppressive heat, both of which had caught Vivaldi's attention. Rather, Honegger has composed music for an unhurried breakfast in the garden, with someone else to do the washing up. It is sleepily rhapsodic, filled with long, lyrical string lines, bird-like woodwind phrases and French horns often sounding as if from very far away. Rather fuller and more varied in shading that was common in standard Impressionism, *Pastorale d'ete* is yet reminiscent of *Daphnis and Chloe* by Maurice Ravel (1875 – 1937). If one comes away wanting to hear more of Honegger, try his Symphony no. 4, "Basel Delights," having many of the same moods on a larger scale.

♪♪♪♪

Piston: *Three New England Sketches* –
    II. Summer Evening

Born in Rockland, Maine, Walter Piston (1894 – 1976) was a grandson of Italian immigrants, whose name had been Pistone. Walter was only ten when the family moved from small town Maine to cosmopolitan Boston, where the youth would graduate from the Mechanic Arts High School. Drafting was his field; however, he earned pocket change playing piano and violin in dance bands and theater orchestras, and soon, music would supplant technical work. Nonetheless, Piston's skills with a pencil paid off in his pristine manuscripts and in his illustrations for his later music textbooks.

Piston retained close connections with Boston. His orchestral scores often premiered with the Boston Symphony, and from 1926 through 1960, he served on the music faculty at Harvard. There, he numbered amongst his students the man who would become the most influential musical figure in the nation, Leonard Bernstein (1918 – 1990).

The *Three New England Sketches* was commissioned by the Worcester County Musical Association in Massachusetts. The premiere, however, was given by the Detroit Symphony with conductor Paul Paray October 23, 1959. Though not strictly a symphony in name or form, it uses symphonic techniques of melodic manipulation and development to increase musical interest and variety.

Each of the three movements bears a descriptive subtitle, though the composer was quick to point out that he had no specific inspirations; rather, it was a case of "chance impressions of realism." Any further visual details are left to the listener's imagination.

The gentle first movement *Seaside* suggests the even-tempered ebb and flow of the waves; the imposing final movement *Mountains* seems more reflective of Piston's native Maine than of Massachusetts, where he spent so many years. Between those two points is the second movement *Summer Evening*. Smooth low strings and French horns provide a backdrop to tremolo effects from upper strings and trills from woodwinds that seem to flutter like bird's or insect's wings. At the head of the page, Piston placed the descriptive term *Delicato* to hint to performers the mood he had in mind.

Summer Evening is brief, scarcely half the length its companion movements. However, perhaps Piston was mindful that summer evenings tend to be short.

♪♪♪♪♪

Hanson: *Bold Island Suite* – II. *Summer Seascape*

Composer/conductor Howard Hanson (1896 – 1981) was handily the most famed of all native sons of Wahoo, Nebraska. Having discovered his love of and skills for music in high school, he went on to study at Northwestern University in Chicago, then taught in Seattle, and ultimately spent decades at the helm of the Eastman School of Music in Rochester, New York, on Lake Ontario. One might begin to suppose that, having grown up on the high plains, Hanson was eager to experience water-side communities, as long as they were located at moderately northerly latitudes.

As for Bold Island, it is near none of those locales. On the contrary, it is a scrap of evergreen-studded rock off the mainland of the state of Maine, not far from Acadia National Park. The composer maintained a summer home there, and in 1961, having a commission from the Cleveland Orchestra, decided to capture the moods of his retreat in music.

Second of *Bold Island Suite*'s three movements is *Summer Seascape*, a title it happens to share with another Hanson work, a piece for cello and orchestra that, other than title, is very different. *Bold Island*'s *Summer Seascape* is largely serene, especially in its opening pages which place English horn in a brief starring role. All builds smoothly on tides of strings and winds until grans central scenes develop. Cautionary remarks from trumpets and trombones announce the approach of a storm, that notion reinforced by swirling phrases from woodwinds and strings. However, calm returns, along with a reminder of earlier grandeur: Bold Island itself does rise rather abruptly and dramatically from the sea. After that recollection, Hanson brings the movement to a close largely as it had begun, though here the serenity is thanks to harp, not English horn. For a man raised in a farming community, Hanson yet managed to capture his seaside vision with remarkably vivid colors: other than the brief storm, summer at Bold Island seems perfect for relaxation and enjoying the views.

♪♪♪♪♪

Barber: *Summer Music,* op. 31

Most often encountered through his deeply mournful *Adagio for Strings* (1938), Pennsylvania-born composer Samuel Barber (1910 – 1981) also wrote for other sections of the orchestra. Sometimes these works use the full orchestra, though Barber sometimes wrote for smaller ensembles wholly lacking in strings.

His wind quintet *Summer Music,* scored for flute, oboe, clarinet, bassoon, and French horn, was written in 1956 for the Detroit Institute for the Arts' Chamber Music Society. The title asserts a seasonal connection, though the quintet was not composed in the summer, and its premiere took place in March. Perhaps a lengthy winter had led Barber to anticipate balmier days.

Summer Music opens with gently pulsing background phrases and short, spirited flourishes, first from flute, but then appearing in the care of other members of the ensemble. The first expansive theme is a serene one for oboe; quite suddenly, jaunty moods arrive with very short rhythmic fragments that lead to much exuberance. These glimpses of serenity, jauntiness, and exuberance return one after another, in varied order and varied character. After a spell, it seems that *Summer Music* will float to a close much as it had begun, though Barber has one more surprise to offer: a few jolly little bassoon phrases, then descending lines for all, ascending ones in reply, and lastly a little fillip of farewell. Throughout, long, flowing lines and dancing ones have shared the page, suggesting a summer day wholly without storms.

Many decades later, Barber's idea of applying a seasonally flavored title to a work for wind quintet inspired another American composer to craft a response. Jennifer Higdon's *Autumn Music* will appear in Chapter Five. As we'll find, she says she had Barber's piece specifically in mind when she set to work.

♪♪♪♪♪

Rodrigo: *Concierto de estio (Summer Concerto)*

When a composer has written the beloved *Concierto de Aranjuez* (1940), he will inevitably be identified with guitar concerti. However, Valencia native Joaquin Rodrigo (1901 – 1999), blind from early childhood and using a Braille writer to compose, did not neglect other solo instruments. His *Concierto de estio (Summer Concerto)* is a violin concerto from 1944 drawing inspiration from Vivaldi: given its title and its solo instrument, it could scarcely be otherwise.

Rodrigo's orchestra is both larger and better supplied with woodwinds and brass than Vivaldi's, though general structural ideas remain. These include not only the number of movements and their tempos, but also having themes that appear first in the orchestra take on greater detail and color when they subsequently move to the soloist's care. Melodic ideas return, at least in fragmentary form, holding the work together without quite wearing out their welcome. Perhaps Vivaldi's ghost would be gratified to know that what worked so well when his *Four Seasons* were published in 1725 still serves over two centuries later.

The first movement *Preludio* opens with charging passagework for the soloist, soon joined by a clock-like tick-tock pulse from the orchestra. Ensemble and soloist exchange phrases, though players other than the solo violin also have spotlights. Plaintive, song-like themes provide contrast, at times keeping the orchestra occupied even as the soloist is intent upon executing torrents of rapid-fire pyrotechnics. Whether driven, restful, or stately, the atmosphere is ever-changing.

In the second movement *Siciliana*, the violin soloist is not the first featured instrumental voice to appear; instead, Rodrigo begins with the oboe, only belatedly handing the spotlight back to solo violin. One might note that in his own Violin Concerto, Johannes Brahms (1833 – 1897) does the same thing. Phrases of the soloist's part often reappear in woodwinds, echoing each other in a call-and-response manner. When the brass instruments have their turn, it is generally in muted form, to better maintain the restful spirit.

For the final *Rondino*, Rodrigo sets different melodies – all of them spirited – in contrast to one another, some themes returning more frequently than others. The soloist's lines race forward against the orchestra's dance-like energy, solo harmonics and double-stops not just adding to the soloist's challenges, but also giving further vibrancy to the musical colors. This relentless motion continues not quite to the last chord. With a short trill and plucked phrase from the soloist and a single orchestral chord, Rodrigo's vibrant *Concierto de estio* has reached its conclusion with flair.

♫♫♫♫♫

Larsen: *Deep Summer Music*

Libby Larsen (b. 1950) grew up in Delaware, but the Atlantic coast is not present in her *Deep Summer Music*. Much of her career has been spent in the Midwest and Rocky Mountain West, with residencies at the Minnesota Orchestra and the Colorado Symphony Orchestra. Of those years, Larsen remarks on having noticed how, in the Plains states, "in the deep summer, winds create wave after wave of harvest ripeness which... creates a kind of emotional peace, and awe." That's what she sought to capture in this deftly shaded orchestral tone poem from 1982.

Deep Summer Music is vividly scored, its wind sections including piccolo, though no tuba, as well as a wealth of pitched percussion instruments, amongst them bells, marimba, and vibraphone. Those choices add a strikingly shimmering character to the music, as of the air shifting on waves of heat. The effect is further reinforced by woodwind trills and string tremolos, with additional color coming from such elements as a gentle French horn solo and muted trumpet, calling as if from quite a distance away. Richer passages appear amidst the general languor, and a short motif arising in the woodwinds become core material for one such surge through full orchestra. However, all will ultimately fade to a close suggestive of the "emotional peace" that Larsen recalls feeling when gazing over late summer wheat fields. The composer says she was seeking to capture a sense of "peace of mind:" most listeners would agree that she achieved her goal.

♪♪♪♪♪

Summer music comes in many flavors, depending on the tastes and experiences of the composer, and on the climate in which that composer may live – or at least visit. Here are six additional suggestions, for which there wasn't room in the main body of this chapter:

- Carl Michael Ziehrer (1843 – 1922): A colleague of the Viennese Strauss clan, Ziehrer was, like they, a master of the concert waltz. His *In der Sommerfrische* (*The Fresh Air of Summer*) is an elegant recollection of a holiday in the mountains near Salzburg.

- Wilhelm Stenhammar (1871 – 1927): The varied moods and energies of his *Late Summer Nights*, op. 33, suggests that late summer in Sweden is a time of romance and adventure, even with only one piano to express the scenes.

- Erkki Melartin (1875 – 1937): The Finnish composer's Symphony no. 4 is a grand orchestral celebration of summer. Exuberant moods, tender ones, and playful celebration appear in turn; the nocturnal third movement includes wordless singing voices to magical effect.

- Frank Bridge (1879 – 1941): Another of the English Pastoralists, Bridge appeared in Chapter Three. However, his orchestral tone poem *Summer* shimmers and sings as vividly as did *Enter Spring*, and would provide a superb next discovery in any exploration of his music.

- Robert Muczynski (1929 – 2010): The Chicago-born composer's *A Serenade for Summer* is a short orchestral tone poem with both leisure and excitement in its heart. It may not be what Mozart would have called a "serenade," but since a serenade can also be a heart-felt rhapsody of praise, the label certainly applies.

- Michael Torke (b. 1961): His saxophone quartet *July* (1995) balances restless moods and leisurely ones, perhaps contrasting the day's activities to the evening's calm. It is a vibrant counterpart to Torke's *December*, which shall be featured in Chapter Six.

Chapter Five: Autumn

With the phrase above prancing along in the care of the first violin, Wolfgang Mozart's String Quartet no. 17 begins. The nimble three-note motifs and bouncy dotted rhythms give it an eager forward motion, one that has sent many minds in search of specific imagery. Some listeners swear those details evoke trotting horses, others counter with the suggestion of hunting horns calling to the hounds. From either viewpoint, the scene is of the hunt – not for waterfowl, but surely deer, or at least foxes. Mozart himself never claimed that such was his intention and the determined urban dweller would only have known of such activities second-hand. However, in listening to the music, one can readily hear the suggestion of outdoorsy scenes.

This chapter of autumn-themed music includes a handful of hunt-themed works: admittedly, one might hunt in other seasons, but surely countless paintings of such robust activities tend to have autumn forest settings. Those copper and amber leaves will also make musical appearances without hunters. We'll even find winsome, song-like melodies and jaunty barn dances.

To some minds, autumn carries a somber mood: alas, they sigh, summer is over. However, for most of the composers featured here, those regrets are soon lightened by brilliant foliage and bright blue skies.

♪♪♪♪♪

Leopold Mozart: *Sinfonia di caccia* (*Hunting Symphony*)

Miloš Forman's 1984 film *Amadeus* would have us believe that Leopold Mozart (1719 – 1787) was quite a humorless and controlling father. Controlling, he may have been: his letters to Wolfgang make clear that Leopold believed father knew best. Humorless: no. Here was a man who, in his own music, vividly evoked the tipsy revelers at a peasant wedding as readily as the shivers and laughter of a sleigh ride. Surely such a man knew how to smile, and not just in music.

Of his *Sinfonia di caccia (Hunting Symphony)*, the elder Mozart could have captured the mood with hearty French horns; that orchestral instrument did derive from early hunting horns. He does that, and much more, too. Not only are there assertive and prominent horn passages, the composer also calls for gunshot effects (well-chosen percussion will serve), shouts of "yo ho," and even barking dogs. How, in the absence of recording technology, he intended to achieve the last of those effects on cue is perhaps best left to the imagination. Leopold Mozart also specified that the horn players should not seek to play with grace, but rather "quite raucously... and as loudly as possible." It is simply not music of humble mien.

The first movement *Allegro* is bold and bright with dotted rhythms that neatly suggest trotting horses. Short, firmly articulated notes perhaps suggestive of gunshots further add to the excitement. By contrast, the second movement *Andante* is slow and gentle, with strings at first dominating, though horns gradually resume prominence. Perhaps here the imagined hunters are seeking refuge from the midday sun.

If so, with the final movement *Menuet*, they are back in action. Although the music has the structure of a ballroom dance, it is a decidedly jolly one quite lacking in powdered wigs. In the opening and closing pages, horns and strings echo each other's musical statements, though at the movement's heart, the focus is strongly upon the horns. In all, it is a work in the highest of spirits, despite its creator's rather dour public image.

♪♪♪♪♪

Wolfgang Mozart: String Quartet no. 17 in B-flat major, K. 458, "Hunt"

In 1785 in Vienna, Wolfgang Amadeus Mozart (1756 – 1791) published a set of six string quartets. Initially, they appeared as his opus 10, simply because Mozart, wary of his music being pirated by others, had withheld from print the great majority of his completed works. In fact, by this point in his career, having been composing before he reached school age, he had completed well over 400 compositions in nearly any imaginable genre.

History has come to know them as Mozart's *Haydn Quartets*, because of an effusive note of dedication in tribute to Joseph Haydn (1732 – 1809), the composer's colleague, lodge brother, and frequent partner for evenings of string quartet playing; Haydn would take one of the two violin parts, though Mozart preferred viola. In sending a copy of the quartets to Haydn, Mozart wrote, "A father who had decided to send out his sons into the great world thought it is his duty to entrust them to the protection and guidance of a man who was very celebrated at the time, and who, moreover, happened to be his best friend... Your good opinion encourages me to offer them to you and leads me to hope that you will not consider them wholly unworthy of your favor. Please, then, receive them kindly and be to them a father, guide, and friend!"

Fourth of the six Haydn Quartets – 17th of what would eventually be 23 string quartets in all – bears the nickname "Hunt." There seems little likelihood that Mozart set out consciously to write a quartet reflective of hunting scenes. However, the rhythmic energy of the opening movement certainly is well supplied with exuberant dotted rhythms, their patterns of alternating short and long notes suggestive of eagerness and motion. Its opening phrase stands at the head of this chapter. Whether representing horses or hunting horns – or neither – it is certainly spirited, especially given the indicated tempo *Allegro vivace assai* (Very quick and lively). Melodic fragments reappear in ever new form, especially notable when the movement's central pages take even very small fragments and develop from them much more elaborate ideas.

The other three movements are less overtly hunt-like in nature, unless one wishes to imagine what else those hunters might have been doing with the rest of their day. The second movement *Menuetto* is gracefully dance-infused; it would have been more according to form to put this movement third, rather than second, but Mozart thought to try something out of the ordinary. Central pages feature a more playful atmosphere, though the movement closes with a revised restatement of the material with which it had opened.

The third movement *Adagio* is a sweet romance, its main theme becoming intricately ornamented in later re-appearances. In the *Allegro assai* finale, Mozart seems mostly intent upon letting his quartet scamper to its close. Being Mozart, however, and never lacking for a few more good ideas, he also includes passages of tender reflection, and when the nimble opening phrases return from time to time, he gives them new energies and colors for the sake of variety. Our hunters, it seems, are off for a high spirited evening of celebration.

♪♪♪♪♪

Coste: *Feuilles d'automne*, op. 41 (*Autumn Leaves*)

It was the Spaniards who first proved the guitar to be an instrument as worthy of serious attention as pianos and violins. However, many of those Spaniards had studied in Paris, so the French were not slow to catch on to this exciting new possibility. Prominent amongst this second generation of guitarist/composers was Frenchman Napoléon Coste (1805 – 1883). Before the age of twenty, he was performing and teaching guitar in Valenciennes near France's border with Belgium. Soon, Coste relocated to Paris in search of more advanced training and broader horizons for his virtuosity. His timing was such that he arrived in Paris not long after that Polish-born master of the piano, Frederic Chopin (1810 – 1849). Before long, Coste had made it clear that, in his hands, the guitar could sing and dance just as well as Chopin's piano.

Coste's *Feuilles d'automne (Autumn Leaves)* is a set of twelve waltzes. Like Chopin's piano waltzes, Coste's were not necessarily intended for actual ballroom use, though they certainly capture the rhythms and spirit of the dance. Also like Chopin – and, for that matter, like Johann Strauss Jr. (1825 – 1899), though at this time, the Austrian was still a boy – Coste does not limit any of the individual waltzes to a single melody. Each juxtaposes at least two waltz themes, some more, and even when an earlier theme re-appears, it usually does so in more elaborate form. Coste also makes use of the multiple layerings of counterpoint; guitars may have fewer strings than pianos, but given a top-notch player, the instrument can still offer music of impressive complexity.

Given the title *Autumn Leaves*, some might expect music of generally melancholy demeanor, as those leaves fade and fall. However, only two of the twelve waltzes – numbers four and ten – spend much time with minor key moods. Otherwise, the waltzes seem to speak more of autumn's beauties. It is music of optimism, not of sorrow at the passing season.

♪♪♪♪

Liszt: two Transcendental Etudes –
no. 8 in c minor, *Wilde Jagd* (*Wild Hunt*)
no. 9 in A-flat major, *Ricordanza* (*Remembrance*)

Franz Liszt (1811 – 1886) was a pianist par excellence. His technique was flawless, his charisma legendary, his ability to possess an audience almost demonic; the technique, at least, is well captured in his *Trancendental Etudes*. The etudes represent a work long in progress: begun in 1826 when Liszt was fifteen, thoroughly revised and published a dozen years later. In that latter form, there were simply called the *24 Grandes Etudes*, though in fact there were only twelve. Only in 1852, in another revised version published in Leipzig, would the Etudes reach their final form under the title "Etudes d'execution transcendante," or, boiled down to the more concise English, *Transcendental Etudes*. The final version was dedicated to Liszt's mentor Carl Czerny (1791 – 1857), a former student of Beethoven, though neither Czerny nor Beethoven would have known quite what to make of these fiendishly varied pieces. It isn't just that few pianists can play them adequately; Hector Berlioz (1803 – 1869), a good friend of Liszt's, observed that no one else could do them justice. These etudes are also generations beyond any solo piano music that predated them and are, indeed, Liszt at his most Lisztian.

Most of the Transcendental Etudes bear nicknames presumably of Liszt's own choosing: certainly, one finds them in the 1852 premiere publication. Eighth of the twelve is *Wilde Jagd* (*Wild Hunt*). The hunting portion of the scene appears in its frequent use of dotted rhythms, short notes alternating with somewhat longer ones in a manner perhaps suggestive of galloping hoofbeats. As for the supposed wildness, the etude opens in thunderous and frenzied mood, with a specified tempo of *Presto furioso (furiously fast)*. Almost unimaginably busy passagework rages up and down the keyboard; counting the notes in a live performance would be an impossible task. A sense of sweet romance appears briefly, though the hurricane promptly returns. In the closing pages, Liszt combines these two distinctly different ideas simultaneously, and a performer must balance the weight and pacing of the different lines, lest one overwhelm the other. In all, it is a virtuoso test of a single pair of hands.

Ninth of the *Transcendental Etudes* is *Ricordanza (Remembrance)*. Liszt does not identify what is being remembered, though the music – with tender moods interrupted by occasional outbursts – suggests it may be a romance in which the waters did not always run smoothly. At the outset, Liszt requests that the music should be played *dolce con grazia (sweetly with grace)*, an instruction that, nonetheless, does not prevent him from including, from time to time, rapid and scintillating passagework: more sparkle than aggression, yet still neither sweet nor graceful. Boldly passionate statements appear late in the etude, though the general serenity of the opening pages returns in time to bring the piece to a close. There may be storms in these remembrances, but those memories are still largely sweet.

♪♪♪♪♪

Josef Strauss: *Herbstrosen Walzer*, op. 232
(*Autumn Roses Waltzes*)

Asked to name a work uniting the words "Strauss" and "waltz," most fine music lovers will immediately cite *The Blue Danube* and may even sing a phrase or two of that widely familiar piece. Here, however, is a different waltz by a different Strauss. Josef Strauss (1827 – 1870) was the middle of three brothers. The eldest, Johann Jr (1825 – 1899), was the intercontinental star; the youngest, Eduard (1835 – 1916), was primarily a conductor. All three boys followed in the footsteps of their father, Johann Sr. (1804 – 1849), who had tried unsuccessfully to divert his sons into careers other than music. Did he fear their competition, or was he merely trying to guide them to better paying professions? Whatever his motivation, he would not succeed: this second generation of the Strauss family carried on in the family business.

Having first rejected a career in the military and then abandoned studies in engineering, Josef Strauss joined Johann Jr. in conducting their father's dance band after Johann Sr. had passed away. Josef often shared concert programs with his brother, and travelled with the Strauss Orchestra on concert tours. However, plagued by poor health, he had neither the strength nor the inclination to demand the spotlight. Nevertheless, even a man too weak to be ever on the road may find the strength to work at his composing desk, and this Josef did frequently enough to ensure that hundreds of his waltzes, polkas, mazurkas, and other dance forms have survived.

One of Josef Strauss' late works is the *Herbstrosen Walzer* (*Autumn Roses Waltzes*). Note the plural: it is not a single waltz, but a sequence of different waltzes linked together into a single danceable tapestry of sound. Johann Jr. wrote waltzes the same way, making more of them than simply an excuse for dancing and thereby creating something that could stand on its own on a concert program. Furthermore, neither brother would launch into such a work with the biggest, most memorable waltz tune at the first downbeat. Instead, the usual Strauss approach tended to favor a slow and thoughtful introduction, hinting at what will come even as it tempts listeners and dancers alike to give closer attention to the music before the actual waltz energy develops. These introductions seem to declare, "something splendid is about to happen."

Dating from 1868, *Herbstrosen* sets peaceful, string-dominated melodies against livelier ones: this might mean bold brass or assertive cymbals, though in *Herbstrosen*, even the piccolo is given an opportunity to shine. The variety is such that, whether or not one is actually dancing, the ear is ever finding new delights, and earlier waltz themes reappear just frequently enough to give a sense of the full work being a cohesive whole. At times, tender transitions might seem suggestive of the faded roses of this autumn season, as the title suggests. Before long, however, the mood becomes vibrant once more; after all, in any season, one may find belles of the ball decked with hothouse blossoms.

♪♪♪♪

Grieg: *In Autumn*, op. 11

The melody at the heart of *In Autumn* by Edvard Grieg (1843 – 1907) began life as a song, and then became a score for piano four-hands; only belatedly did it take on the orchestral form in which one might encounter it today. Throughout the process, Grieg kept the basic tune he'd crafted as early as 1866, as well as much of the way in which it developed. If one were to hear the song and then the 1886 orchestral score, one would likely recognize the connection. Perhaps it had taken Grieg twenty years of professional development to come to the point of realizing that what the music had needed all along was grander treatment and more vivid expression.

The original song, *Efterårsstormen* (*Autumn Storms*), set a text by Danish poet Christian Richardt (1831 – 1892), in which one finds both fearsome winds tormenting the fall leaves and also musings upon the season that will pass and spring that shall return. So it is far more than just the death of summer. Removing the words and giving the musical materials over to orchestra, as Grieg has done, allows splendidly varied coloring. The orchestral piece opens with stern chords and sweet phrases appearing in turn, long before an outburst of brass and percussion propels the orchestra into a turbulent storm scene. Determined dotted rhythms beneath the action may suggest someone hastening toward shelter, or more abstractly, the clouds themselves powering into view. Less urgent passages reimagine those rhythms, making room in places for pastoral French horn spotlights.

At last, gentle strings and woodwinds lead the way to a nimble theme of 6/8 meter; it's quite new to *In Autumn*, though not, perhaps, to Grieg's original listeners, as he seems to have borrowed it from a Norwegian folk dance. Joyful exuberance dominates these last few pages, reflective, one imagines, of the last lines of Richardt's poem: "How sweet to watch the first blossom in the last snow!" Here is an autumn-titled piece that, in fact, begins in late summer and continues to the following spring. Given the latitudes at which the Norwegian composer spent his life, one supposes that progression would be an encouraging image.

♪♪♪♪

Chaminade: *Autumne, Fileuse et Tarantelle –*
Concert Etudes, op. 35, no. 2, 3, & 6

It helps to have influential neighbors. When Cécile Chaminade (1857 – 1944) was growing up in Paris, her parents ensured that she studied piano, as was considered suitable for elegant young upper class ladies such as Cécile. A career in the arts, or, indeed, university studies of any type, would <u>not</u> have seemed suitable, so Cécile's music training might have ended there. However, the Chaminades were neighbors of Georges Bizet (1838 – 1875), at that time not yet composer of *Carmen*, but still known and respected for his stage works. Upon hearing the girl at the piano, he persuaded her parents that it would be a loss to the musical world if she did not have the chance to study at the Paris Conservatoire, and so she went.

Mademoiselle Chaminade would go on to a successful career as both pianist and composer. That she happened to be an attractive and fashionable woman may have helped; certainly, her publishers were fond of putting her photograph on the cover page of her music. Yet the essential quality still needed to be there, and critical commentary at the time agreed that she was not just a woman who composed, but rather a true composer – and a fine performer, as well.

Chaminade's *Concert Etudes* of 1886 strike the perfect balance of beauty and fervor, as gentle, lyrical passages alternate with others more markedly emphatic. Each etude bears a descriptive title suggesting, if not necessarily the composer's original intention before she put pencil to paper, then certainly the general character of the ultimate result. Only one of those titles is seasonal in nature. However, matching it with two others of contrasting moods results in an entrancing concert suite for autumn.

Second of the six etudes, *Autumne* begins in tender, song-like demeanor with more rapid passagework developing beneath the main theme. So far, all is gently wistful, as if the leaves are falling, but not yet driven away by storms. In the central pages, those storms arrive, driven into the scene by turbulent phrases and pounding chords, distinctly different from the opening mood. This alternation of sweetness and storms occurs once more, though it is with one final statement of the delicate opening theme that Chaminade's *Autumne* concludes.

Chaminade's third *Concert Etude* is *Fileuse* (*Woman at the Spinning Wheel*), sparkling with cascades of six-to-a-beat figurations, one after another. The specified tempo is not overly fast, but with so very many notes per beat, the activity level is still high. Even the comparatively reserved contrasting melody still has those active phrases, now as accompaniment to a song-like melody. Perhaps the spinner is humming as she works, in contrast to the spinning of the wheel itself in the faster passages; whatever the image, the overall result is purely scintillating.

Last of the six *Concert Etudes* is *Tarantelle*, capturing the frenetic energy of a Neapolitan folk dance. Rapid triplets power along above a steady, lower-pitched pulse, suggesting the combined effect of swirling skirts and tapping toes. A more restful contrasting melody appears midway, though the dance resumes promptly, and Chaminade develops her musical materials for even greater intensity. The tempo she has specified is nearly twice that of *Fileuse*: 192, rather than 108 beats per minute. Admittedly, *Fileuse* has shorter note values, so the player's fingers are still racing along. Nonetheless, *Tarantelle,* having more accents and dynamic variation, makes for a highly dramatic conclusion to the set.

Chaminade's *Concert Etudes* demand far more evolved artistry than one might find in pretty little salon pieces. Few of those elegant debutantes of the young Chaminade's early acquaintance would have dared to try them, but her male colleagues were impressed.

Lyapunov: *Chant d'Automne* in f-sharp minor, op. 26
    (*Autumn Song*)

A product of the Moscow Conservatory, pianist/composer Sergei Lyapunov (1859 – 1924) was a classmate of Peter Tchaikovsky (1840 – 1893). Despite their age difference, their studies coincided due to the elder man having pursued a career in law before taking up music. Lyapunov, perhaps in part due to an earlier start, was the better pianist of the two, in fact, better than most of his generation.

Lyapunov enjoyed a thriving international career as a concert pianist, ending his days teaching piano in Paris; in his own compositions, the piano often features prominently. Few composer/pianists would have dared to face comparison with the mighty Franz Liszt (1811 – 1886). However, that's exactly what Lyapunov did when, at the turn of the century, he published, as his opus 11, a set of piano pieces that he daringly titled *12 études d'exécution trancendante (Transcendental Etudes)*. Liszt had used that title fifty years before; two of his *Transcendental Etudes* appear earlier in this chapter. Lyapunov was confident he had something to contribute to a truly magnificent legacy.

When Lyapunov's opus 26 came to print in 1906 in Leipzig, it bore a French title, *Chant d'Automne (Autumn Song)*. For generations, French had been the language of Russia's educated and cultured class. Moreover, giving it a French title would be better for foreign sales than giving it one in Russian.

Spanning almost ten minutes, *Chant d'Automne* opens with a delicate phrase that falls and then rises again. That gentle wave-like motion continues, beginning to overlap with itself as the phrase is stated both by the pianist's right hand and simultaneously by the left. Before long, the "song" theme arrives in the higher pitches of the right hand, while lower-pitched left hand lines further develop that opening phrase. Fuller, more passionate moods arise, with occasional rather spare transitions, as if Lyapunov had chosen to focus briefly on what visual artists call "negative space:" the open areas between more obvious statements. This *Autumn Song* closes in wistful mood, though, despite its minor key, at no point does it become despairing. It is a restful tribute to autumn, not one regretting that summer has run its course.

♪♪♪♪

MacDowell: Orchestral Suite no. 1 in a minor, op. 42 –
I. Haunted Forest; III. In October, V. Forest Spirits

Edward MacDowell (1860-1908) was born in New York City. His parents loved fine music and started him on the piano by the age of eight. When Edward was fifteen, his mother took him to Europe for advanced training. MacDowell studied in France and Germany for about a dozen years, earning favorable notice not only for his piano playing – not every young American would have dared to play music of Franz Liszt (1811 – 1886) for the man himself – but also for his compositions, which were finding both audiences and publishers. Pianists were playing his solo works for American audiences even before MacDowell himself returned in 1888.

MacDowell composed a great quantity of solo piano music, though also piano concerti and purely orchestral scores. When an orchestral work is grand of scale and structured in several movements, these possibly linked thematically, it would often be called a symphony. However, this word appears nowhere in MacDowell's catalog. He preferred instead the term "suite," a choice that gives a composer a much more open canvas. Time-honored expectations of how a symphony should manage forms and tempos are set aside in favor of the composer's own ideas of what he or she might choose to express, with or without specific imagery. Clearly, MacDowell appreciated the free-form nature of suites. His musical imagination could go wherever it wished, and including descriptive subtitles for the individual movements served to hint to listeners as to what the scene might be.

Most of MacDowell's Orchestral Suite no. 1 was written in 1891, though the third of its five movements came along later; the work as a whole did not reach the public until a premiere by the Boston Symphony in 1895. In addition to the usual suspects that tended to characterize a 19th century orchestra – strings; timpani; pairs of woodwinds, horns, trumpets, and trombones – the composer added piccolo, one extra trombone, one tuba, two more horns for a total of four, and percussion including bass drum and crash cymbals. They don't all play in every movement. On the contrary, MacDowell draws upon those that, in his view, were best suited to the mood at hand. So *October* is a spectacle of horn timbres, but *Forest Spirits* require a touch of piccolo.

In the first movement, MacDowell gives us *The Haunted Forest*, apparently, not only haunted, but also ominous. Its central pages are of anxious mood, though calmness develops for the last lines; perhaps whoever was lost in that forest has escaped to safety.

The third movement *October* suggests hunters galloping about on horses, using their horns to call boisterously to one another. Restful interludes occur, notably one with a prolonged solo for clarinet, though cheerful moods and buoyant energy remain the principal ideas.

With the fifth and last movement, *Forest Spirits*, MacDowell returns to the forest: no longer haunted, or perhaps it is a different forest entirely. Here, one finds a sparkling, dance-like energy, driving along on a 6/8 meter, suggests the play of fairies, particularly when piccolo and strings are in the spotlight. Brilliant brass passages also have their time as the movement – and, thus, the suite – nears its close. Having crafted a suite that is pastoral in all but name, MacDowell seems determined to close in a most optimistic mood.

The Orchestral Suite no. 1's gentle second movement *Summer Idyll* and tender fourth movement *Shepherdess Song*, well infused with bird-song-like woodwind phrases, have subtitles less suggestive of autumn. However, these movements are as deftly crafted as the others; taken as a whole, the suite proves that MacDowell, an influential representative of the late 19th century American Romantics, had as much to say in music as his more immediately famous European counterparts.

♫♫♫♫

Delius: *North Country Sketches* —
   I. *Autumn: The Wind Sighs in the Trees*

Frederick Delius (1862 – 1934) was that rather rare beast: an English Impressionist. Long before he took up residence in France, he was leaning toward the subtle shading of the French artistic movement; he was, after all, a contemporary of Claude Debussy (1862 – 1918). Delius' musical leanings confused his father, a prosperous businessman and wool merchant, but delighted his friends and colleagues. One prominent person on both halves of that latter statement was the Norwegian composer Edvard Grieg (1843 – 1907), who appears earlier in this chapter.

Despite years in his youth living in Florida, where his father had sent him to manage an orange grove, and an even lengthier time on the European continent, Delius never entirely forgot the land of his boyhood. In 1913, he began an orchestral suite flavored by the Yorkshire Dales. The result, *North Country Sketches*, premiered in 1915 under the direction of the respected English conductor Thomas Beecham (1879 – 1961). Not quite a symphony, for it avoids the expected structures of a work with that name, it is, on the contrary, a symphonic suite in four contrasting movements in which shifting orchestral color is used to portray a sequence of scenes. Here, those sights and feeling reflect the north of England, its open moors dotted with sheep, scattered villages, and a generally pastoral pace of life.

Autumn, the first movement of *North Country Sketches*, opens restfully, with mellow French horn that might suggest a call ringing out from the far side of the Dales. Background strings pulse gently, reminiscent of the second portion of the movement's subtitle: *The Wind Sighs in the Trees*. Clarinet joins, and then oboe rising over the background of strings. Midway, richer tonal colors and fuller textures develop; the sun, it seems, is higher in the sky and beaming warmly upon the scene. Woodwinds and French horn remain prominent, the latter sometimes in full-throated, chorale-like mood. Everything, however, rides upon a sublime tide of strings, long, languid phrases suggestive of open countryside. Delius' *Autumn* is no lively harvest scene, but rather a cool afternoon tinged with bronze.

The second movement of *North Country Sketches* moves on to a shivery *Winter*, the third an eager, though nameless *Dance*, and the last a rapturous *March of Spring*. It is nearly a full calendar reflection, though Delius reserved his summer reflections for several single movement works, one of which appears in Chapter Four. English composers of Delius' generation tended to be moved by scenes of nature's beauty, turning frequently to the gentle English countryside for inspiration, and resulting in a style known as English Pastoralism. However, no English composer was more inclined to lean in this direction than Delius. Perhaps it was his fondness for mellow Impressionist harmonies, so ideally suited to giving musical expression to natural beauty.

♪♪♪♪♪

Marx: *Feste im Herbst* (*Autumn Festival*)

When Joseph Marx (1892 – 1964) was growing up in Graz, Austria, his homeland was still a political and musical powerhouse. Resisting the legal profession advocated by his father, Marx took up composition in his early twenties, and by 1914 was teaching upper-level music theory in Vienna. Alas, war was then in the immediate future, and before long, that which had been the mighty Austrian Empire would occupy a very different place in the world order.

Nonetheless, even in the new Austria, music remained important and Marx continued to pursue a respected and successful career. Some of his elder colleagues – Anton Webern (1883 – 1945) and Alban Berg (1885 – 1935) amongst them – were pressing forward on the cutting edge of music, with radically new concepts of melodic and harmonic structure. Marx, on the other hand, had conservative tastes; his music brings Romantic styles only a very few steps into the new century, a point of view reflected in his side career as a Viennese music critic. If one ever wished to find a cross between Brahms and Debussy, Marx might be just the man to explore.

Marx's grand orchestral tone poem *Feste im Herbst* (*Autumn Festival*) dates from 1946. Reworked from the last movement of his perhaps overly monumental *Herbstsymphonie* (*Autumn Symphony*) of 1922, it is a splendid work in the manner of the symphonic poems of Richard Strauss (1865 – 1949), with no specific plot line but much room for application of imagination.

From the vibrant opening passages to the tenderly fading sunset colors of the finale, the work suggests myriad autumn moods in rather less than half an hour. There are celebrations with bold brass statements, languorous romances for woodwinds and strings, festive folk-flavored energies, suggestions of not-quite-Viennese waltzes, and much else along the way. Grace, splendor, and subtlety were all within Marx's reach, particularly having supplied his orchestra with harp, piano, and glockenspiel, as well as most of the usual choices. From harvest feasts to lovers strolling amidst the changing leaves, it's all here, vividly crafted and offering rewards for curious listeners.

♪♪♪♪

Bax: *November Woods*

Sir Arnold Bax (1883 – 1953) was English born, a product of the Royal College of Music and Master of the King's Music for King George VI. However, he was also fascinated by Celtic history and culture, and adopted an Irish pen-name, Dermot O'Byrne, for his published fiction. Whether his tone poem *November Woods* reflects English origins or Irish sympathies, in either case, the latitudes in question are northern ones, so it might be a frosty scene of frozen ponds and naked boughs in the British Isles. Then again, given that he composed the work in 1917, he might equally well have been imagining the war-torn woods of France. Nonetheless, the music seems more natural in affect than martial, so a forest in autumn it is.

Mysteriously shaded opening lines, rising and falling in waves, gain urgency from brass and ornaments from flute and clarinet. Drama mounts, with themes heroic or rhapsodic by turn. Respite arrives with a peaceful, nocturne-like passage and a solo spotlight for violin, before the storm returns, just as urgently as before. The next pause in the action features not violin, but oboe and clarinet before another period of tumult. At last, an enduring peace takes root, with violin, clarinet and French horn exchanging the spotlight as all drifts to a drowsy close.

Bax has cast his score with a richly varied assemblage of instruments, including piccolo, English horn, bass clarinet, contrabassoon, trombones, tuba, two harps, and celesta, along with the usual complement of instruments. Often, leading players in the various sections are given brief solo lines, drawing attention to the different colors that can arise from one instrument or another. As the bronze of one tree's foliage might contrast with the amber of the next, even as the softer tones of evergreens appear here and there, so Bax's deftly populated orchestra allows for diverse color combinations. His *November Woods* is more vibrantly shaded than one might otherwise expect of a late autumnal forest vision. Bax seems less concerned with dry leaves blown away on the wind than with the overall scene and what feelings it might inspire: thoroughly fulfilling for composer, performer, and listener alike.

♪♪♪♪♪

Prokofiev: *Autumnal Sketch*, op. 8

As he grew into his musical career, Sergei Prokofiev (1891 – 1953) developed a reputation for restless rhythms, strong energy, and astringent harmonies: not dramatically avant garde, but surely moving beyond styles of the previous generation. However, that compositional personality did not develop instantly; some of his early works barely admit that the 20th century has arrived, and only hint at the new directions in which he would soon drive the musical world.

Prokofiev's *Autumnal Sketch* (1911) dates from late in his studies at the St. Petersburg Conservatory. The work premiered in Moscow that summer, the young composer himself conducting. Some composers might choose to evoke autumn as a time of unsettled weather. Prokofiev, however, is working with orchestra of strings and harp, pairs of woodwinds, an additional bass clarinet, four horns, and only a single trumpet, thus few of the usual tools generally required for storms and tumult. Instead, he opts for generally restful moods and flowing phrases, with only mildly progressive harmonies. Central pages are comparatively more eager in motion, having passages of lush grandeur, as if of glorious sunshine on brilliant fall foliage. However, the restful themes soon return, allowing the short tone poem to fade to a peaceful close. The boldly dramatic side of Prokofiev's musical persona is yet in the future; here, he is familiarizing himself with orchestral tools, and showing that he is already comfortable with his craft.

♪♪♪♪♪

Sowerby: *Comes Autumn Time*

Born in Grand Rapids, Michigan (across Lake Michigan from Milwaukee), and spending most of his career in Chicago, Leo Sowerby (1895 – 1968) was a thorough Midwesterner. In and of itself, that makes him stand out in American fine music, a field in which the great majority of composers of his time and before were New Englanders. Sowerby and Howard Hanson (1896 – 1981) of Nebraska (see Chapter Four) were not the only Midwesterners, but they did represent a rather limited contingent. Spending 35 years as organist at Chicago's Episcopal Cathedral, Sowerby frequently drew upon that experience, writing for organ, whether alone or in ensemble. However, he also explored other genres, from symphonies to folk song arrangements, and it was for his cantata *Canticle of the Sun* that he won the 1944 Pulitzer Prize for Music. Sowerby's musical gifts stand as evidence that, even without Boston or New York City prominent in one's resume, one can still contribute to the rich heritage of American fine music.

Sowerby's works often display colorfully varied musical textures, a tendency ideally suited to his tone poem *Comes Autumn Time*. Initially a solo organ fantasy, the piece was composed rather quickly in October 1916, when Sowerby learned that an organist colleague had announced a recital that would, according to the advertisements, include something new by Sowerby – something the colleague had quite neglected to request of the composer. An orchestration would soon follow when the original version proved immediately popular.

From the first notes of *Comes Autumn Time*, it is clear that Sowerby adores the season. Not for him wistful regrets of summer's passing: rather, his music revels in amber oaks and crimson maples. The opening is as eager as an autumn festival. Calmer moods follow, but, after all, one might sometimes relax amidst those glorious colors, or simply muse upon the gentler backdrop of a blue sky. These two ideas – boldly outspoken and sweetly reflective – appear in turn, even just a few phrases at a time, the better for variety. Ultimately, *Comes Autumn Time* surges to a close in musical colors no less vivid than those of the changing foliage.

The organ version of the piece and the orchestration are largely similar in phrasing and melodic structure. Sowerby included in his orchestration piccolo, bass clarinet, harp, chimes, cymbals, glockenspiel, and celesta, along with the usual orchestral forces. However, a fine pipe organ is perfectly able to express the voices of orchestral instruments of nearly all types and, when required, of doing so nearly as loudly as any large orchestra. The orchestral parts are sometimes quite elaborate in the way they are layered against one another, but an organ can do that as well. That the orchestral version is somewhat longer than the organ version may be due to a wish to spotlight as many members of the orchestra as possible. Whether one wishes to explore the original organ version, or the later orchestration, in either setting, Sowerby allows one to dive wholeheartedly into autumn's brilliance.

♪♪♪♪♪

Finzi: *The Fall of the Leaf*, op. 20

Despite the Italianate family name, Gerald Finzi (1901 – 1956) was born in London and raised in Yorkshire. His father, whose own ancestors had come from Italy in the 1700s, was a businessman who started Gerald on music studies when the boy was only 13. This first burst of musical exploration was interrupted when young Gerald's first music teacher died in combat during World War I. The passing of his father and three elder brothers subsequently turned the youth to an introspective slant of mind, which can be sensed in his mostly thoughtful, often pastoral compositions: songs and instrumental works alike.

Finzi's *The Fall of the Leaf* is a surviving portion of an unrealized plan that was intended as a full musical celebration of the seasons. Subtitled *Elegy*, the piece first reached the public in 1929 as a piano duet. Finzi revised it again and again. Ultimately, he decided it would be best suited to symphonic forces and began to orchestrate it. Alas, at the time of his early passing from Hodgkin's disease, he had not yet finished; the task of completion fell to his musical executor Howard Ferguson. The final orchestral version premiered in 1957 with conductor Sir John Barbirolli (1899 – 1970) and the Hallé Orchestra.

This piece opens and closes in restful mood, with oboe and flute particularly prominent over smooth textures of strings and horns. In the central pages, one finds more brightly colored passages; here, bass and an abundant complement of percussion (including gong and crash cymbals) drive the action. More often than not, however, gentleness is the dominant spirit. After all, Finzi intended a sort of elegy: neither a funeral march nor a victory parade, only a somber tribute. Just because the orchestral forces are resplendent does not mean that continual high drama is required.

According to his publisher, Finzi borrowed the title from a keyboard piece found in the Elizabethan-vintage Fitzwilliam Virginal Book. However, one might wish someone had introduced him to the poem *The Fall of the Leaf* by Henry Thoreau (1817 – 1862), who, amongst many other reflections, observes:

> Far in the woods these golden days
>   Some leaf obeys its maker's call,
> And through their hollow aisles it plays
>   With delicate touch the prelude of the fall.

Thoreau's Walden bore little resemblance to Finzi's Yorkshire. Nonetheless, the American's verses are suffused with much the same autumnal mood.

♫♫♫♫♫

Alwyn: *Autumn Legend*

Northampton-born William Alwyn (1905 – 1985) was a composer, flutist and painter. Perhaps those facts, together with his colleagues in the circle of composers in the so-called English Pastoralism style, influenced the moods of his *Autumn Legend*. The work premiered July 22, 1955, by the Hallé Orchestra with conductor Sir John Barbirolli.

Scored for solo English horn and string ensemble, *Autumn Legend* might almost serve as the central movement of a concerto for English horn. However, it was not a virtuoso showpiece that Alwyn had in mind. He headed the score with a few lines from *Blessed Damozel* by London-born poet Dante Gabriel Rosetti (1828 – 1882):

> Surely she lean'd o'er me – Her hair
> Fell about my face...
> Nothing: the Autumn fall of leaves
> The whole year sets apace.

So the vision is less seasonal than romantic; the fact that Rosetti also crafted his own oil painting to capture the scene in rich auburns and forest greens, makes this abundantly clear. Nonetheless, the gentle melancholy of Alwyn's work seems to suit either view, and the richly mournful voice of the English horn provides perfect contrast to mellow strings.

Autumn Legend begins with strings, though their phrases soon reappear, in gradually expanding form, in the care of English horn. Greater motion develops, with turns and trills to ornament the otherwise sedate mood. However, Alwyn never gives way to high drama. *Autumn Legend* is a musical canvas painted in soft tones: comparatively vivid in places, yet still largely mellow in character. The sweep of the lady's hair may remind Rosetti of autumn leaves, but neither the hair nor the leaves are driven by fearsome winds.

♪♪♪♪♪

Peggy Stuart Coolidge: *New England Autumn*

When an American composer shares a generation with Samuel Barber (1910 – 1981) and Leonard Bernstein (1918 – 1990), it is all too easy to be overlooked. Add the further complication of being a woman at a time when musically gifted ladies were accepted as pianists or singers, but rarely as composers, and one understands why the name of Peggy Stuart Coolidge (1913 – 1981) is less familiar than her skills merit.

A graduate of the New England Conservatory, Coolidge – then still Miss Stuart – had planned a career as a concert pianist before discovering her compositional abilities. It is one thing to understand the rules and tools of composition; it is quite another to have ideas worth expressing through those techniques. Coolidge excelled at both understanding and ideas, producing songs and piano pieces, chamber works, a ballet, concertante works, and a number of orchestral scores, these often earning premieres with the Boston Pops and its maestro Arthur Fiedler (1894 – 1979).

Amongst Coolidge's orchestral scores is *New England Autumn* (1971). A two-movement tone poem scarcely a quarter hour in length, the piece begins with *Dawn Over the Mountain,* a sunrise scene of mostly leisurely moods. Gradually, the coloring brightens, thanks in part to deft juxtaposition of woodwinds over strings, particularly English horn combined with harp. Brass instruments have their opportunity as well, adding a further dash of brilliance to this dawn.

With the second movement *Country Fair*, languor is set aside in favor of a spirited country dance, with snare drum and triangle driving the action forward. Occasional passages of sweetness might suggest romantic interludes on the verges of the crowd. As the movement concludes, first more spacious melodies, and then vibrantly high spirits, might lead one to suppose this lively country fair is taking place under the brightest of sunny skies.

♪♪♪♪♪

Rautavaara: *Autumn Gardens*

Helsinki-born Einojuhani Rautavaara (1928 – 2016) got his big break thanks to the best-known name in Finnish fine music, Jean Sibelius (1865 – 1957). In 1955, the American-based Koussevitzky Foundation decided to honor Sibelius' 90th birthday by offering a Juilliard scholarship to any young Finnish composer whom Sibelius might name. His choice fell to Rautavaara, who then spent two years living in the US for studies both at Juilliard and at the Tanglewood Music Center. By the age of thirty, Rautavaara was back in Europe for further studies and a teaching position at the Sibelius Academy. Yet academic activities did not prevent him from working on his own compositions. His catalog includes eight symphonies, eleven operas (most to his own librettos), eleven concerti, short orchestral works, chamber music, solo piano pieces, and much choral music.

Frequently in his works, Rautavaara played with subtle shifts of musical colors, new shades and moods emerging often calmly from the previous idea, so that one atmosphere quite gradually becomes the next. Such is the general spirit of his 1999 orchestral tone poem *Autumn Gardens*. One could observe that, in his native Finland, a garden in autumn might be a barren place; however, Rautavaara's creation is far from sparse in its shading. He uses instrumental resources so that one shade of muted green drifts to another and then another, with diversions to the most vivid shades of gold and bronze when required.

The first movement *Poetico* draws melodic material from Rautavaara's opera *House of the Sun*, borrowing a phrase sung to words referring to a butterfly in an autumn garden. Serene legato lines of shimmering demeanor are juxtaposed to more nimble phrases, the energy rising and falling in gentle waves. It is not, it seems, a purposeful march through the garden, powering on to the next required task; rather, the music suggests a leisurely stroll, with pauses along to way to admire some particularly striking view.

Poetico ends with mellow French horn phrases and string tremolo, but there is no definitive close; rather, Rautavaara wished to move without interruption, in an *attacca* fashion, on to the following *Tranquillo* movement. Here, the scene is more peaceful yet, with long sustained strings, flowing woodwind phrases, and a touch more French horn (the only brass instrument used in *Autumn Gardens*). Apparently, the decision reached while strolling along in the first movement was that one ought stroll less and observe more.

The final movement is marked *Giocoso e leggiero*, that is, "humorous and light." A dance-like mood arises, with rolling triplets for strings and high woodwind phrases. Colors become ever more vivid, like sunshine upon autumn foliage. Calmer interludes appear, though the overall mood is of sweet rapture with occasional bursts of brilliance. Ultimately, the energy calms, leading to a closing with all the gentleness of drifting off to sleep. Rautavaara himself observed that he viewed autumn as "a time of leaves falling," and here, it seems, those leaves find places to rest.

Of the title, and aware that some observers would find gardens and autumn to be almost mutually exclusive, giving the changing weather of the season, Rautavaara remarked that saw parallels between gardening and composing: "In both processes, one observes and controls organic growth rather than constructing or assembling existing components." He expressed a greater fondness for the more informal English-style garden than the tightly controlled French approach. In the easy motion from one idea to another that one hears in Rautavaara's *Autumn Gardens*, one might sense that relaxed connection. Rautavaara's musical blossoms don't grow in tidy geometric rows; they are mixed together, their blended colors and shapes bringing gentle variety to the scene. Grays and greens and golds all come together to create a tenderly shaded autumn vision.

♪♪♪♪♪

Higdon: *Autumn Music*

Jennifer Higdon (b. 1962) composed her *Autumn Music* on commission from the Pi Kappa Lambda national music honorary society; the work premiered in 1994 at the organization's annual convention. Pi Kappa Lambda had specifically requested a wind quintet scored for the standard complement of flute, oboe, clarinet, bassoon, and French horn. Training as a flutist before taking up composition and having played in wind quintets in college, Higdon jumped at the chance to write for a combination she knew well.

The title is in homage to *Summer Music,* a wind quintet composed in 1956 by Samuel Barber (1910 – 1981). Higdon played that work while studying at Barber's alma mater, Philadelphia's Curtis Institute of Music. The composer herself attests, "When Pi Kappa Lambda commissioned the work, asking for a woodwind quintet, I thought, why not write a work that is a response to the Barber?"

The composer describes it as "a sonic picture of the season of brilliant colors," and the instruments allow her to delve deeply into those colors, shading them vividly or subtly, as the mood strikes. Woodwind trills suggest leaves fluttering in the breeze, while long tones from French horn provide a mellow undercurrent. Solos appear for each player, some nimble, others restful, as eager moods yield to peaceful ones.

Higdon's *Autumn Music* closes serenely, though with a subtle surprise, as the oboist and the clarinetist switch to the more wistfully toned English horn and bass clarinet. So this quintet uses five players, but seven instruments. Higdon has remarked that, in addition to the splendor of the season, she also sees a certain melancholy in autumn; the shift to the two lower-pitched and more richly voiced instruments smoothly underscores that closing point. "The season is moving towards winter," Higdon says, and reflecting that fact, musical colors take on a measure of regret.

Higdon's *Autumn Music* came to life a long generation after Barber's *Summer Music*, which was featured in Chapter Four. However, the musical resources are largely the same, just used differently. Together, the two composers – products of the same conservatory – have proved that one can write music of a seasonal nature without it sounding at all like Vivaldi, indeed, without a violin being anywhere in the room. Let the winds have the day!

♫♫♫♫

Whitacre: *October*

Eric Whitacre (b. 1970) has principally found attention as a composer and conductor of choral music, and will appear in that role in Chapter Seven of this survey. However, he is not opposed to using instruments in his music, and even has composed entirely instrumental scores with no voices whatsoever. These include orchestral pieces, as well as works for wind ensemble, some existing in both formats.

Such is the case with Whitacre's *October* (2000). Initially, it was written for and dedicated to Nebraska high school band director Brian Anderson. Then, Whitacre reworked it for string orchestra. In both forms, one finds delicate, bell-like percussion adding some extra shimmer to the musical vision of what the composer has declared to be "my favorite month."

His *October* begins with smooth flowing lines to which is added a serene, song-like melody (oboe or violin, depending on whether one has the wind ensemble score in hand or the string version). A gently pulsing energy develops, still restful, as if suggestive of a leisurely stroll along a woodland path surrounded by the colors of autumn. From time to time, more outspoken moods arise: perhaps a particularly brilliant scene has come into view.

Another solo spotlight gives attention to baritone horn (or cello), and this pattern of calm alternating with more effusive passions continues, ensuring that Whitacre's score will be as determinedly varied as the season itself. Ultimately, *October* comes to a tranquil close on two sustained chords. Might they represent "the end" or perhaps "amen?" Either would suit.

In all, Whitacre's *October* has the blissful tranquility of the finest composers of the English Pastoralism style, including Delius, Bax, Finzi, and Alwyn, all appearing earlier in this chapter, but also Ralph Vaughan Williams (1872 – 1958), whom we shall encounter in Chapter Seven. Whitacre, however, gives the concept an American accent.

♪♪♪♪

What else can one say musically about autumn? As it happens, there is a substantial amount, often of quite varied moods. Here are six other suggestions, mostly smaller-scale works that contrast well with the grander offerings featured earlier in this chapter:

- John Thomas (1826 – 1913): The Welsh-born official harpist for Queen Victoria, Thomas captured the spirit of the season in *Autumn*, his scintillating solo harp rhapsody. It brilliantly proves that music for a single instrument need not necessarily require a piano.

- David Popper (1843 – 1913): The Czech-born cellist/composer's *Im Walde*, op. 50 (*In the Forest*) is a six-movement cello/piano suite replete with song-like and dance-like melodies. Movement subtitles and the energy of the music suggest an autumn day of varied experiences.

- Frank Bridge (1879 – 1941): Structured in two movements, the solo piano piece *In Autumn* begins with "Retrospect," mostly thoughtful in mood, though occasionally anxious. Its livelier second movement is the fluttery "Through the Eaves," suggestive of leaves in the breeze.

- Percy Grainger (1882 – 1961): His gentle *Harvest Hymn* exists in myriad arrangements; these include solo piano, chamber ensemble, chamber orchestra, full orchestra with chorus, and more. Australian-born/British resident/

eventually American citizen Grainger believed in making his music available for almost any imaginable performing forces.

- William Grant Still (1895 – 1978): The African American composer's *Wood Notes* (1947) is a charming orchestral suite offering visions of a singing river, a shimmering autumn night, serene moonlight, and a cheerful whippoorwill.

- Margaret Brandman (b. 1951): The Australian composer's *Autumn Rhapsody* for solo piano is thoughtful, largely serene, and quite beautiful. Perhaps she'll get around to adding three more movements for a full seasonal survey.

Chapter Six: Winter

Midway through Tchaikovsky's *The Nutcracker,* young Clara and her Nutcracker Prince set off for the Land of the Sweets, which apparently lies on the far side of a snowy forest. At least, the composer says it's a forest, and then adds a waltz for snowflakes. Midway through that waltz, he decided that orchestral instruments were not quite enough for the effect he had in mind: voices were required as well. As it happens, it is voices without words, as the composer only wants them to sing the syllable "ah" on gentle phrases that flow up and down, as seen at the head of this page. He asked for soprano and alto voices; either women or a children's choir will serve, though given inevitable crowds of kids both amongst the dancers and in the audience, most performances of *The Nutcracker* opt for a children's choir.

The Nutcracker is more often thought of as a Christmas piece than strictly wintery; after all, the entire first act takes place around a Christmas tree. However, these transitional scenes are winter visions. As for the other works in this chapter, we'll have sleigh rides, ice skating, winter dances, and even a reflection on New Year's.

♪♪♪♪

Oswald: *Floral Suites* – winter sonatas

Folk songs and ballroom dancing both featured in the career of Scottish composer James Oswald (1710 – 1769). Initially, he worked as a dancing master before taking up composition. At first based in Edinburgh, he made his way to London where, in 1761, he was named chamber composer to George III. His works for the monarch, as well as those for the general public, might not have been profound, but their grace and elegance was undoubted and clearly appreciated. Sometimes Oswald crafted arrangements of Scottish folk tunes, which enjoyed much popularity, even south of the border. Evidence suggests that some of the melodies were in fact his own, not of folk origin, but the Scottish flavor was always there, so few found reason to protest.

Oswald's several dozen *Floral Suites* are short chamber sonatas for solo instrument – flute, oboe, or violin, as one chose, all having interchangeable keys and largely similar ranges – together with cello and harpsichord accompaniment. Each is in two or three movements of different tempos; their individual titles refer to garden flowers and are linked to seasons in which Oswald imagined that flower was most likely to be encountered. Whether the music actually sounds like those specific flowers, or whether his winter flowers would appear in winter anywhere other than Oswald's Scotland, depends on one's point of view. However, it is certainly music ideal for drawing room settings and even small recital halls.

The four sonatas designated by Oswald as "winter" are *Golden Rod, Heart's Ease, Snow Drop*, and *Hawthorn*. The first of those is related to the aster family, the second a cousin of the pansy, the third a delicate perennial bulb flowing in late winter, and the last a berry-producing evergreen shrub. *Golden Rod* is cast in alternately tender and eager moods. *Heart's Ease* and *Snow Drop*, though having different melodic material, both tiptoe through their first movements and scurry in their second movements.

Longest of the four winter sonatas, *Hawthorn* opens with a slow, ballad-like movement, followed by a dance-infused second, and a third of quite driven spirit. It is the most folk-like of the four winter sonatas in its rhythmic energy, though the four sonatas together allow performers and listeners alike to explore subtle contrasts in expressive moods, even with only three musicians and scarcely a quarter hour of music. Here are no grand statements, but much elegant expression.

♫♫♫♫

Leopold Mozart: *A Musical Sleigh Ride*

Best remembered as the father of the genius Wolfgang, Leopold Mozart (1719 – 1787) had a successful career of his own long before his son was born. Augsburg-born Leopold was a violinist and composer attached to the music establishment of the Prince-Archbishop of Salzburg, and also published a violin instruction treatise that would soon be in wide usage.

Once it became clear to all that Leopold's younger child was a musical talent for the age, the elder Mozart put his own professional career largely on hold as he set about promoting the youth's gifts to wider audiences. That this mission began when the boy was barely of school age means that relatively little of Leopold's own music survives. However, that which exists provides intriguing evidence of what Salzburg's musical circles were hearing before the next generation came into its own.

Leopold composed several hundred works, including numerous symphonies, much sacred music, and chamber pieces, as well as concerti, dance music, and serenades. This last category includes *A Musical Sleigh Ride*, composed in 1755, just months before Wolfgang's birth. It is an unusually early example of so-called "program music," attempting to tell a story through purely instrumental resources. The idea here is that a group of friends gathers for a sleigh ride, arrives at a village dance, warms up with dancing, and then heads home again.

Leopold tells the tale in six deftly varied movements, some stately and elegant, others perky and spirited. In the third movement, the subtitle declares that young ladies are shivering with cold, a scene that Leopold sets with minor keys and string tremolo effects. Along with the string ensemble, Leopold includes oboe and brass, as well as trumpet fanfares, jingling bells, cracking whips, and even occasionally barking dogs have been included in the boisterous movements by imaginative conductors – or their recording engineers.

Many of those same effects, other than the bells and whips, appear in Leopold Mozart's *Sinfonia da caccia*, a hunting-themed work that appears in Chapter Five. Both are bright and charming, gracefully crafted, and fine evidence of the musical roots from which the unsurpassed talents of Wolfgang arose.

♪♪♪♪

Wolfgang Mozart: German Dance in C major,
    K. 605, no. 3, *Sleigh Ride*

In December, 1787, Wolfgang Amadeus Mozart (1756 – 1791) obtained the only official post he would ever hold at Vienna's Imperial Court. Officially, he became composer of dance music, for which effort he was to receive 800 gulden annually, scarcely one third of what the previous occupant of that post, Christoph Willibald Gluck (1714 – 1787), had earned. Of the salary, Mozart remarked in a letter to his family that it was "too much for what I do, too little for what I could do" Lesser minds might have reacted by putting minimal effort into the job, but, when it came to music, Mozart was very far from a "lesser mind." He put his highest level of craft into even simple assignments, and though one might suppose the dancers in the court's ballroom little noticed the excellence of the music, at least Mozart and his professional colleagues recognized his mastery.

Amongst the works arising from this court position are the Three German Dances that musicologist Ludwig Koechel (1800 – 1877) would later label K. 605. Mozart's own hand recorded on the manuscript that it was completed February 12, 1791, about six weeks before Easter, nicely timed for Carnival celebrations. The dances are scored for strings, pairs of flutes, oboes, bassoons, and horns, along with piccolo, trumpet, timpani, and sleigh bells. It is thanks to this last item that these dances have continued to attract attention. All three are gracefully balanced, stately, gentle, or airy in turn, not using all instruments at all times, thus providing opportunity for varied musical expression.

Only with the last of the three dances, *Sleigh Ride*, do the sleigh bells appear, brightly marking the beat in the second of two alternating themes. With trumpet calls also appearing, one can readily envision dancers being summoned to the sleighs and then setting forth on a spirited winter excursion. It is a simple scene, but when the composer is Mozart, listeners can rely upon the most being made of the musical materials.

♪♪♪♪♪

Waldteufel: *Les Patineurs* (*Skater's Waltz*)

Thanks to the Strauss clan, appearing in Chapters Five and Seven, the Viennese get much of the credit for inventing the waltz. Nevertheless, the dance was not entirely their own. It derived from Austrian folk dances, and at first scandalized society matrons, who were shocked that couples, rather than just touching finger-tips, actually embraced on the dance floor. By the early 19th century, the dance had gained a devoted international following; one French master of the art form was Emil Waldteufel (1837 – 1915).

Born in Strasbourg near the German border (a border that had shifted from east to west over numerous generations), Waldteufel brought his Germanic family name to Paris for studies at the Conservatoire and would spend his career in that city, playing piano for the diversion of Empress Eugenie and writing music for the entertainment of all. Much of that music was intended for the ballroom, and more often than not, was set to the rhythms of the waltz.

Best known of Waldteufel's waltzes is *Les Patineurs* (*Skater's Waltz*), the graceful flow of which would be equally suited to a ballroom or an ice rink. As his rival Strauss would have done, Waldteufel offers not a single waltz melody, which might outstay its welcome, but rather a sequence of contrasting waltz themes, some serene, others exuberant.

Borrowing a technique from the Viennese masters, Waldteufel does not choose to have the music waltz from its very first notes. Instead, he begins with a stately introduction that serves as a kind of call to the dance floor, music that returns near the close of the work. As for the wintry image implied by the title, listen for jingle bells to appear in the percussion midway through the score. A bold coda concludes the whole with the flair of dancers bowing and curtseying at the close of the dance. Those fond of the effusive elegance of *Skater's Waltz* (1882) will find many of the same endearing features in Waldteufel's *Soirée d'ete*, appearing in Chapter Four.

♪♪♪♪♪

Tchaikovsky: Symphony no. 1 in g minor, op. 13, *Winter Dreams*

When a Russian writes a symphony and names it *Winter Dreams*, one might suppose he knows a thing or two about the subject. Certainly, the climate could provide some inspiration. However, when that Russian is a 25-year-old music professor, recently embarked on his second career after having given up on the law, one might then wonder if he would have the skills required to write a symphony at all, regardless of winteriness.

Nonetheless, if the Russian is Peter Tchaikovsky (1840 – 1893), the innate skill is there, and possessing as he did the support of his supervisor at the Moscow Conservatory, Russian pianist and conductor Nicolai Rubinstein (1835 – 1881), there is at least the chance that the musical world will notice. Tchaikovsky's Symphony no. 1 in g, op. 13, *Winter Dreams*, came to life and to the public in part because it was Rubinstein's idea: not the winter theme; just the thought of writing a symphony at all.

Tchaikovsky began his Symphony no. 1 early in 1866, many weeks before his 26th birthday, which would not come until May 1. His correspondence from the time reveals that he felt ill-prepared for the task, and fear of failure led him to proceed only slowly on the ambitious new score. Once it was finally completed late that year, he dedicated it to Rubinstein, and that maestro included the third movement – only the third movement – on a concert given before New Year's.

Two months later, the second and third movements were heard together, but it was not until February 1868 that the complete symphony was performed. Although it was well-received, Tchaikovsky, ever uncertain of his skills, decided that the audience was mistaken and set about revisions, not allowing its publication until 1875.

Tchaikovsky provided descriptive subtitles for two of the four movements: *Dreams of a Winter Journey* for the first and *Land of Desolation, Land of Mists* for the second. However, the "misty desolation" of a winter journey on the Russian steppes is not to be heard. Here, despite the minor key, one finds Tchaikovsky in general optimistic demeanor.

Perhaps mindful of being a rookie in the world of symphonies, Tchaikovsky chose standard orchestral forces: pairs of woodwinds and trumpets, four horns, timpani, and strings. The complement is no more progressive than what Beethoven would have used sixty years earlier, though the treatment of those forces is largely Tchaikovsky's own.

The first movement *Allegro tranquillo* opens peacefully with flowing lines from woodwinds and shimmering ones from strings. Gradually, energy builds to a burst of bold brass, seemingly announcing that this *Winter Journey* is underway. Languid contrasting passages appear, especially for strings, though the overall mood is of outspoken exuberance. Apparently, this dreamed-of winter journey is one in which adventure and delight are both anticipated. The movement closes with gentle recollection of its opening measures.

The second movement *Adagio cantabile ma non tanto* (Restful, song-like, but not too relaxed) is less frosty than the composer's subtitle of desolation and mists might suggest. From piccolo to bassoon, woodwinds are sing, and cellos, too, enjoy a prominent role. Later in the movement, there is a heroic surge of horns, though this passage also takes on sweeter colors. A general mood of restfulness continues to the final phrases.

Much of the material for the third movement *Scherzo* – specifically its opening and closing pages – Tchaikovsky borrowed from his early Piano Sonata in c-sharp minor. It begins with a playful, swirling exchange between woodwinds and strings, spirited and danceable in its energy. The central pages bring, at first, ominous shadows, which, before long, resolve into sweetness. The eventual restatement of the opening material is accomplished gradually, hints of its phrases beginning to sneak in the door en route to an assertive closing.

Tchaikovsky chose to begin the final movement with a slow introduction, to which he gives the tempo marking not only of *Andante*, but more descriptively *Andante lugubre*: slow and lugubrious, and, as it happens, rather sober. That sobriety will not last long. The tempo increases and the music builds, powering toward celebratory brass and percussion, launching festivities for all. If this is a Russian winter, then it must be time for a winter carnival, with boisterous crowds skating to folk-like rhythms and laughing as the sunshine sparkles on the snow. Tchaikovsky will end his *Winter Dreams* symphony with brilliant fireworks.

♪♪♪♪

Tchaikovsky: *The Nutcracker*, op. 71 –
  Scene in the Forest and *Waltz of the Snowflakes*

The Nutcracker is handily the most famous and most performed of all ballets. However, it has always been rather unusual in the world of dance. Its first half, set at a Christmas party, has as much graceful strolling around the stage as actual dancing, and its second half is almost entirely lacking in plot. Those facts have never prevented the work from being adored.

Last of three ballets by Peter Tchaikovsky (1840 – 1893), *The Nutcracker* premiered in St. Petersburg on December 18, 1892 (December 6 according to the old style calendar then used in Tzarist Russia). Coming that late in his career, it contains some of his most magical music; after all, he'd had a quarter-century before critical audiences and observers to hone his skills. Even without dancers, it is music that stands brilliantly on its own – something that cannot be said of all famous ballets.

Occupying the transition between *The Nutcracker*'s two acts are the *Scene in the Forest* and *Waltz of the Snowflakes*. The young leading lady and her Nutcracker Prince are journeying through the snow to The Land of the Sweets where they will be entertained by a divertissement of vaguely international dances. All of those scenes will be quite short. For more expansive musical expression, however, Tchaikovsky allowed himself this wintery interlude, shading the two scenes with a generally light touch of the brush.

The *Scene in the Forest* opens with a rising harp arpeggio leading to flowing phrases for strings. These become both richer and more expansive as winds join, building to rapturous moods. Bold brass and cymbals dominate the central pages, expanding upon previous ideas. A cymbal crash then signals a return to the delicacy of the scene's opening, leading directly in the *Waltz of the Snowflakes*.

For the waltz, solo flute warbles over strings, the two elements echoing one another. These ideas grow into the main waltz theme, flute and harp prominently on display. As the music grows fuller, a wordless chorus joins in with a new theme evolved from the earlier flute material; the opening phrase of this melody appears at the head of this chapter. Tchaikovsky gives them no words to sing, only the syllable "ah." They are there not for plot, but for color. Quicker tempos and fuller colors, complete with brass, lead to a spacious harp solo, then hastening strings, with brass and cymbals driving the forward charge. Once more, voices join in, leading to a delicately starlit coda that might suggest an ethereal closing. In fact, Tchaikovsky has one more surprise in mind: a few powerful chords that drive his *Waltz of the Snowflakes* to its close.

One can scarcely imagine a more sparkling vision of winter snows. Perhaps it required a Russian, such as Tchaikovsky, to bring it to life. Certainly, it is a vividly crafted vision of the scene. This former law clerk had spent decades perfecting his craftsmanship.

♫♫♫♫♫

Ysaÿe: *Chant d'hiver,* op. 15 (*Winter Song*)

Belgian-born Eugène Ysaÿe (1858 – 1931) was the son of a violinist and before the age of eight was studying at the Liège Conservatory. Before many years passed, he developed a reputation for blending a nimble technique with a lyrical, flowing line. Another great Belgian, Cesar Franck (1822 – 18890) was a firm admirer, and composed his own Violin Sonata in D major in celebration of Ysaÿe's marriage; Ysaÿe gave its first performance in 1886, and ever since, violinists of any nationality have given thanks for the piece inspired by the friendship of these two countrymen.

When time permitted, Ysaÿe himself also composed; he never studied formally, but instead used techniques learned through playing, flavored with his own free-spirited approach. His compositional catalog includes a set of six fiendishly difficult sonatas for utterly solo violin with no piano accompaniment, a quintet, a trio, and a variety of virtuosic violin showcases, both with piano accompaniment and with orchestra, for use on his own concerts and recitals. Some of those programs were given in the US, where he served as music director of the Cincinnati Symphony from 1918 – 1922.

Ysaÿe's violin showpieces exploited his own performing technique, readily able to manage both the most intricate passagework and the gentlest, songlike lines. The former may be more flamboyant, but the latter is no less challenging to pull off, particularly with consistency of phrasing and evenness of tone.

Ysaÿe's *Chant d'hiver* (*Winter Song*) exists in two forms: violin with orchestral support, or, alternatively, with piano. In either case, the solo lines are often calm and reflective, as if this "song" is mostly concerned with placid views of snowy landscapes. However, anxious moods develop, as do yearning phrases: somewhere out there in the snow is the beloved. Storms arise, though all settles back into restfulness. Ultimately, his *Chant d'hiver* drifts to its close on long sustained tones that fade to silence. This song of winter, it seems, becomes a song of a winter night.

♪♪♪♪♪

Rimsky-Korsakov: *The Snow Maiden* (*Snegurochka*) – orchestral suite

Properly speaking, *The Snow Maiden* is not entirely a wintery tale. Fifth of fourteen operas by Nicolai Rimsky-Korsakov (1844 – 1908), the fanciful story derives from a play by Alexander Ostrovsky (1823 – 1886) about the daughter of the Frost King. Recklessly ignoring her father's advice, she sets out in search of human love that she has been told will kill her. She finds love with an honest fellow who means her well, though the acceptance of that love causes Snegurochka to melt into away. Rimsky's opera has scenes set in springtime, and even carries the subtitle *A Spring Fairy Tale*. Nonetheless, one might imagine it as a winter morality play: had Snegurochka taken Dear Old Dad's advice, she might have remained ever safe in a wintery world. Her passing frees the people of Tsar Berendey from an overlong winter.

Given the challenges of presenting a staged production of any Russian-language opera – other than Tchaikovsky's *Eugene Onegin* – in American and Western European opera houses, Rimsky's *The Snow Maiden* is generally encountered in the form of an orchestral suite. Fortunately, the suite's four selections represent some of the most vividly colored music in the entire opera. Throughout, one finds evidence of the composer's familiarity with and fondness for the timbres of wind instruments, which in his memoir he credits to his experience as Director of Navy Bands.

The *Introduction/Prologue* is drawn from the scene with which the opera as a whole begins, one of Nature awakening in the forest under a full moon. One finds quiet elegance with smooth string textures and phrases passed around amongst the woodwind instruments. As the tempo picks up, piccolo starts to hint at motifs that will become predominant in the second movement *Dance of the Birds*. Gradually, the *Prologue* grows fuller with peaceable French horn phrases.

Also from Act One, the *Dance of the Birds* is light on its feet and fluttery with readily recognizable cuckoo calls from the clarinet and other birds elsewhere in the orchestra; Rimsky attests that young merlins are heard. An exuberant frolic develops, becoming ever fuller in coloring, though the bird-like phrases remain. Here, there is nothing but good cheer and high spirits, and, after all, as anyone who has kept a bird-feeder stocked all winter can attest, even wintery weather will not necessarily keep song birds from being lively.

The suite's third movement, *Cortege*, derives from Act Two's Procession of Tsar Berendey: a grand scene having much potential for on-stage splendor. Short phrases anticipate fanfare-like trumpet calls, leading to a regal marching theme. This is no military parade: it is a stately procession of courtiers. Those little phrases that had preceded the trumpet calls return again and again in ever new character, bring further variety to what is yet the shortest movement in the suite.

Last of all comes Act Three's *Dance of the Clowns/Tumblers*, jolly of mood and swirling of energy, with frequent contributions from percussion, including triangle and cymbals. It brings *The Snow Maiden* suite to an effervescent close, drawing upon the various sections of the orchestra for ever more vibrant coloring. Soon, Rimsky would be at work on a textbook on the subject of orchestration, and here, his delight in instrumental effects is on full display. That treatise is still available, and makes clear his facility for instrumental coloration.

One also finds *The Snow Maiden* in the catalog of Rimsky's colleague Peter Tchaikovsky (1840 – 1893). Tchaikovsky, however, had written not an opera, but only incidental music to accompany a staged production of Ostrovsky's play. Moreover, it is Rimsky who gave to the musical world the beloved sounds of playful birds and exuberant tumblers from *The Snow Maiden*'s magical world. Nonetheless, the two works make an intriguing pair, as one reflects on how two great masters reacted differently to the same tale.

♪♪♪♪♪

Debussy: piano suite for winter

Bless those imaginative Impressionists! Thanks to their fondness for descriptive titles, one can craft a winter piano suite from the music of Claude Debussy (1862 – 1918) despite the utter absence of the French word "hiver" (winter) in his catalog. The composer may not have chosen to specifically name the season, but he often alluded to aspects of that coldest time of the year. Taken together, they make a splendidly varied little journey through a winter landscape.

Rather than beginning with something outspoken and dramatic, let's consider something more subtle, *De pas sur la neige* (*Footsteps in the Snow*). Sixth of the twelve items in Debussy's Preludes – Book One (1910), the music implies that whoever is making those footsteps is neither trudging through a gale nor stepping lightly across the lawn. The action is cautious, though not exactly fearful. *De pas sur la neige* is all tentative delicacy, with a recurring two-note pattern perhaps suggestive of placing one foot ahead of the other, then pausing to consider one's next move.

At times, contrasting phrases more flowing in nature stand juxtaposed against those footsteps. These elements descend in pitch, but do so gradually, more like snowflakes falling than a person swept off his feet. Note that Debussy's chosen title specifies footsteps, not footprints. It is the process of making those steps, not prints left earlier in the snow.

Greater motion, even if not yet surging energy, appears in the second of twelve pieces in Book Two of Debussy's Preludes (1913), *Feuilles mortes* (*Dead Leaves*). Admittedly, "dead leaves" might be doing almost anything, from lying damply on the forest floor to swirling frenetically in the wind. However, Debussy chooses neither extreme. Poignant chords punctuated by short passagework suggest the last few leaves drifting to the forest floor. Particularly in the central pages, there is rather more action, though gentle not urgent, and the melodic flow never strays far from a central point. It is music of gray melancholy, not black despair. If winter comes, can spring be far behind?

A brighter view of winter comes with *La neiges danses (The Snow is Dancing),* from Debussy's *Coin des enfants* (*Children's Corner*) written in 1908 and dedicated to the composer's toddler daughter Claude-Emma (familiarly known as Chou-Chou). In this fourth of six movements, a short phrase rising in pitch is repeated again and again, occasionally punctuated by serene chords. More exuberant motion is implied in the comparably fervent central pages, though the movement will close largely as it had begun. It is music full of smiles, leading one to suppose that little Chou-Chou loved to play in the falling snow.

For a brisk finale to our imagined winter-themed piano suite, let us return to the Preludes, this time Book One (1910), where we began. Here, as third of the dozen pieces, one finds *Le vent dans la plaine* (*The Wind on the Plain*). The music suggests that this wind, though relatively steady, is not of gale force. Something, be it leaves or snow or small resident creatures, is moving along with the wind, but it is nimble action, scurrying in nature, rather than racing desperately along. Firm chords occur from time to time, though not so frequently as to suggest a continual force, let alone a formidable one. *Le vent dans la plaine* (*The Wind on the Plain*) makes for an energetic, though not overly dramatic, conclusion to our ten-minute solo piano suite for winter. Thank you, Debussy, for some delightful wintery impressions!

♪♪♪♪♪

Fučík: *Winterstürme Walzer*, op. 184 (*Winter Storms*)

Julius Fučík (1872 – 1916) was the Czech John Philip Sousa (1854 – 1932). Like the American "March King," Fučík is best known for composing martial music, but actually had a diversified career. Born in Prague, Fučík studied composition with Antonín Dvořák (1841 – 1904), then joined a military band. Four years later, Fučík returned to civilian life to perform with orchestras in Eastern Europe, but soon the world of military bands again beckoned, this time as a conductor. Throughout Fučík's active performing career, he composed hundreds of short works, mostly marches and waltzes, although also more ambitious pieces, including a requiem. The parallel between Fučík and Sousa lies not merely in marches and conducting. Both men, due in part to their great compositional productivity, developed an interest in the publishing business. In Fučík's case, that led to the founding of the music publishing firm, Tempo Verlag.

Fučík's *Entry of the Gladiators* may be his most famous march; few can have escaped hearing it in cinematic circus scenes. However, his *Winterstürme Waltz* (*Winter Storms*) offers more of in the way of fine craftsmanship. It begins with an ominous brass fanfare, soon joined by the full orchestra with much percussion. Its threatening mood suggests a formidable tempest. More wistful contrasting passages imply a gentler side, not only to the weather and to the voices of brass, but also to Fučík's own artistry. So far, none would suspect that a waltz is in the offing. However, Johann Strauss Jr. (1825 – 1899) had long earlier popularized the notion of prefacing waltzes with dramatic introductions, and that's exactly what Fučík has in mind. Ultimately, a waltz theme appears, unusually, one in a minor key, as if the ballroom is filled with tense thoughts about the storm outside. However, sweeter passages begin to appear and ultimately, *Winterstürme* becomes bright and festive, driving spiritedly into its final chords. Music, it seems, can keep the storms at bay.

♫♫♫♫

Holst: *A Winter Idyll*

It is with his orchestral suite *The Planets* (1920) that Gustav Holst (1874 – 1934) seized the attention of the musical public. Ambitious both in scope and in inspiration, that work came to represent Holst's compositional voice to colleagues and audiences alike, a fact that the shy composer ultimately regretted. His other works were closer to his heart, as Holst was not a man fond of the spotlight.

Rather more representative of his retiring personality is his early tone poem *A Winter Idyll* (1897). Here is pastoral side of Holst's musical personality, enamored of a strong English trend to celebrate natural beauty – especially that of the nation's gentle countryside – in music of peaceable character. *A Winter Idyll* suggests a fresh and sunlit day, with perhaps a bit of snow lying over the fields, but not so much as to prevent smiles. On the verge of graduation from the Royal College of Music, Holst apparently wanted to put his newly learned skills to the test.

A few stern, brass-driven chords open *A Winter Idyll*, though these promptly yield to flowing strings and then brighter moods, some lyrically song-like and others eagerly dance-like, especially when in the care of woodwinds. Those two musical ideas appear in turn, often in close succession, and phrases pass from one orchestral section to another, gaining new colors and moods with each shift. Grander statements develop, some complete with almost Wagnerian brass outbursts, though the playful side of winter is never far absent. This is, after all, an "idyll," not a heroic adventure. Holst's piece is more vibrant than determined, and he clearly knew how to make much of his orchestral forces, which here include an English horn and various percussion choices, along with the usual suspects. He was not yet a household name, but an attentive listener can already find the signs of Holst's fine craftsmanship, here just emerged from the bud.

♫♫♫♫

Dohnányi: *Winterreigen (Winter Rounds)*, op. 13

Early in his career, Bratislava-native Ernst von Dohnányi (1877 – 1960) – or Ernö Dohnányi, to give the name its Hungarian form – enjoyed the support of Brahms. Throughout his life, Dohnányi continued to compose in a somewhat Brahmsian manner, rather than mimicking his own generation. His contemporaries were welcome to find new and different ways to fling the rule book out the window. However, Dohnányi preferred to show how the old ideas still worked in a modern age, traditional structures and means of achieving balance leavened with only a dash of late 19th century harmonies.

Dohnányi's *Winterreigen (Winter Rounds)* dates from 1905, when he had recently left his previous home-base of Vienna to accept a teaching position at Berlin's Hochschule für Musik. It is a set of ten short solo piano pieces, each of varying personality, exactly the sort of thing that the previous generation would have called "character pieces." German master composer Robert Schumann (1810 – 1856) was especially fond of the genre, even going so far as to try to evoke in each piece specific personal friends. Dohnányi does much the same thing, heading each of the eight central movements – those other than the prelude and postlude – with the name of someone he knew. As for the Schumann connection, that gentleman's *Papillons (Butterflies)* provides the delicate main theme of Dohnányi's introductory *Widmung (Dedication)*, the melody recurring more assertively in the final *Postludium*, neatly framing Dohnányi's work.

Winterreigen's eight central pieces provide a cornucopia of varied moods. The second movement *March of Cheerful Comrades* is as forthright as its title suggests, though with contrastingly relaxed central passages. The third movement *To Ada* is light and elegant, with the lady's name spelled out over and over in musical notes: A – D – A. *Friend Victor's Mazurka* is by turns jaunty and graceful, whereas *Music of the Spheres* – which the composer attested was inspired by a hot air balloon ride – is floating in nature, with Impressionistic chords and a brief appearance of high drama in its central lines.

Valse amiable, the sixth movement overall, is a rather abstract dance, with themes yielding peacefully to one another. Movement number seven, *At Midnight*, is all stormy motion, with firmly surging phrases in the low pitches for the left hand, while the right hand is busy with sparkling cascades of high pitched notes. The *Jolly Companions* of the eighth movement are a boisterous bunch, though with playful passages providing levity. Last of the scenic movements is *Morning Shadows*: the title may suggest ominous clouds, though the music itself reflects more of a restfully songlike atmosphere. Together, the set is a tribute not only to the specific friends whom Dohnányi identified by name, but also to his own musical craftsmanship and imagination.

The title *Winterreigen* (*Winter Rounds*) alludes not to the travels of a courier on the move, but rather to a similarly named poem by Victor Heindl, the same fellow to whom Dohnányi dedicated the fourth movement *Mazurka*. In that context, a "round" is a particular sort of dance, and in his poem, Heindl suggests a group of friends escaping their worries on a starry winter night:

"Ye friends, reach out your hand to the splendid dance! ... Such a beautiful fairytale dream!" "Ade," the poet ultimately declares: not the lady's name "Ada," but a Germanic twist on "Adieu." These letters (A – D – E) Dohnányi spells out in musical terms in the *Postludium*, just as earlier he had rendered Fräulein Ada's name. With that gesture, he brings *Winterreigen* to a close, bidding it farewell rather as one might imagine he had waved goodbye to this set of friends, not being sure if he would see them again.

♪♪♪♪♪

Bloch: *Hiver-Printemps (Winter-Spring)*

In recent realms of creative expression, one finds two men with remarkably similar names, who unfortunately led contemporaneous lives, thus causing a degree of possible confusion. These were Ernst Bloch (1885 – 1977) and Ernest Bloch (1880 – 1959). Ernst was a German philosopher, Ernest a Swiss-born composer who moved to the US and took American citizenship. Although Ernst once wrote about how the hopes of mankind are expressed through music, it was Ernest who actually undertook that expression himself.

Composed in 1905, Ernest Bloch's *Hiver-Printemps (Winter-Spring)* speaks vividly of that transitional time when the gentle weariness of late winter moves onward, even as the burgeoning life of early spring steps into the light. The first of the two movements is serene and moody with barely tense chromatic harmonies. Flowing string lines, restful brass and woodwind phrases, as well as particular focus upon violin, clarinet, harp, and English horn ensure that the atmosphere, though definitely hesitant in its forward motion, never becomes too dark.

As for the second movement dedicated to spring, one could scarcely imagine anything further from darkness. Bright flute, piccolo and distant brass motifs alternate with passages of increasing eagerness. From time to time, one might be certain that one is hearing the sounds of spring sweetly spread across the landscape with all the musical hope for the future that one could desire for such a scene. Those fond of the ballet *Daphnis and Chloe* by Ernest Bloch's shorter-lived near contemporary Maurice Ravel (1875 – 1937) will find in Bloch's music a similarly splendid tapestry of orchestral color.

♪♪♪♪♪

Korngold: *The Snowman* – ballet

In the 1930s, his music would become the soundtrack to the swashbuckling adventures of Errol Flynn, but Erich Korngold (1897 – 1957) started out far from Hollywood. He was born in what is now Brno in the Moravian region of what has become the Czech Republic. At the time, it was part of the Austrian Empire and Erich's father Julius was an eminent music critic whose opinions could make or break the success of works even by the greatest composers. The elder Korngold saw to it that the lad received not only training in piano playing, but also in composition.

Even before Erich reached his teens, his compositions were earning favor from the great names of the day, from Giacomo Puccini (1858 – 1924) to Gustav Mahler (1860 – 1911) to Richard Strauss (1864 – 1949). Skeptics might suggest that those gentlemen dared not cross swords with the elder Korngold. However, in other contexts, they were happy to speak their minds, and besides, young Erich's music reveals no faults that one might even credit to lack of experience. He could turn a musical phrase and make the most of it, whether it was best suited for chamber music or the operatic stage: Erich Korngold was the Mozart of his time.

One of his earliest compositions, praised by all three of the master composers named above, was the ballet *Der Schneemann* (*The Snowman*), telling a tale derived from the folk-theater form *commedia dell-arte*. Its first performance – by piano four-hands and solo violin – was given April 14, 1910; not quite having reached his teens, the young composer was one of the two pianists. Interest arose to have it orchestrated for performance at the Vienna Opera House. Here, young Erich, or at least his father, hesitated briefly. The youth had only just begun formal study of composition with respected composer Alexander Zemlinsky (1871 – 1942), and insiders wondered if Erich was quite ready for such a big step. Zemlinsky agreed to take on the task himself, crafting an orchestral version of his student's chamber work. This reached the public October 4, 1910; perhaps the instrumental selections were not young Korngold's own, but melodies, harmonies, and overall structures, even the lissome violin solos, were entirely from his imagination.

As a whole, *The Snowman* is alternately rapturous and lyrical with a certain tendency to waltz, sometimes gently, at others spiritedly. One finds bouncy folk-like passages, an often playful energy, and, at times, forthright, rather ominous scenes. The solo violin passages are song-like in a sweetly romantic manner. One can readily imagine these as Pierrot serenading his adored Columbine, long before he is chased off by children armed with snowballs. The snowman of the title serves as a diversion allowing Pierrot to sneak into the house and run off with Columbine blissfully on his arm. There is nothing epic here, but it is surely lovely music, worthy of any composer, let alone of a twelve-year-old Korngold.

♪♪♪♪

Finzi: *New Year's Music*, op.7

For a set of three simple words, *New Year's Music* is remarkably non-specific in meaning. To some, it might imply noisy, public, champagne-infused festivities. Others may imagine an intimate one-on-one evening, while yet others see only loneliness. The music that would accompany any of those three visions would ill-suit either of the others. However, in the case of his *New Year's Music* (1928), English composer Gerald Finzi (1901 – 1956) helpfully provided an answer as to his inspiration. The composer attested that what he had in mind was the essay *New Year's Eve* by English writer Charles Lamb (1775 – 1834).

Lamb's work has nothing to do with parties, and only touches passingly on intimacy and loneliness; he is more concerned with musing in "sober sadness" (his phrase) upon the passage of time and how the close of the year might bring such thoughts to the forefront of one's mind. According to Finzi, his *New Year's Music* was his own reflection upon Lamb's ideas. Thus, its inspiration is not wintery per se. However, as both Lamb and Finzi were Englishmen, any New Year's reflections would have been seasoned with shorter days, colder temperatures, and perhaps a chance of snow. So let the work stand here amongst our winter selections.

Finzi's ten-minute tone poem on the subject begins in very reserved mood, with low strings and winds; textures do not so much build as gradually emerge from the mists. Phrases rise and fall in a wave-like fashion, and before long, solo passages for muted trumpet and then, even more prominently, English horn, emerge. It might suggest a solitary walk along a quiet road on a frosty, starlit night. Richer, more passionate passages develop, becoming at times truly splendid with timpani rolls and cymbal crashes, though before long, the peaceable opening moods return. These will last to the final page. At the close, English horn takes the spotlight again before all fades away. It is a restful closing, not a grim one, and one could say the same of Lamb's essay. As the writer observed, "New Year's Days are past. I survive, a jolly candidate for 1821." If Finzi's music is not exactly jolly, it is yet exquisite music of endurance and hope.

♪♪♪♪♪

Anderson: *Sleigh Ride*

A first-generation American, son of Swedish-immigrant parents, Leroy Anderson (1908 – 1975) was born in Cambridge, Massachusetts, and pursued higher education at Harvard, both in music and in languages; his World War II military service would be as a translator. At Harvard, he arranged some pieces for the college band, and when these earned the attention of Arthur Fiedler (1994 – 1979), the revered conductor began promoting the young man's music, playing it with his Boston Pops orchestra. Soon, Anderson was coming to international attention, a spotlight he would not surrender for another half century.

Anderson cared not for grand orchestral statements, never bothering to write symphonies or operas. However, few could match his unerring ability to craft light, imaginative orchestral pieces. From *Bugler's Holiday* to *The Syncopated Clock*, from *The Typewriter* to *The March of Two Left Feet*, he kept pops concerts and radio programs well supplied, and even earned a star on the Hollywood Walk of Fame for his contributions to the recording industry. Anderson was also elected to the Songwriters' Hall of Fame. Both honors came after his death, but at least he had had ample opportunity to observe that his music was well-received by generations of diverse audiences. If, as Mozart once observed, "above all else, music must be pleasing to the ear," Anderson achieved that goal in no uncertain terms.

Like much of his music, Anderson's widely beloved *Sleigh Ride* (1948) exists in multiple arrangements: for string orchestra, full orchestra, symphonic band, and any of those with or without additional chorus. He well understood the practicality of making his music available to diverse ensembles. It is bright and festive with sleigh bells and wood blocks reinforcing the scene. Each time the central melody recurs, it becomes a bit bigger and more exuberant, until by its last appearance, it has acquired syncopation and bluesy color, telling us that this wintry journey is an exciting occasion. On the final page, a four-note pattern repeats, rising in energy, until Anderson wraps up the scene with solo trumpet evoking the whinnying of a horse. It is a colorful and imaginative way to end a sleigh ride, and trumpeters delight in having the final spotlight.

♪♪♪♪♪

Tower: *Snow Dreams*

Snow Dreams by Joan Tower (b. 1938) was written in 1983 at the request of guitarist Sharon Isbin and flutist Carol Wincenc. Isbin had recently come to know Tower's music, and being given, as she describes it, an "opportunity to premiere a new work for the two of us [herself and Wincenc] in concert," she directed the offer to Tower. Twenty-five years later, the work is still in their repertoire and enjoys a devoted following, in part because, as Isbin observes, "both instruments are given equally strong roles and are showcased in solo passages as well." There is also the fact that *Snow Dreams* is quite beautiful and often exciting.

Snow Dreams opens with guitar quite alone, offering a short rhythmic motif that expands and contracts. As the guitar line broadens, the flute joins in, gently and very low in its range, to quite haunting effect. Busier passages begin to appear, first for one instrument, then the other, with more spacious phrasing and more restless energy, though the thoughtful character of the opening lines returns regularly. Some listeners will notice a four-note musical fragment, three short notes followed by one longer one, which may remind them of Beethoven's Symphony no. 5, though here far more subtly expressed.

In *Snow Dreams*, both players have substantial solo passages, making the resumption of the other person's participation especially notable. Tower says she opted for these alternating solo passages so the guitar would not be overwhelmed by the flute. Waves of urgent activity develop; as Isbin observes, "it is remarkable how Joan achieved a new 'third instrument' by combining the virtuosity of both instruments in blazing 16th notes played together." At last, calm is restored, with a shimmering guitar tremolo, flute trills, rhythmic fragments, and a single long, sustained tone bringing the piece serenely to a close.

Of the title *Snow Dreams*, which the composer herself chose, Tower remarks that the word "snow" may imply many images: "light snow flakes, pockets of swirls of snow, rounded drifts, long white plains of blankets of snow, light and heavy snowfalls, etc." She also observes that, though one might find many of those images in *Snow Dreams*, one need not necessarily look for them at all: the music can stand on its own. Indeed so, though given the work's character – initially sparse, then gaining complexity and intensity, before fading to a close – one might readily imagine a developing, then passing snowstorm. One might also simply hear *Snow Dreams* as a tapestry of musical expressions that shift in character, the better to explore the voices of her chosen instruments: that approach also offers delights.

Tower was born in suburban New York City, but raised in Bolivia, where her engineer father's professional commitments took the family. Given the prevalence of both guitars and flutes in music of the Andes, the commission that resulted in *Snow Dreams* may have been ideally suited for Tower's leanings.

♪♪♪♪

Daughtery: *American Gothic* – II. Winter Dreams

It may be the most iconic image in all of American art: a dour pair posed in front of an equally solemn house, the fellow grasping a three-tined pitchfork, the woman not meeting the painter's gaze. It's *American Gothic* (1930) by Grant Wood (1891 – 1942), loaning not only its title, but also imagery to this orchestral work by Michael Daughtery (b. 1954). An Iowa native, as was Wood, the composer was well familiar with the artist's down-home approach to modernism. Daughtery thought Wood's visions would be the perfect theme for a commission he had from Orchestra Iowa; his *American Gothic* premiered May 4, 2013.

The last movement of the orchestral suite bears the title *Pitchfork* in reference to that so-very-famous canvas. The first, *On a Roll*, recalls Wood's evocations of Iowa cornfields. Between the two is *Winter Dreams*, characterized not only by the slower tempo found in many middle movements, but also by gentler energy and magical instrumental colors. Daughtery attests that he was thinking of two particular Wood canvases, *January* and *February* (both 1940). The former captures an array of haystacks plastered on one side by wind-blown snow. The latter has horses, rather than haystacks, each standing in the snow and facing toward a barbed wire fence, the flow of their manes and tails implying a substantial breeze. Both have the austerity of winter on the High Plains. Just because Wood grew up in the countryside and Daughtery in the comparatively urban community of Cedar Rapids does not mean that both might not be familiar with the feeling of an Iowa winter day.

The *Winter Dreams* movement opens with lonely, very low-pitched phrases from alto flute, accompanied by shimmering strings and triangle. The music shivers as an observer might were one standing amidst those haystacks. Solo spotlights arrive for violin and oboe, amongst others: mellow spotlights, more meditative than virtuosic. Before long, Daughtery adds sleigh bells and glockenspiel, so perhaps those horses standing in the field are now trotting down the lane to some more congenial place. By the closing pages, that delicate opening mood has returned, largely as before, with alto flute and strings, bringing Daughtery's *Winter Dreams* to a peaceful close.

♫♫♫♫

Torke: *December*

The music of Milwaukee-born Michael Torke (b. 1961) tends to be vividly colored, using instrumental forces – often grand ones – to convey varied and diverse images. Here, after all, is a composer whose catalog includes works titled *Ecstatic Orange* and *Bright Blue Music*, and who, upon writing a work for the 1996 Atlanta Summer Olympics and athletically naming it *Javelin*, then admitted the title might also relate to the American muscle car of the same name.

His *December* (1995) was not originally an attempt to give musical expression to the last month of the year. A composition starts to come into shape, and as it is in process, Torke begins to realize what images and memories it brings to mind for him. In the case of *December*, originally titled *Rain Changing into Snow*, it was memories of his childhood paper route, specifically in early winter with the first snow dusting newly strung Christmas lights. The often shimmering music makes clear that, for Torke, this is a positive reminiscence.

His *December* opens with playful, dance-like themes built of melodic fragments that grow and evolve. A contrasting middle passage is slower and more restful, as if our paperboy is lingering over a cup of cocoa at a friendly neighbor's home. Then, the opening theme returns, with much buoyant action, though not nervous tension. Reflecting on the work's original title, perhaps the temperature has fallen enough that the rain has changed to gently falling snow; the precipitation no longer drenches the scene, but instead gives it sparkle. *December* ends with a pair of chords that seem to say "the end," or perhaps "I'm home." If one wished for evidence that modern music can charm the ear, without launching an aural assault, here it is.

♪♪♪♪♪

Ellisor: *Blackberry Winter*

Many composers have flavored their works with folk traditions. For Béla Bartók (1881 – 1945), that meant the spirited rhythms of Hungarian dance; for Ralph Vaughan Williams (1872 – 1958), it was the harmonic flow of English traditional songs. Coming of age in a melting pot, American composers face a different challenge: choosing which of countless cultures one might capture. The compositions of Conni Ellisor, a Juilliard-trained violinist who began her professional career in the violin section of the Denver Symphony before relocating to Nashville, are often influenced by the connection that latter home has with bluegrass and country music, blended with her classical roots. Those influences come together in *Blackberry Winter*, a chamber concerto for mountain dulcimer and Tennessee music box with string ensemble. The specific inspiration would have been startling for Bartók and Vaughan Williams, but not the motivation, nor the elegance and energy of the result.

Commissioned by the Nashville Chamber Orchestra, *Blackberry Winter* (1996) was inspired in part by David Schnaufer, a gifted artist on both chosen solo instruments. Ellisor structured the solo part so as to best utilize those folk instruments' ranges, timbres, and techniques, while remaining mindful of the fact that, if she was going to modulate to a different key mid-movement, the soloist would need time to retune his instruments.

The mountain dulcimer, sometimes known as the Appalachian dulcimer, is a finger-plucked fretted instrument with three or four strings and a long, narrow sound box. Unlike the guitar or members of the violin family, the mountain dulcimer has essentially no neck, the instrument's body reaching nearly from end to end. By contrast, the Tennessee music box is rectangular in form, an open box usually strung with four strings, which one might play either by plucking or with a bow; it is often set upon a table top to play. The two sound quite different from one another, and also from standard orchestral instruments. However, being characteristic of the same musical heritage, they are congenial companions when paired in a single work.

As Ellisor was at work on the piece, Nashville experienced a late spring frost, the sort of weather that folk tradition terms a "blackberry winter," reflecting the fact that such conditions may trigger abundant blackberry crops the following summer. Hence the work's title, as well as Ellisor's decision to reference in the first movement, the old bluegrass tune *Blackberry Blossom*. So the title is both a tribute to a central melody and to the season.

Structured in three movements, none of which bears a specific heading, the work opens with the string ensemble in gentle demeanor. The dulcimer joins, its light, almost brittle voice given generally downward flowing lines. Before long, more eager moods develop for ensemble and soloist alike, as the tune *Blackberry Blossom* appears. In places, quick moving passages are juxtaposed directly against more smoothly flowing phrases, and Ellisor takes care that the soloist is not given all of the fun: the string ensemble, too, has opportunity to prance.

For the second movement, the dulcimer is set aside in favor of the haunting voice of the Tennessee music box, as the music takes on the flavor of a gently melancholy ballad. An extended string ensemble passage midway allows the soloist not only to switch back to dulcimer, but also to re-tune the dulcimer for the key now at hand. However, the music box will return in time for the movement's close.

Liveliest of all is the closing movement, vibrant with the spirit of a country square dance. Dulcimer and string ensemble take turns with flowing phrases and more intricately detailed ones, occasionally having short statements that punctuate the broader passagework. Midway in the movement, a calm interlude appears, but high spirits will take center stage once more, driving Ellisor's *Blackberry Winter* to its final chord. To a certain extent, it is a mix of bluegrass and Baroque, a more felicitous blend than one might at first expect.

Were one lacking dulcimer and Tennessee music box, one could still perform *Blackberry Winter* by using as soloists harpsichord and the parlor organ known as the harmonium. Alternatively, a synthesizer or digital sampler could cover both solo parts. Any of those choices could offer a distant similarity of timbre; admittedly, the folk connection would be lost, but the music itself speaks for that heritage, even without the specific – and, regrettably, rare – solo instruments.

♪♪♪♪

Even setting aside distinctly Christmas-inspired works – after all, in the Southern Hemisphere, Christmas is not a winter occasion – there is still an abundance of material to celebrate winter. Here are six further suggestions to consider:

- Josef Strauss (1827 – 1870): In his *Wintermärchen Walzer,* this middle brother of the Viennese waltz dynasty brings his artistry to "winter tales." It is not, presumably, Shakespeare's *A Winter's Tale*, as that play would require more sobriety and less waltzing.

- Peter Tchaikovsky (1840 – 1893): The Russian master already has two articles in this chapter, but don't forget his *The Snow Maiden*. An expansive sequence of dances, songs, and entr'actes, it was intended not as an opera, but as incidental music for the original play.

- Eugene Ysaÿe (1858 – 1931): The Belgian violinist/composer's *Neiges d'antan* (*Snows of Yesteryear*) is in part a reflection on the season, though also muses upon Medieval French poet François Villon. In either case, it makes for a gently thoughtful showpiece for violin and orchestra.

- Georgy Sviridov (1915 – 1998): The Russian composer's orchestral suite *The Snowstorm* (1964) is inspired by a Pushkin story. Sleighrides, waltzes, romances, reminiscences, a march and a wedding scene: it offers a bit of everything in vivid and colorful fashion.

- Kenneth Leighton (1929 – 1988): The Oxford graduate was a gifted pianist who, in the seven movements of his *Winter Scenes* proves how much can be accomplished with a single keyboard instrument in the right hands. It isn't exactly Impressionist, but certainly does a fine job of hinting at various moods of the season.

- Kenji Bunch (b. 1973): Recall the fairy tale of the beautiful but evil Snow Queen, who freezes the heart of the young boy Kai, leaving his friend, valiant Gerda, to rescue him? Oregon-born Bunch gives it ballet form, balancing delicate beauty, nervous tension, and splendid success, as the story progresses.

Seasonal Music Insights: Vivaldi and Much More

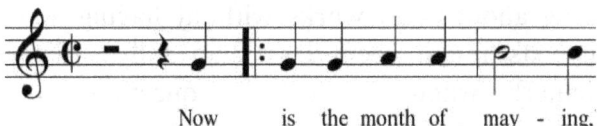

Chapter Seven: Seasonal Songs and Choral Works

"In the Spring, a young man's fancy lightly turns to thoughts of Love:" so observed Victorian poet Tennyson (1809 – 1892) in his *Locksley Hall*, but the idea did not originate with him. Centuries before Tennyson, poets and composers alike, perhaps with an eye to birds in their nests, began to equate spring with romance; put words and music together, and it might result in ebullient songs of love. Certainly, that is true of the music above, the opening line of a Thomas Morley madrigal. Merry lads and their lasses are playing in the grasses: surely it must be spring. As we have seen in Chapter Three, one could celebrate the occasion with instrumental sounds, but adding voices allows for quite specific imagery.

Other seasons, too, may find their most vivid expression through song. Relaxing summer evenings, entrancing autumn colors, gentle blankets of snow over the fields: all have their place. If spring happens to get more attention, perhaps that is due in part to the tuneful nature of birds singing to their mates. Recall that such was part of Vivaldi's springtime vision explored in Chapter Two: music that will recur here, at least in small part.

Reading about vocal works without having access to their texts might seem less than fully satisfactory, particularly when the texts in question are in a language other than English. Many texts – and, when necessary, translations by this author – can be found in Appendix Two, with short references to some of the texts in the following articles. For reasons of space and, in some cases, copyright laws, readers will not find 100% of the texts and translations provided here. However, in the source lists in Appendix Five, digital links to vocal music texts are provided.

♪♪♪♪♪

Morley: three springtime madrigals

English composer Thomas Morley (@1557 – 1602) knew well the advantages of attracting favorable attention from persons of influence. Born in Norwich in eastern England, he was barely thirty when he joined the musical staff at London's St. Paul's Cathedral. Soon, Morley's musical gifts caught the ear of Queen Elizabeth. She invited him to join her musical establishment and then, in 1598, granted him control of all music publishing in England. The honor ensured that Morley's music would readily come to print and also placed him in a position of influence over his colleagues.

With his cathedral background, Morley wrote much sacred music, though also secular works. Both in chronology and popularity, Morley was the first major

English composer of madrigals. The art form had developed early in the 16th century in Italy, and came to England in Morley's own time. Intended for ensembles of singers unaccompanied by instruments, madrigals employed compositional techniques of sacred works without the religious component. Melodies are often given to higher voices, with lower ones usually providing harmonic support; sometimes several vocal lines are occupied with different melodic material at once, a practice known as "counterpoint."

Most often, madrigals had to do with love. Italian madrigals might admit that love, when unrequited, can be a mournful subject, but Morley apparently thought happy love songs would attract a larger audience, and, perhaps, sell in larger quantities. So like the vast majority of his madrigals, *Now is the Month of Maying* is as merry and dance-like as one could wish. Its "fa-la-la" refrain should suggest to many listeners the famed Christmas carol *Deck the Halls*, its seasonal words set to quite ancient music. English madrigals were the pop songs of their day, and their melodies remained in the nation's musical memory for generations.

Of a different type is Morley's *April is in My Mistress' Face*: no fa-la-la-ing, and rather more somber colors. Appearing in his *First Booke of Madrigals* (1592), the song compares the sweetheart in turn to April, July, September, and December. The tender first of those months may be her face, but the heated second is her eyes, the hearty third her bosom, and the frosty last her heart. So it seems the waters of this musical romance do not run smoothly, and Morley has crafted music of gentle regret.

Optimism returns in Morley's *It was a Lover and His Lass*, its text borrowed from Shakespeare's *As You Like It*, Act V, Scene III. Morley's madrigal came to print in 1600, a fact that Shakespeare scholars use to date the play itself to 1598-1599. When the play was on stage, Shakespeare intended to incorporate song settings of portions of the text; one can easily suppose that a contemporary audience might have heard Morley's madrigal as part of a stage production. Like the text the poet had provided for his sweethearts Touchstone and Audrey, Morley's music is sunny and cheerful, with lines intertwining in a manner suggestive of the dance, or even an embrace. "With a hey, and a ho, and a hey nonino... sweet lovers love the spring:" all is well for these sweethearts, and Morley's music laughs aloud.

Texts in Appendix Two (pages 278 – 279)

♪♪♪♪

Vivaldi: "Dell'aura al sussurrar," from *Dorilla in tempe*

Even the most devoted opera lover is quite unlikely to have seen a staged production of *Dorilla in tempe*, Vivaldi's 1726 drama of ancient Greece. Only portions of the original score have survived, and though one might complete it by inserting selections from other composers' works, as has been done at times, Baroque love stories of mythological flavor rarely attract much attention. However, one would not need to be a Baroque opera devotee to hear the work's opening chorus and declare it to be thoroughly familiar – other than the presence of the singers.

Finding himself confronted with a tale set in the countryside in springtime, Vivaldi decided that the best method of evoking that setting was to borrow from one of his own violin concerti: the ever-adored *Spring* from *The Four Seasons* (1725). That work had been recently published, and Vivaldi, either wanting to capitalize on its popularity or to perhaps further drive its acceptance, set the very first vocal music of the opera to what is clearly the beginning of the first movement of that instrumental work. There's no solo violin, but all the melodies and most of the harmonies are right there.

In this opening scene, the chorus remarks gleefully upon the tender murmurs of spring, welcoming the new season with song. Flowers and nightingales are lauded, and if the words are new to those myriad fans of the concerto, the music itself is yet familiar. Vivaldi makes only small divergences from the original form, largely to accommodate the rhythm of the text at hand. By the last page of the chorus, he introduces new melodic phrases, though even these are so much in the spirit of the concerto that the transitions are more intriguing than startling. The scene welcomes spring in the most vibrant fashion, and Vivaldi, not wanting to leave his favorite instrument long out of the spotlight, even manages to include a short solo passage for violin. "Dell'aura al sussurrar" (The whispering atmosphere) is a joyous tribute to the season.

Text/translation in Appendix Two (pages 280 – 281)

♫♫♫♫♫

Wolfgang Mozart: two vocal selections for spring

- *Schon lacht der holde Frühling*, K. 580
 (*Noble Spring Already Laughs*)

As distinct from an opera aria, a concert aria is a free-standing showpiece for singer and orchestra, one not belonging to a specific opera in which, theoretically, it would provide plot and character development. As it happens, *Schon lacht der holde Frühling* is both. However, the opera for which it was composed is not one of Mozart's own. On the contrary, he wrote it for a German-language Viennese staging of *Barbiere de Siviglia*, written in 1782 by Italian composer Giovanni Paisiello (1740 – 1816): the very same tale Gioacchino Rossini (1792 – 1868) would set in another quarter century. Mozart's contribution of an additional aria for the leading lady was cut from that production; perhaps the soprano found its bubbly nature beyond her skills. So the aria, no longer having an operatic reason for existence, joined instead the concert repertoire.

Its orchestral opening, scored for strings with pairs of clarinets, bassoons, and French horns, is bright and eager, generally rising in pitch, like rising hopes upon the advent of spring. The vocal melody derives from this orchestral prelude, though substantially more ornamented, and soon acquiring much coloratura, with a great many short, quick notes occurring in close order, requiring the most nimble of vocal chords. Certainly, it makes demands upon a singer's technique, but one could scarcely imagine a better way of communicating the sparkle of a spring morning.

The first two verses are fully joyful. With the third verse, music and text alike take a tearful turn, as the young lady admits a longing for her absent sweetheart. However, after that verse concludes, Mozart returns to the top of the page (the musical term being "da capo") to revel again in spring's beauties. The words are the same as they had been initially, and the melody similar. This time, however, there is even more intricate detail, musical embroidery making the utmost of the opportunity to celebrate the season.

- *Sehnsucht nach der Frühling*, K. 596 (*Longing for Springtime*)

For Mozart, January 14, 1791, was a day of songs. According to his own meticulous catalog, on this date he wrote three songs, all for a friend's upcoming publication of songs for young audiences. Given the purpose, Mozart's contributions are not suffused with imposing drama. Rather, they are sweetly unassuming, and two are visions of spring. It was winter at the time, but publication was yet some months away; moreover, one might imagine that in the days before central heating, thinking of spring during the winter might be good for morale. The third of the songs has to do with children's games, and is appropriately light of spirit. Just because Mozart was a musical genius does not mean he was incapable of expressing simpler ideas in music. Moreover, he was well able to do so without short-changing his own musical imagination.

The first of these songs, *Sehnsucht nach der Frühling* (*Longing for Springtime*), sets a poem by Mozart's contemporary, Christian Adolf Overbeck (1755 – 1821). A salute to flowers and birdsong – though with one central verse admitting that there is also joy in snow and sleigh rides – the original poem has five verses, of which Mozart set the first, second, and fifth. Some performers, likely wishing to make more of the song, repeat the music of the second verse to include one or the other of the omitted verses.

For Overbeck's words, Mozart crafted a vocal line of gentle smiles and a piano accompaniment that flows sweetly. Each verse has a piano postlude that is more ornamented than the basic accompaniment and has much in common with his more light-hearted piano sonatas. The vocal line remains largely consistent, with only small changes. However, a talented performer can give it nuance with decorative trills and turns, as would have been standard practice in Mozart's time.

Mozart apparently had a special fondness for the song, or at least for its melodic heart. Its vocal melody also appears in his Piano Concerto no. 27 in B-flat major, K. 595, which immediately precedes the song in the Koechel catalog. Did the melody originate with the song or with the concerto? Almost certainly with the song, as it fits the given text so perfectly. However, a gifted musical mind such as Mozart's was always able to see broader musical potential in his materials.

Texts/translations in Appendix Two (pages 288 – 289)

♪♪♪♪♪

Schubert: a seasonal song cycle

No important composer made more significant, not to mention numerous, contributions to the repertoire of art songs than did Franz Schubert (1797 – 1828). In a tragically brief life, he produced over 600 such works for solo voice and piano, creating inspired settings of poems both great and small. Clearly, Schubert had an inclination for poetry and how one might best bring it to musical expression; he also had a number of gifted singers amongst his circle of friends, persons who frequently brought him specific poems of which they wanted musical settings. A German-speaker such as the Vienna-born Schubert would have called them "Lieder" (pronounced LEE-der), though in English, the term is "art songs." The "art" part of that term serves to distinguish them from folk songs, drinking songs, and the like: this is music with more ambitious standards.

Apparently, none of those singing friends ever said, "Franz, how about a cycle of songs depicting the seasons?", as there is no such thing in Schubert's catalog. However, he composed individual seasonally-flavored settings frequently enough that one can easily assemble such a collection, even without drawing upon his *Winterreise*, D. 911. Written in the composer's last year, that cycle is more about the wintery chill that has taken root in a broken heart than it is about the snowy landscape in which the gloomy traveler finds himself tramping along the roads. So let us instead draw upon four songs with more cheerful views of nature.

Im Frühling (*In Spring*), D. 882, is one of regrettably few Schubert works to come to print (as opus 101, no. 1) during his own life. The song dates from the spring of 1826 and uses a text by Ernst Schulze largely on the subject of the buds and blossoms of the season, set against blue skies. A sweet piano prelude presents the main theme on which the vocal lines elaborate. Wistful colors arrive with admissions of unmet desires, but reflection upon a little warbling bird on the branch restores the simple joy with which the song had begun. Spring, it seems, is not a time for sorrow.

If one had never before encountered the name of poet Ernst Schulze, that will surely not be the case with the poet whose words inspired Schubert's *Ständchen* (*Serenade*), D. 889, setting, as it does, Shakespeare's *Hark, hark, the lark* from Act Two, Scene 3 of *Cymbeline*. The play itself is rarely produced, but this portion of the text, sung by a fellow hoping to win a young lady's heart, is a favorite in compilations of Shakespeare's poetry. Schubert opens with a light and cheerful piano phrase evocative of bird song: perhaps the lark soars against the summer sky. The vocal lines offer new rising phrases set against similar rhythms. All is sunny and bright, becoming bolder for the closing statements of "Steh auf!" (Arise! Awake!). A short piano postlude recalls the prelude, bringing the little song full circle. That the fellow to whom Shakespeare gave the song does not succeed in his wooing may be due to him not having had at hand Schubert's inspired setting of a German rendition of the text, composed in 1826, but not coming to print until 1830, two years after Schubert's death.

Mond in einer Herbstnacht (*Moon on an Autumn Night*), D. 614, was composed in 1818, though not published until 1832, yet another Schubert work that only belatedly reached the public. The gifted but chronically timid composer simply could not bring himself to promote his own works, a task that fell to Robert Schumann (1810 – 1856), himself never reluctant to bring attention to music he judged to be worthwhile. Setting a text by Aloys Wilhelm Schreiber, the song opens with two largely carefree verses paying tribute to the moon. Then, the mood becomes more tenderly regretful, with reflections upon lost love, though hope returns amidst nature's beauty. The fifth and final verse is, in part, one of regret, with musings upon moonlight not reaching beyond this life, though all ends not in despair, but in tenderness.

One feature that sets *Herbstnacht* apart from many Schubert songs is its length: seven minutes or so, rather than the three-to-four that he usually uses. That extra space may be due to the original poem being longer than usual. However, Schubert takes advantage of that fact to explore a wider range of feelings, and to ornament phrases differently when they reappear.

Also more generously proportioned is our winter selection. Written early in 1828 and coming to print in 1835, *Winterabend* (*Winter's Night*), D. 938, sets a text by Karl Gottfried von Leitner. The first verse reflects upon the quiet of a winter landscape lying under its blanket of snow, evoked with restful vocal phrases and only slightly more active piano lines. After a piano interlude comes the longer second verse, in which Schubert introduces a new theme that echoes between piano and singer, the singer's phrases rather more detailed than those of the pianist, as the text muses contentedly upon the moonlight slipping into the room like a welcome visitor. Another piano interlude leads to the final verse. Here, the music becomes rather more outspoken, at least briefly, as the text remembers "eine schöne verschwund'ne Zeit" (a lovely, vanished time). However, it seems there is consolation in moonlight, and Schubert closes *Winterabend* with music not of tears, but of tender sighs. It may be a lonely winter night, but it is not one of despair. *Winterabend* serves to close out our seasonal Schubert song cycle in peace.

Texts/translations in Appendix Two (pages 290 – 297)

♫♫♫♫♫

Berlioz: *Les nuits d'été*, op. 7

It is through his highly charged orchestral works that one most often encounters the music of Hector Berlioz (1803 – 1869). However, the Frenchman had diverse intellectual and musical interests. Having been given a broad liberal arts education, Berlioz was devoted to literature and forged connections with Parisian literary circles. Such a background will often lead a composer to the realm of art song, and Berlioz was no exception. Poet Théophile Gautier (1811 – 1872) shared Berlioz' neighborhood in Paris. Soon after Gautier's poetic collection *La comédie de la mort (The Comedy of Death)* came to print, the composer was at work on setting some of the poems to music.

When Berlioz first wrote these songs in 1840 and '41, he intended them for mezzo-soprano or tenor with piano. After completing six, he decided to rework their keyboard accompaniments into orchestral parts, a process not completed until 1856. The very low opus number reflects the appearance of the first version, not the much later date of the final revision. At that time, the songs were published together under the collective title *Les nuits d'été (Summer Nights)*. The title is mildly puzzling, as summer is not really the topic at hand; rather, love and, at times, the loss thereof is a recurring theme. Perhaps the composer imagined the music as entertainment to be sung at a summer soirée. Nonetheless, the first song, the dance-like *Villanelle* is, at least, a celebration of spring, and the last, *L'île inconnue (The Unknown Isle)*, an exuberant vision of a journey with the beloved, is at least a suitable scene for pleasant weather.

Villenelle offers delicate vocal lines over a gently pulsing accompaniment. There are six verses, the odd numbered ones all musically similar to one another, the even numbered ones of a different, though still unified, character. Spring is welcomed, with frequent reference to birdsong, flowers, and other natural delights, as well as to romance. A sparkling vision of sharing a spring day with the person nearest to one's heart, *Villenelle* is an effervescent opening to the cycle of songs.

The second song, *Le spectre de la rose (Specter of the Rose)*, is a dreamy reflection of a rose pinned to a lady's ball dress. As the lady sleeps, the rose reflects upon the experience, first tenderly, then with building passion. The third song, *Sur les lagunes: Lamento (On the*

Lagoons: Lament) has tears of sweet remembrance, building in drama as the text reflects that such a love can never be found again: the dear one is in her grave.

The fourth song, *Absence,* is also mournful, though here, it seems there is still hope that the beloved may yet return. Vocal lines are yearning, not despairing, and at times, the accompaniment (whether piano or orchestra) echoes the singer's phrases, underscoring the expressed wish of a reunion. No such denouement can be expected of the fifth song, *Au cimentiere: Clair de lune* (*At the Cemetery: Moonlight*). Here, gentle regrets are, at times, overcome with deeper sorrow. Berlioz tends to keep accompanying lines rather subdued, perhaps to keep the words clear, though he may also wish to suggest that only the human voice can express such pain.

For a return to good cheer, consider *L'ile inconnue* (*The Unknown Isle*), the sixth and last song of *Les nuits d'été*. In spirited fashion and with breathless urgency, Berlioz sets verses in which a young fellow seeks to tempt his sweetheart to set off on a journey with him. It may be an imaginary journey, angel's wings not being the most practical of sails, but the breeze is rising, and he wishes to be off, as long as she will join him. "Tell me, young beauty, where you wish to go:" the phrase is boldly and passionately set. She asks for a place where love is everlasting. What is "unknown" about this isle? Its location, or that a place where love endures forever does not exist at all? Gently, perhaps regretfully, the fellow suggests that she choose another place.

Les nuit d'été has little in common with Berlioz's masterpiece, the sometimes overwhelming *Symphonie fantastique* (1830). Even in its orchestrated form, the song cycle proves he can also paint with a more delicate brush: rather than commanding one to participate, it whispers an invitation to glance through the door. Here is Berlioz exploring the notion of subtlety.

Texts/translations in Appendix Two (pages 298 – 301)

♪♪♪♪♪

Mendelssohn: *Sechs Lieder im Freien zu singen*, op. 48
(*Six Songs to Sing in the Open Air*)

Many music lovers know of the solo piano pieces called *Songs Without Words* of Felix Mendelssohn (1809 – 1847). Here, by contrast, are songs <u>with</u> words, and <u>without</u> a piano. Although Mendelssohn also composed songs for solo voice and piano, here are works for a cappella vocal ensembles; it's a genre known as "part songs" for the presence of several vocal parts, in this case, soprano, alto, tenor, and baritone.

Mendelssohn composed several dozen part songs, using texts by poets both famous and little known. Often rich with natural imagery, the part songs offer moods ranging from bright and buoyant to wistful and poignant, depending upon the requirements of the words. Voice parts are often interestingly intertwined, without being so virtuosic as to stand beyond the talents of a local chorus. Mendelssohn could, and, on other occasions, did write for professional singers, but here he clearly wanted to reach the masses and let them experience the delights of performing music with a larger group. Nearly all German towns had an amateur chorus, and Mendelssohn happily gave them music worth singing.

Mendelssohn's second published set of part songs, *Sechs Lieder im Freien zu singen* (*Six Songs to Sing in the Open Air*), was published in 1839 as the 20-year-old composer's op. 48. It set texts by Ludwig Uhland (1787 – 1862), Nikolaus Lenau (1802 – 1850), and Joseph von Eichendorff (1788 – 1857), all German poets who could be relied upon to express the influence of nature upon mankind. The descriptive title of the full cycle, that these are not necessarily songs for drawing room entertainment, when one might take them outdoors, underscores the crucial nature of that interaction.

The first song, *Frühlingsahnung* (*Spring Sensation*) is tender and playful, sometimes having soprano voices sing alone, at others just tenors, at yet other times everyone all together; its last line, reminding listeners that soon the violets shall bloom, is gently repeated, almost like a prayer. The second song celebrates a different flower, *Die Primel* (*The Primrose*), serenading it in sunny fashion with men's and women's voices sometimes echoing one another; the notion of welcoming the primrose as a messenger of spring recurs to close the song. Third comes *Frühlingsfeier* (*Spring Celebration*), a serene tribute to this "Süßen, goldner Frühlingtag" (sweet, golden spring day); for its final measures, Mendelssohn emphasizes the lines advising that one "ruhn und beten" (rest and pray).

The fourth song, *Lerchengesang* (*Song of the Lark*) opens with just the ladies in rather ebullient mood; once the opening lines repeat, the men join in as well, they having simpler lines while the ladies provide more nimble ornamentation. The phrase "zur Sonne" (to the sun) provides a rich and vivid concluding passage. The fifth song, *Morgengebet* (*Morning Prayer*) is calm and appropriately reverent in mood, with gentle motion and smoothly flowing phrases and harmonies. The text is, perhaps, more a hymn to the Lord than one to the season itself, though Mendelssohn's music seems to emphasize the idea of whence spring had sprung.

The sixth and final item in Mendelssohn's op. 48 cycle, *Herbstlied* (*Autumn Song*) still speaks to spring, though now as a farewell, its blossoms having been driven away by autumn's power; summer is quite overlooked in these reflections. The first three verses have wistful, minor-key colors, details and energy gradually evolving. By the final verse, however, the composer recalls the smiling beauty of spring with cheerfully relaxed phrases, the soprano part moving quite high in pitch. The new leaves, he reminds us, bring "neues Hoffen" (new hope), an idea that apparently required the music to rise in pitch, like rising hopes. In all, the six opus 48 part songs are a sweet tribute to the power of nature's beauty, with neither late frosts to trouble the gardener nor soaking rains to dampen the spirit.

Texts/translations in Appendix Two (pages 302 – 305)

♪♪♪♪♪

Johann Strauss Jr.: *Frühlingsstimmen*, op. 410
(*Voices of Spring*)

In the world of waltz music, the Strauss family functioned as a royal dynasty. The combined efforts of Johann Strauss Sr. (1804 – 1849) and his sons, Johann Jr., Josef, and Eduard, led to the creation of perhaps a thousand compositions, with waltzes and polkas (also folk-derived, although in duple, not triple, meter) most numerous on the list. Of the four men, eldest son Johann Jr. (1825 – 1899) was the most influential. He took a dance form at that time intended mostly for the ballroom and deftly raised it to concert-hall status, producing compositions almost symphonic in expressive power, making substantial demands on both his orchestra and himself. His influence in the musical world was so pronounced that, at the composer's passing, Vienna's most influential music critic, Eduard Hanslick (1825 – 1904), who more frequently devoted energy to boosting Brahms symphonies and blasting Wagner operas, wrote a laudatory obituary praising Johann Jr. as the city's "most original musical talent."

In 1883, nearly twenty years after the justly famed *On the Beautiful Blue Danube*, Strauss added yet another waltz to his collection, this, unusually, including a solo singer with the orchestra. *Voices of Spring* has a text by writer Richard Genée (1823 – 1895) that revels in the joys of spring, particularly from an avian point of view. As the coloratura soprano, appropriately bird-like in the lightness of her voice, sings "All trouble has fled!... All laughs and awakes." This joy, she declares, is as true of humans as it is of larks and nightingales.

Like all Johann Jr.'s best waltzes, *Voices of Spring* has numerous contrasting waltz themes, some brisk, others languid, all graceful in their own way. Short phrases, suggestive in themselves of birds' voices, serve as basic material for more expansive lines, and the soaring lark music of the opening phrases returns from time to time, even granted pride of place as the theme which will draw *Voices of Spring* to its joyful conclusion.

A purely orchestral version of *Voices of Spring* of much the same character also exists. It is somewhat shorter than the vocal version, and what would otherwise be the soprano's lines are given to woodwinds, often clarinet. Using clarinet rather than the more obviously avian flute allows the orchestral version to retain one of the most charming effects that Johann Jr. used in the original: letting the soprano and the flute echo one another's phrases, as if the singer and the lark are engaged in a duet to celebrate the season.

Text/translation in Appendix Two (pages 306 – 307)

♪♪♪♪♪

Fauré: four seasonal songs

When it comes to art songs – those expressive musical settings of poetry, generally scored for one singer and one pianist – Austrians and Germans seem to get much of the attention. Admittedly, they were remarkably productive in the field, with Franz Schubert (1797 – 1828) alone composing over 600 such pieces.

Nonetheless, the French, having a poetic heritage as vibrant as that of German-speaking lands, were not laggard in the field. Gabriel Fauré (1845 – 1924) composed roughly 100 songs, as well as a quantity of incidental music for stage productions, in which songs feature prominently. Moreover, the French language, being abundantly supplied with vowels of subtly varied shading, virtually begs for musical expression, and Fauré was pleased to oblige.

Fauré composed roughly 100 art songs, or "chansons," as he called them, generally publishing several under each opus number. Reaching the public in 1880, his opus 18 included three songs, the last of which was *Automne*, setting a poignant text by Armande Silvestre. Flowing vocal lines over restless piano raptly observe upon the melancholy beauty of dawns and sunsets, before tenderly reflecting upon enchanted slopes where the observer had spent his youth. By the last verse, the tone is one of tender sorrows at forgotten memories.

Two decades would pass before, in the opus 85 set of 1902, Fauré composed a more optimistic vision of autumn, *Dans la forêt de Septembre* (*In the Forest in September*). Here, the view is reverent, rather than regretful; melancholy thoughts are soothed by the good forest, and though winter is coming, there is still green foliage to admire. Perhaps the poet here, Catulle Mendès, was more kindly inclined to the changing season than Silvestre had been. Certainly, Fauré provides melodies and harmonies alike that are tender and thoughtful in demeanor, more expressive of sweet smiles than of tears.

Standing chronologically between those two autumnal points, one finds reflections upon spring and summer amidst the songs of *Le bonne chanson* (*The Good Song*), op. 61. The cycle sets selections from the twenty poems in the collection of the same name published in 1863 by Paul Verlaine (1844 – 1896); at the time, Verlaine was soon to be married, which may have influenced the generally bright character of the verses. Fauré chose nine of the poems, scoring them for voice and piano, in which form they came to print in 1894. Soon afterward, he reworked the cycle, still for solo voice, but adding a string quartet to the piano, allowing for even fuller and more varied timbres.

Appearing seventh in *Le bonne chanson* is *Donc, ce sera par un clair jour d'été* (*And So, It Shall Be on a Bright Summer's Day*). The three short verses rhapsodize about sun, sky, breezes, and lovers' delights. The vocal line floats serenely over accompaniment so fluttery in character as to suggest that the breeze might be rustling in the leaves. The last verse is gentler yet, as it is now evening, and the lovers are gazing at the stars, a shift of atmosphere that Fauré has masterfully communicated in his music.

Last of the nine songs in *Le bonne chanson* is *L'hiver a cessé* (*Winter has Ended*). "The saddest heart," Verlaine declares, "must give way to joy... and all my hopes at last have their turn." Fauré, setting the first, third, fourth, and fifth verses of Verlaine's original poem, balances playful moods with more inwardly emotive ones. "Immense joy" is given passionate expression, laughter under blue skies is dance-like in spirit, and closing reflections on how all seasons are dear, though less outspoken, are shaped with delicate grace. Fauré was one of the most gifted of French art song composers, and given verses of romance and natural beauty, he was at his best.

Texts/translations in Appendix Two (pages 308 – 313)

♪♪♪♪♪

Mahler: *Lied von der Erde (The Song of the Earth)*

Das Lied von der Erde is more-or-less the Symphony no. 9 of Gustav Mahler (1860 – 1911). Certainly, he had finished eight symphonies before it, and might have labelled this one no. 9, had the deeply superstitious composer not felt dread at the fact that the mighty Beethoven – as well as Schubert and Dvořák – had died after composing exactly nine symphonies. So he gave instead a more descriptive title to this symphonic song cycle inspired by his reading of *The Chinese Flute,* a collection of Chinese poems in German translations. The poems vary in subject matter, from pretty scenes of young love to exuberant drinking songs to wistful verses of loneliness and death, but the general theme is of the eternity of nature contrasted with mankind's more temporary existence.

It is an unusual work, and not just because of its pseudo-Chinese inspiration. *Das Lied* is scored for a massive orchestra, its forces including two harps, two piccolos, English horn, three types of clarinet, contrabassoon, celesta, and mandolin, along with the usual forces. Moreover, there are two vocal soloists: one tenor and one contralto (or baritone). Mahler had included voices in symphonies before, most magnificently in his Symphony no. 2, *The Resurrection*, though also in his Symphony no. 4. However, the latter of those two works had premiered in 1901, most of a decade earlier. Much of the intervening time Mahler had spent conducting opera, but audiences had not always responded well to his hybrid choral symphonies, and it was perhaps a bit bold to try again something that had produced more skepticism than acceptance. However, the poetry had spoken to Mahler. He completed *Das Lied* in 1909, but a conducting post in New York City prevented its immediate premiere, and then serious health problems intervened. By the time *Das Lied* premiered November 20, 1911, in the care of his disciple Bruno Walter, Mahler had been in his grave for four months.

Das Lied is filled with reflections upon life and nature, and thus a certain amount of musing upon the seasons. The second of its six movements, designated for the contralto (or baritone) soloist, is subtitled *Der Einsame in Herbst* (*The Lonely One in Autumn*). Its text, of golden leaves and chilling winds, draws parallels between the season and the heart, not, perhaps, just a lonely heart, but possibly one that is beginning to fail; Mahler had recently received a diagnosis of a serious heart condition that would, indeed, ultimately prove fatal. The music, though often plaintive, is undeniably lovely, serene and thoughtful throughout, with particular prominence given not only to the vocal soloist, but also to the oboe, which takes the spotlight nearly as often as does the singer. Phrases rise and fall, with rapt passions and weary sorrows in turn. The leaves are falling, and so, it seems, are tears, though always with music of sweet reflection.

By stark contrast, the fifth movement, arriving about a quarter hour later (the entire symphony is nearly an hour in length), is not only a different season, but also an utterly different atmosphere. *Der Trunkene im Frühling* (*The Drinker in Spring*) brings a splendidly exuberant solo for tenor, often declaiming in playful, if bold manner. "Listen!" he announces, "a bird is singing in the trees." Better yet, wine is flowing into the glass, and newborn spring has arrived. Mahler seems to take particular delight in that bird, using piccolo and other woodwinds to convey its warbling and its laughter. Often, one finds the tenor soloist engaging in duets with violin, alternately in dance-like and song-like mood. It is music of the very highest spirits.

One might only wish that Mahler had chosen to use the same voice for the autumn movement as for the spring one, so that one might imagine that the poor lonely soul of earlier had found new happiness in springtime. However, it is the spring vision that remains strongest, not only because he places *Der Trunkene im Frühling* after *Der Einsame in Herbst*, but also because, in the sixth and last movement of *Das Lied*, he reminds one again of the season of rebirth. It is the contralto who is assigned the restorative task of intoning that, in spring, all becomes new, forever and forever. Ultimately, Mahler concludes *Das Lied* with a message of hope – for nature and for the individual alike.

Texts/translations in Appendix Two (pages 314 – 317)

♪♪♪♪♪

Delius: two summer songs – *Midsummer Song* and *To Be Sung of a Summer Night on the Water*

"On midsummer day, we'll dance and we'll play!" It's a sentiment that could hardly be expressed in somber colors, and Frederick Delius (1862 – 1934) gives it all the joy one could require. Having begun with a German song that he translated himself into English, he made small changes along the way, but retained the meter so his new words would still fit the melody. For example, in the German, we do not dance and play, but "wir tanzen zu zweit" (we dance in pairs); Delius' version, though not quite exactly literal, found the best means of capturing the sense of the scene without drastically altering the rhythm itself. Besides, he needed "play," so it would rhyme with "day."

In Delius' care, *Midsummer Song* (1908) becomes an a cappella part song for eight-part chorus: two parts each of sopranos, altos, tenors, and baritones. The choir needn't necessarily be double-sized, just divided into twice as many sections. It is light and lilting, and frequently one part of the chorus is occupied with musical material rather different from that of the others. A "la-la-la" refrain appears between the two short verses, the second of which he chooses to set in rather fuller, richer fashion, as if the singers have gained even more enthusiasm for the celebration. The second verse closes not with more "la-la-las," but rather with repeated statements of "Heigh-ho:" arguably an even more outspoken response to the season. Clearly, Delius regarded midsummer as a time for good cheer.

For *To Be Sung of a Summer Night on the Water*, Delius wants not eight sections, but only six: one each of sopranos and altos, though two each of tenors and baritones. Amongst those tenors must be one of solo skills: not necessarily virtuosic, just able to carry a line distinct from and rather above the others in pitch.

Dating from 1917, when much of Europe was torn by war, the resolutely peaceful nature of these two little songs might have seemed out of touch with the times, though if a tormented public had begged for something soothing, here it is. The first song moves gently in waves, with generally short phrases but rather longer individual notes. Sopranos have the most active lines, though still with a mood of relaxation. In the second song, the tenor soloist is set gracefully "la-la-lahing" over smooth harmonies from the ensemble. One finds, perhaps, rather more forward motion than in the first song, though neither evidences a particular hurry to be anywhere other than simply here on the water.

There is, essentially, no text to *Summer Night on the Water*. The entire first song is sung to the syllable "Ah;" the second is simply "la." It was unusual to write choral music with no words of specific meaning, but perhaps Delius hoped to focus more closely on subtle variation of vocal colors than on any particular words: words might have been a distraction from the musical craftsmanship. Being wordless, the blending of voices becomes all the more noticeable.

Text for *Midsummer Song* in Appendix Two (page 318)

♪♪♪♪

Richard Strauss: *Four Last Songs* –
  I. *Frühling* – II. September

Richard Strauss (1864 – 1949) loved writing songs. His wife Pauline was a highly regarded soprano; moreover, as an opera conductor, Strauss was well-acquainted with vocal repertoire and with practitioners of that art. Give him a text he admired, and he would create a perfect musical setting of it. Lacking a text, he sometimes crafted music lines, then set out in search of words to suit the rhythms and moods he had just written. His *Four Last Songs*, a title chosen not by the composer, but by his publisher Ernst Roth, are a fitting valedictory statement to a field that was long close to Strauss' heart.

The songs were begun in the winter of 1947-48, when the aged composer and his wife were living in exile in Switzerland, waiting for the post-war political situation to stabilize in their German homeland. Having encountered the poet Hermann Hesse (1877 – 1962) there in Switzerland, Strauss began setting several of Hesse's poems to music, and three of those resulting songs – *Frühling* (*Spring*), *September*, and *Beim Schlafengehen* (*Going to Sleep*) – found their way into this final set. One further song, *Im Abendrot* (*At Evening Light*), used the words of Joseph Eichendorff (1778 – 1857). Although Strauss often composed songs for solo voice and piano, at other times, he chose the fuller option of orchestral accompaniment, and such is the case here.

Frühling opens in reflective manner: this is not yet the sparkle of a spring morning, but rather dreams of an expected spring to come, dreams that will be realized. References to birdsong bring not only trills in the vocal line, but also in the woodwind parts; before long, as spring "lies revealed," Strauss' music builds to rapt and wondrous splendor. Spring beckons, and with a sigh, the song eases to its tender close.

By contrast, *September* has the garden mourning as flowers sag beneath rainfall, Strauss' melodic phrases similarly tend downward in pitch. All, however, is not sorrowful; golden leaves and summer smiles are still present, or at least gently recalled. The garden, we are told, longs for rest, and with much ornamentation of the simple word "weary" (less simple in German, in which "müdegewordenen" has six syllables), the vocal line suggests the roses are falling into sleep. With a restatement of the singer's final line from the French horn, Strauss bids a gentle farewell to autumn.

Strauss may not have originally intended the four songs as a single set. However, stylistically and thematically, they fit splendidly together, so his publisher's decision to join them together seems inspired.

Incidentally, Richard Strauss and Johann Strauss Jr., featured earlier in this chapter were not related. Richard was Bavarian, Johann Viennese. The name Strauss is rather common in German speaking lands.

Texts/translations in Appendix Two (page 318 – 319)

♫♫♫♫♫

Vaughan Williams: *Folk Songs of the 4 Seasons*

In the late 19th century, two young ramblers took to the walking paths between rural English communities. One was a bear of a man; the other, slender and bespectacled, was half his friend's size, but both shared a devotion to their nation's folk music and a wish to preserve it. Encroaching urbanization was placing that musical heritage in danger. The smaller man was Gustav Holst (1874 – 1934); the larger was Ralph Vaughan Williams (1872 – 1958). Long before their serious musical works attracted attention, the Royal College of Music classmates were trekking from village to village, writing down all the music they could find.

Of the hundreds of songs and dances that found a place in their notebooks, many subsequently reappeared in instrumental and vocal compositions. One particularly famed example from Vaughan Williams' catalog is his *Fantasia on Greensleeves* (1934). Less well-known, though ultimately more ambitious, is his choral cycle *Folksongs of the 4 Seasons*, fifteen movements with prologue and spanning the better part of an hour complete. Scored for four-part women's chorus (two sections each of sopranos and altos) with instrumental accompaniment, the collection was long a work-in-progress, not reaching its final form until 1949. Each movement features several songs with texts and moods suitable to their assigned seasons. Basic melodic materials arose from folk tradition, though these specific musical settings reflect Vaughan Williams' own compositional tastes and talents.

The opening Prologue is a festive treatment of the song *To the ploughboy*. Given a text that makes frequent use of the phrase "Let's sing and be merry withal," this portion of the cycle is all good cheer and festive high spirits, ensuring that the overall sequence of songs begins with a broad smile on its face.

The subsequent movements proceed through the year, with three or four songs per season. Thoughtful moods and spirited ones occur in turn, so that no season is typecast as being only bright or only dark. At times, those contrasting colors appear in a single song. Consider, for example, a pair of avian-inspired songs found in the spring and summer sections. Spring's *The Lark in the Morning* sets gently flowing vocal lines against more fluttery phrases in the accompaniment, both expressive elements gaining more elaborate detail in the final verse. Even more marked contrast appears with the first of four summer songs. After beginning with the jaunty, bouncing energy of *Summer is a-comin' in*, Vaughan Williams shifts to the smoother flow of *The Cuckoo*, though for the closing page, *Summer is a-comin' in* makes a jolly return.

Autumn brings both melancholy moods and cheerful ones, the latter idea especially represented in *John Barleycorn* a jaunty, march-like melody that Vaughan Williams liked so well as to also use it in his *English Folk Song Suite* (1923) for wind ensemble. Winter's songs are rather Christmas-flavored, though not always sacred in tone. The festive *Wassail Song* has more to do with holiday revelry than with babes in mangers. Here, despite implicit quaffing of alcoholic beverages, Vaughan Williams offers impressively intricate music, often setting two distinctly different melodic ideas in direct juxtaposition to one another. It would have been an exuberant way to conclude the *Folk Songs of the 4 Seasons*, though as it happens, Vaughan Williams has yet more tricks up his sleeve. Just because his source material comes from humble roots does not mean the composer cannot make something substantial of those musical building blocks.

♪♪♪♪

Orff: *Carmina Burana* – Part One: Spring

Carmina Burana by Carl Orff (1895 – 1982) is not exactly music of springtime. Drawing upon Medieval German and Latin poems found in an ancient Bavarian monastery, the "scenic cantata," as its composer called it, has more to do with how mankind may be tested by the trials of fortune and by man's own lustful nature. However, the first of the work's three main sections bears the heading *Spring*, and is, to a certain extent, the most optimistic music of the whole piece.

The *Spring* portion of *Carmina Burana*, which, as a whole, premiered December 8, 1937, in Frankfurt, Germany, follows the thunderous O *Fortuna* prelude to the complete work and also the gruff second movement men's chorus *Fortune plango vulnera* that laments the wounds of fortune. Now, with the third movement *Veris leta*, good cheer appears for the very first time. Piccolo and glockenspiel set a crystalline backdrop, soon joined by almost reverent vocal lines punctuated by chimes. Spring, we are told, has vanquished winter, inspiring Orff to set very high-pitched phrases in direct juxtaposition to very low ones, for maximum contrast. Floral imagery, nightingales, and joyous maidens provide reassurance that spring is a happy time, and Orff's music has an occasionally magical quality that underscores sparkling imagery.

The next movement, *Omnia sol*, is a baritone solo, introduced by four bell tones before the voice joins with long, flowing lines in plaintive mood. April, it seems, sets a man thinking of love, even though he is not yet certain the love is mutual. Love me faithfully, he pleads, as I am faithful to you. It is not music of a broken heart, but one that has yet to receive the balm of shared affection, and the music to which Orff sets those lines is more yearning than confident.

Third of the movements of the *Spring* section (fifth overall) is *Ecce gratum*: behold pleasant spring! The movement begins with a bold statement of those two words, four syllables total, leading to music of smoothly swaying motion. Winter, we are reminded, has fled, spring has arrived, and summer is coming, all being reason for celebration. It is graciously danceable music in three balanced verses, each introduced by a four syllable declamation on the same pitches to which we first heard "Ecce gratum." Brass and percussion outbursts occur, but otherwise, the movement is vibrant and joyous. In spring, love is hopeful, without yet taking on the abandoned colors it may bear later in the year. Rejoice in spring, and in love.

♪♪♪♪♪

Barber: *Knoxville: Summer of 1915*

> ... It has become that time of evening when people sit on their porches, rocking gently and talking gently and watching the street... People go by; things go by. A horse, drawing a buggy, breaking his hollow iron music on the asphalt; a loud auto; a quiet auto; people in pairs, not in a hurry... talking casually, the taste hovering over them of vanilla, strawberry, pasteboard and starched milk...

The reflective words, and paragraphs more, were written in 1938 by American author – and native of Knoxville, Tennessee – James Agee (1909 – 1955). It is a vision of a subtler time, slower paced, softly reminiscent, a time recalled visually in photographs of sepia tones, aurally in the music of some of America's finest composers. Combine the skills of one of those composers with Agee's words, and the results may be magic.

Agee's prose poem *Knoxville: Summer of 1915* had the good fortune to come to the attention of Samuel Barber (1910 – 1980), a man perhaps ideally suited to the task of bringing these lyrical phrases to life. Born in West Chester, Pennsylvania, Barber grew up in a small town environment similar to that which had inspired the writer. Also, having begun his conservatory training as a singer (Barber had a fine baritone voice), and with a maternal aunt, Louise Homer (1871 – 1947) who sang regularly at the Metropolitan Opera, he was unusually well tuned to the fine are of expressing words through music.

In 1947, an esteemed colleague of Barber's Aunt Louise, Metropolitan Opera soprano Eleanor Steber (1914 – 1990) asked Barber to compose for her not a full opera (this he would do in 1958 with *Vanessa*, also for Steber), but rather a concert work that she might perform in recital with orchestra. The choice fell upon Agee's exquisite Knoxville text. The composer himself later recalled, "Agee's poem was vivid and moved me deeply, and my musical response was immediate and intense... The summer evening he describes... reminded me so much of similar evenings when I was a child at home... It expresses a child's feeling of loneliness, wonder, and lack of identity in that marginal world between twilight and sleep. "

Knoxville: Summer of 1915 premiered April 9, 1948, with Miss Steber joining conductor Serge Koussevitzky (1874 – 1951) and the Boston Symphony. The music, like the text it seeks to convey, is often gentle and lyrical, though a palpable sorrow underlies that quiet mood. The dreamy woodwind-flavored pastoral of the opening lines and the gradual variations on those initial motifs contrasts elegantly with the curt and restless energy as streetcars intrude on the quiet of the evening. Reflections of lying in the damp grass with family are set tenderly, with rapture for "my mother, who is good to me," and anguish when times of trouble are recalled. Barber closes his *Knoxville* with ultimately calm lines, only briefly interrupted by assertive phrases.

Although *Knoxville: Summer of 1915* may be new to some listeners, it may yet sound somewhat familiar. It moves from the serenity that opens his Violin Concerto (1940) through the tragedy that infuses his *Adagio for*

Strings (1938) and back to calm resolution. Barber has brought his vision of this imagined summer evening full circle, thereby achieving what one may suppose is essentially an optimistic ending. It is Barber at his best.

♪♪♪♪♪

Laitman: three seasonal songs

Despite occasional generic usage of the word, an opera is not simply a type of song. In classical music, a song – usually called an "art song" – is a short setting of a poem for singer and pianist. It may have a bit of a story to tell, but the musical focus is on brevity of expression. An opera is quite a lot more than that: dramatic, multi-faceted, and often highly emotional. Some composers have excelled at both art songs and operas, and Richard Strauss (1864 – 1949) is the most prominent of these. Of the current generation, consider Washington D.C. based composer Lori Laitman (b. 1955).

Having composed hundreds of art songs and several operas, Laitman says of her approach to vocal works, "I try to compose music that is kind to both singer and audience... I work from the words out: the music is in the service of the text... Approaching the composition from this angle allows the words and music to become completely entwined." That debate between music and words has persisted for centuries. One can hope that those composers of the past who have wrestled with it would be impressed by the solution Laitman has reached and the results she has achieved.

Dear March is from Laitman's song cycle *The Perfected Life* (2006), setting three poems by Emily Dickinson (1830 – 1886). Dickinson is a favorite of Laitman, who admires the poet's world view, and also finds the pacing with which she phrased her poems ideally suited for vocal settings. In *Dear March*, Dickinson welcomes spring, not only for its colors and birdsongs, but even more crucially as a treasured and long absent friend now come to visit. Laitman describes the poem as "conversational," and chooses generally sprightly lines for voice and piano alike. At times, upward sweeping passages reflect the excitement of the words, though there is also much tenderness; ultimately, *Dear March* closes in almost reverent fashion.

Laitman's *The Apple Orchard* (2004) is equally spring-flavored, though from a different point of view, more lyric and less chatty. The text, by American poet Dana Gioia (b. 1950), recalls his own memories as a self-proclaimed "city boy" consumed by the beauty of flowering apple trees. Such a sight might have been well familiar to Dickinson, whose native Amherst was hardly short of fruit trees. However, being of a different time and place, Gioia brings forth the wonderment in what might otherwise have been an ordinarily pretty day. Laitman sets the opening lines in a gentle, sweetly smiling mood, though enthusiasm builds as the song approaches a phrase that she says initially attracted her to the poem, "spring's ephemeral cathedral." The vocal line ends with reflections upon how some things pass too quickly, and Laitman's song closes with the piano alone, recalling phrases from the song's opening.

Earliest of the three Laitman songs considered here is *Early Snow* (2003), the title song of a three-song cycle setting poetry of Mary Oliver (b. 1935). The song opens with tender, very light piano; initially quite high in range, these lines begin to move downward, suggestive of falling snow. Similarly, the vocal lines are at first rather high and floating. As *Early Snow* continues, the voice falls somewhat in pitch, even as its phrases become gradually broader with somewhat richer piano support: perhaps the snow is beginning to accumulate. Particularly vivid lines of the text are given striking musical coloring, as in the splendidly vivid phrase "wonderful and refreshing," and especially the song's closing words: "white, glittering sublime." Recall that Laitman says she works "from the words out:" one could hardly present the idea of glittering sublimity in shadowed tones.

Texts in Appendix Two (pages 321 – 324)

♪♪♪♪♪

Whitacre: *Winter*

Few composers have ever been as inventive in their outreach and inspirations as Eric Whitacre (b. 1971). Long a devotee of choral music, thanks to having sung in his college choir, he has written a great number of vocal works, often a cappella. Not only have these attracted much attention amongst choral ensembles, but even with amateur singers. Consult YouTube or other online sources for Whitacre's multiple Digital Choir projects, in which he accepted videos from individual singers performing one of his works and then edited them together to create, both visually and aurally, a grand international choral performance.

Sometimes, Whitacre takes additional step of supplementing his choirs with instruments and sound sources from outside the usual choices. His *Cloudburst* (1995) includes a thunder-sheet, the better to evoke the storm. As for his *Winter*, rather than opting for stereotypical sleigh bells, Whitacre chose to support and expand the SATB chorus with string orchestra, harp, and sitar. Indeed: the Asian Indian distant cousin of the guitar. The composer says that, upon reading a winter poem by Edward Esch (b. 1970) – one in which the sitar is certainly never mentioned by name – he was struck by how what the composer describes as the "sparse, static nature" of the poem reminded him of Indian music he'd heard in college. So it is the haunting voice of that exotic instrument that opens Whitacre's *Winter*, even before a single word is sung.

Esch's poem *Winter* is in three verses, though Whitacre sets them in a single, uninterrupted sweep of music rather less than a quarter hour in length. The sitar begins with short rhythmic fragments derived from the traditional ragas and talas of India, while a low droning tone provides foundation. The string ensemble adds falling phrases and high, shimmering tremolo, all setting the stage for what will follow. Once the harp has joined the mix, so do the voices, peacefully intoning "the snow." The sitar provides additional detail, its isolated notes perhaps suggestive of the sun glinting on individual snowflakes.

More outspoken, rapturous passages appear, especially in the middle lines, when the voices speak of gold and silver. Later lines return to more delicate imagery. A single snowflake "shimmers," both in words and music, and though sitar and harp have been silent for several minutes, both rejoin for the closing pages. Murmuring voices evoke the idea of that single snowflake disappearing, and small motifs from the sitar add a final bit of sparkle.

Whitacre's unusual mix of performing forces proves ideal for the text at hand allowing for musical visions that sparkle and shiver, just like the snow and those who might be strolling through it. His *Winter* has been recorded, though, as of summer 2018, the work is not yet published: choral directors hoping to add it to their own programs may need to be patient.

♪♪♪♪♪

As this chapter is devoted to vocal music for any (or all) of the seasons, a wealth of further suggestions is at hand. These six, including three for spring and three for winter, though none for summer or fall, rose to the top thanks to their strikingly vivid coloring.

- Carl Nielsen (1865 - 1931): *Springtime on Funen* is a short cantata that remembers the composer's birthplace, a pastoral island off the mainland of Denmark. If the general mood of the songs and choral scenes is to be believed, it's a place of good humor and high spirits.

- Ottorino Respighi (1879 - 1936): Another small scale cantata, though from an Italian viewpoint, is *La Primavera (Spring)*, not to be confused with Respighi's instrumental piece *Primavera* (see page 87). Its joyous reflections upon this season of love may be influenced by the fact that Respighi and his wife Elsa had just been wed.

- EJ Moeran (1894 - 1950): Few can beat the English Pastoralist composers for seasonal reflections. In this case, however, Moeran gave himself a head-start, basing his *Songs of Springtime* on verses by Shakespeare: few laments, much rejoicing, and a measure of wine and daffodils.

- Georgy Sviridov (1915 – 1998): The Russian composer's *Snow is Falling* is a short cycle for chorus and orchestra setting poems by Boris Pasternak (1890 – 1960) of *Dr. Zhivago* fame. Sviridov provides haunting reflection upon snow, moody musings upon the challenges faced by mankind, and finally effusive joy at a winter night.

- Karl Jenkins (b. 1944): To a certain extent, the Welsh composer's *Stella Natalis* is a Christmas cantata, though with influence from Hindu and Zulu traditions as well as Biblical ones. Jenkins also includes vividly wintery verses by contemporary poet Carol Barratt, such as the prancing *Wintertime*, complete with sleigh bells and snow balls.

- John Rutter (b. 1945): The English composer has written countless choral settings of carols, both ones long familiar and also new ones of his own. However, one might here consider the purely wintery *When Icicles Hang* (1973). Good ale, winter winds, and convivial gatherings have their place, along with magical moods for light glinting upon frozen water. In any hemisphere, those are scenes of winter.

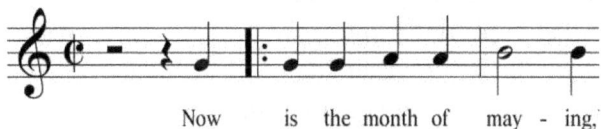

Chapter Eight: Shakespearean Diversions

The music above may be the most widely familiar of all Shakespearean-inspired compositions; certainly, it is the most frequently performed of all such works and one for which the great majority of listeners would be able to state in what sort of situation they first heard it, even if the composer's name didn't instantly come to mind. It is the first notes of the *Wedding March* from Mendelssohn's *A Midsummer Night's Dream*. Whether presented only on organ, or, as Mendelssohn himself first imagined it, with the full splendor of brass, woodwinds, strings, and a bit of percussion, it is featured at the close of the great majority of weddings, both formal and casual, sending countless couples into a new life together.

However, neither the *Wedding March* itself nor the full *Midsummer* music are very summery. In the entire length of the play, the season is scarcely mentioned: one single time by the workman-like Quince and a handful of times by the Queen of the Fairies, Titania, who also mentions the other three seasons in one of these same monologues. So the play is not really <u>about</u> summer, even though one might suppose its outdoor settings to be best suited to that season.

Nonetheless, with the word "summer" so prominent in the title and the enduring fame of Mendelssohn's music for the play, one can scarcely escape including it in any survey of music on seasonal themes. Its absence would be otherwise notable, and certainly few are likely to protest its presence.

In Shakespeare's time, it was conventional to incorporate songs and perhaps dances into a stage work; he would provide texts for the songs and indicate in the body of the play where he expected them to be inserted. Not being himself a composer, he was yet acquainted with enough such persons to have his dramatic requirements met. Music written to accompany live performance of a staged play is known as "incidental music," in that it is an incidental part of the dramatic creation. It was for exactly that situation that Mendelssohn composed most of his *Midsummer Night's Dream* music, and the same is true of Lars-Erik Larsson's *A Winter's Tale*, also featured here. *Winter's Tale* is a less famous play than *Midsummer*, but no less worthy of attention, though its script, too, has not much to say on the specific subject of winter.

One might also write an opera on Shakespeare's seasonally-titled plays, and one such appears in this chapter. Then, there's the thought of composing something that isn't intended to be joined to the play itself, but might be inspired by compelling lines and imagery from the plays. A fine recent example of that approach will be found in this chapter as well. All are musical expressions of *A Midsummer Night's Dream* and *A Winter's Tale*.

♪♪♪♪

Mendelssohn: *A Midsummer Night's Dream* –
overture, op. 21, and incidental music, op. 61

For Felix Mendelssohn (1809 – 1847), *A Midsummer Night's Dream* is both an early work and a late one. The overture itself he wrote as a stand-alone work at the age of seventeen, the remaining selections – including the ever-famed Wedding March – fully another seventeen years later. Such is what happens when a teen is inspired by Shakespeare, and then an emperor asks him to pick up the subject once more.

As an elder son of wealthy parents devoted to the performing arts – not just music, but also theater – young Felix had grown up with German translations of Shakespeare. *A Midsummer Night's Dream*, with its blend of love, wit, and philosophy, was especially well-suited to the young man's sensibilities, and he decided to express his feelings for it in music. In its initial form, his *A Midsummer Night's Dream* (1826) was for two pianos; both he and his elder sister Fanny (1805 – 1847) were talented pianists, and they performed it for an invited audience at the Mendelssohn family home. A full orchestration by Felix himself followed the next year and became an immediate success throughout Europe.

The overture opens with four gently dreamy long tones from woodwinds before scurrying strings seem to evoke the magical fairies of the forest. Bold colors and prancing dotted rhythms develop, leading to a lush, romantically flowing theme for the play's pairs of human lovers. Before long, Mendelssohn introduces a falling hee-haw pattern reflecting the character Bottom's sudden acquisition of donkey's ears, so along with the lovers and the fairies, the workers also have a musical role. Central pages of the overture toy with all those musical elements, giving them new colors and different moods, before the four long tones return and all sets off again much as before, though with somewhat more space for expansion. The overture closes with same four chords with which it had begun, here serving as a kind of benediction to the tale.

Despite the popularity of the overture, Mendelssohn did not go further with this Shakespearean theme at the time, and indeed might have never approached it again of his own accord, since a thriving conducting career began to limit his time available for composition. His return to the subject came at the request of the Prussian emperor, Frederick Wilhelm IV. The ruler had always loved the overture and, indeed, all of Mendelssohn's music. In 1842, he invited the composer to teach at a newly-founded music institute in Berlin, and, as part of the job, requested Mendelssohn's incidental music to accompany an upcoming production of *A Midsummer Night's Dream*. Unfortunately, there was no incidental music other than the overture.

Not wishing to decline the honor, Mendelssohn set to work anew, drawing in part upon themes borrowed from the overture. So, amongst much else, he crafted in short order a Fairies' Scherzo derived from that scurrying string theme and a Clown's interlude based on the hee-haw passage. As the incidental music came along so many years after the overture, it bears its own distinct opus number: op. 61 instead of op. 21.

There were also songs for the fairies, one as a lullaby for fairy queen Titania, surely the only reference in all of Mendelssohn's catalog to hedgehogs and spotted snakes, which Shakespeare fairies (sung here only by women's voices) command to keep their distance. This same music reappears in altered form in another chorus late in the play as the fairies dance off into the night. Rather than supposing that Mendelssohn hadn't had time to think of a new melody for this later chorus, one can reasonably suppose that he wanted the two scenes to reflect one another. It is fairy music: let it represent the fairies, and thereby remind listeners who has just stepped on stage.

Between those points, one finds a dreamy Nocturne rich with French horns, and the resplendent energy of the Wedding March. Those who know the March only from its appearance in wedding ceremonies may be startled to find how much of it there actually is. The glorious opening theme (appearing at the head of this chapter) is contrasted by smoother, more flowing themes from which crash cymbals are entirely absent. One might suppose that the director of the production at the emperor's palace had informed Mendelssohn that he wanted time for quite a substantial procession. Conversely, perhaps Mendelssohn himself thought the scene would benefit from more music, and simply expected the director to make the most of the available time. One way or the other, it is both exciting and beautiful, its glories undiminished by its familiarity.

♪♪♪♪♪

Britten: *A Midsummer Night's Dream* – opera

To most musical minds, *A Midsummer Night's Dream* is largely identified with Felix Mendelssohn (1809-1847), whose musical *Midsummer* came to life in 1842. That famed score was intended to accompany a live performance of the play, in which context there is significantly more spoken text than music. Benjamin Britten (1913 – 1976) took a different approach, making the play into an opera with virtually every word sung, not spoken, and thus a much larger quantity of music.

One cannot simply sing all the words of a play. Singing takes more time than speaking; singing a three-hour play would result in a five-hour opera. So for this twelfth of his seventeen operas (the first and only to derive from Shakespeare), the English composer had to trim the original text. Working together with his life partner, the esteemed English tenor Peter Pears (1910 – 1986), Britten streamlined the play, adding only a very few new words to facilitate edits, and making those edits only when necessary to keep the story moving while still providing enough time to sing.

The one non-singing character is the impish Puck, which Britten makes a spoken role. However, everyone else sings, and Britten sought to reflect their characters in his music. So the fairies are sung by a children's choir, young voices being particularly light in tone. Their rulers, Oberon and Titania, are written very high in pitch, she as a coloratura soprano, and he as a countertenor. Britten's decision served to make his fairies sound rather ethereal, perhaps even otherworldly, in coloring. Let the human characters have the more grounded music, as the fairies reach for the sky: such is Britten's approach.

Of his human characters, he wrote the four lovers for lyrical, Puccini-esque voices and the "mechanicals," as Shakespeare called them – down-to-earth, working-class fellows – as less lyrical, almost conversational in singing style. These fellows are the principal comic relief of the tale, and Britten apparently thought it was best if their singing was not particularly flamboyant. However, one of their number, Flute by name and written as a tenor, is a male character who, in the context of the play-within-a-play, pretends to be a young woman, at which point Britten provides notes in a very high falsetto range. For the premiere production, Pears sang Flute. Pears was, perhaps, beyond the age to sing one of the young lovers, and didn't have the countertenor range to sing Oberon, but his falsetto was beyond compare.

Then there's the orchestra, which also tends toward higher pitches. In addition to the usual suspects, one finds piccolo and harpsichord (or at least celesta), no tubas, and only one trombone and one bassoon. The percussion section Britten supplies with triangle, tambourine, vibraphone, glockenspiel, xylophone, wood blocks, and various other tools, in addition to the standard complement that even Mendelssohn might have used. Britten's goal was to create musical colors reflective of this imagined interface between the fairies' world and that of the humans: his instrumental choices support that intent as well as the voices do.

Britten's initial intention – to write an opera, not a set of incidental music – is utterly different from that of Mendelssohn. Thus, the fact that they are of different nationalities and also different centuries no longer really matters, and comparing one work to the other is not particularly useful. Britten's opera doesn't even have a wedding march, as the original Shakespeare has no grand wedding scene, and his "overture" is forty seconds of introduction to a fairy song. However, Britten's music is ideal for the scenes he is setting. Music for the fairies is often accompanied by haunting string phrases that roll upward and downward in pitch, sometimes joined by delicate touches from xylophone or one of the other mallet instruments. Broader phrases for strings and winds tend to be used for human characters, and his nocturnal interlude features sustained string lines with woodwinds and harp; Mendelssohn had opted for French horns, but Britten, it seems, preferred a lighter touch at this point in the tale. His evening music is more fairy-like than human.

Of all Shakespearean operas, Britten's *A Midsummer Night's Dream* remains most faithful to the original Shakespeare. No offense is intended to Frenchman Charles Gounod's *Romeo et Juilliette* (1867) or Italian Giuseppe Verdi's *Otello* (1887), but apparently, it took an Englishman to keep the details of the tale authentic, while still crafting a compelling evening of musical drama. Britten's opera premiered June 11, 1960, at the composer's own Aldeburgh Festival, near England's North Sea coast, a summer event still in business these many decades after the composer's passing. Non-classical events are also offered, though Britten and his music retain pride of place.

♪♪♪♪♪

Larsson: *A Winter's Tale* suite

Shakespeare's *A Winter's Tale* is not an exceptionally wintery play; the action shifts from place to place, and other than a passing reference to tales told to pass the time during winter evenings, it has little to do with the season. However, like most Shakespeare, it contains cleverly crafted dialog and certainly the opportunity for directors to make something of its two disparate halves: the first highly dramatic, the second rather more comical.

Swedish composer Lars-Erik Larsson (1908 – 1986) first composed for *A Winter's Tale* in 1937 when he was asked to provide incidental music for a staged production. Then the following year, as part of his continuing work with Swedish Radio, he found himself providing music for a broadcast series concerning poetry and music; in that context, *A Winter's Tale* emerged once more. Being on a short timetable and finding himself faced with the same literary subject, Larsson chose to recycle some of his music for the earlier stage production, crafting a ten-minute suite of four short movements, all scored for a studio-sized orchestra.

The first movement *Siciliana* borrows the graceful action of that vintage ballroom dance, here with oboe and strings, initially in gentle demeanor, though gradually becoming fuller and richer in character. The subsequent *Intermezzo* is all light and playful strings.

For the third movement *Pastorale*, Larsson provides danceable lines for woodwinds, juxtaposed against more smoothly flowing strings.

He concludes his *A Winter's Tale* suite with a rather somber *Epilogue*, in which woodwind solos – particularly for oboe – are again accompanied by strings. One might imagine that the regretful moods of these closing pages reflect the challenges suffered by several of the play's characters, or perhaps a general sense of melancholy when a glance out the window confirmed that spring has yet to arrive. The music may not be exceptionally wintery, but even without the play that inspired it, Larsson's *A Winter's Tale* makes for a graciously Neoclassical listening experience.

♪♪♪♪♪

Torke: *A Winter's Tale* – cello concerto

Michael Torke (b. 1961 in Milwaukee) has often specialized in brilliantly colored scores, sometimes single movement works, for full orchestra. However, familiarity with the orchestra does not preclude an understanding of its component parts, so Torke's catalog also includes a large number of concerti. Woodwind instruments and keyboards are his most frequent choices for the solo spotlight, but there are also concerti for string instruments, one such being the cello concerto *A Winter's Tale* from 2014, written on commission from the Albany Symphony.

Torke himself says that, though the title originated in Shakespeare, the work was never intended to accompany the play in question, the moods of which range from what the composer describes as "destructive jealousy" to forgiveness. The concerto simply would not serve for incidental music for a stage production. However, Torke attests that the concerto is "nevertheless inspired by lines from the play: from moody winter thoughts, through warmer and more redemptive springtime feelings." That connection provides Torke's *A Winter's Tale* with all the drama and variety of mood that one might require of an instrumental work spanning rather less than half an hour. At times, the solo cellist feels almost like a narrator relating Shakespeare's tale.

The first movement *Allegro* is restless and driving in nature, with flowing lines for the cello soloist interrupted again and again by short, gruff orchestral statements. Skipping dotted rhythms, in which short notes lead to longer ones, appear frequently. In places, Torke brings vibraphone into the equation and even allows for a brief exchange between solo cello and bassoon.

The two *Andante* movements, appearing second and fourth out of five, both bear subtitles referring to a specific character from the play, Perdita. A lost princess rejected in childhood, she has been raised by shepherds and is of simple tastes, preferring the flowers of the fields to the jewels of the court. Act IV/Scene III finds her reflecting upon her surroundings:

"Here's flowers for you:
hot lavender, mints, savoury, marjoram;
the marigold, that goes to be wi' the sun
... daffodils that come before the swallow dares,
and take the winds of March with beauty."

That tender spirit is reflected in the two *Andante* movements of Torke's work that bear her name. In *Perdita's Flowers I*, short, tender orchestral phrases broaden when handed to the solo cellist; a grander interlude subsides into calm as the movement nears its close. *Perdita's Flowers II* is rather more energized in nature. Two features found in both movements are solo cadenzas for the cellist and a recurrence of those dotted rhythms from the first movement.

Standing midway in Torke's *A Winter's Tale*, between the two Perdita scenes, is the serene third movement *Largo*. Here, French horn first takes the spotlight before handing focus to the cellist. Central pages share attention all around, providing a gently nocturnal atmosphere, before the movement closes with a renewed focus upon cello and French horn.

The concluding *Allegro* movement is largely of spirited, even danceable, energy. As in the first movement, the orchestra sometimes punctuates the solo cello's phrases, and dotted rhythms are still evident. Middle pages suggest the brilliance of a sunny day. A solo cadenza, in which the orchestra speaks up at times, lasts nearly, though not quite, to the final chord. Torke's *A Winter's Tale* ensures that audience attention will be focused until the end.

♪♪♪♪♪

One might further expand this selection of seasonally-shaded Shakespearean works, even on these same two plays. Certainly, some song settings of his poems have seasonal connections, as related at times in Chapter Seven. As for instrumental works, Czech composer Josef Suk (1874 – 1935) crafted incidental music for *A Winter's Tale* and Italian composer Mario Castelnuovo-Tedesco (1895 – 1968) wrote concert overtures for both *A Winter's Tale* and *A Midsummer Night's Dream*, as well as several others. Concert overtures are not intended to accompany the play itself; on the contrary, they are free-standing instrumental works inspired by the characters and moods of the play. Mendelssohn's *Midsummer* music had begun as a concert overture, and only belatedly drew closer to dramatic usage. As for other examples of Shakespeare in fine music, whether seasonal or not, that is a topic for another day.

♪♪♪♪♪

Spring flowers, summer breezes, autumn leaves, winter frosts: none of it is of epic scope, whether in the care of Shakespeare or Beethoven or anyone else. However, surely therein lies part of the appeal. Daffodils are neither fearful nor fear-inspiring, and in an ever more complicated world, "a host of golden daffodils... fluttering and dancing in the breeze," as William Wordsworth (1770 – 1850) memorably described them, can be a soothing sight. Lend that imagery to a gifted composer, whether a past master or one still working today, and the aural element increases the effect.

Seasonal imagery in music might provide reassurance or exhilaration or nearly any other feeling one could name. Music may not actively sound hungry, but if it suggests a harvest celebration, one might, in imagining the accompanying feast, long to be amongst those at the table. Give it a boisterous spirit, and perhaps add some percussion details that could almost be glasses clinking together in a toast, and the scene becomes vividly clear, even to the appetite.

Then again, for some composers, there might be a particularly personal aspect. In the second movement of Beethoven's Symphony no. 6, the *Pastorale,* he calls upon woodwinds to evoke very specific birdcalls. However, by the time he began work on the symphony, his hearing was already failing, and in a heart-wrenching passage from a letter written to his brothers October 6, 1802, Beethoven observes upon the "humiliation" (he uses the German word "Demütigung") he feels when those around him remark upon the sounds of nature that he can no longer hear. Yet the music for what Beethoven labels *Scene by the Brook* does not sound humiliated. Perhaps putting the notes on the page allowed Beethoven to remember vanished sounds, or at least to prove to observers that the memory endured. As listeners, we can take it as just a pretty scene, or imagine its creator's trauma that he seeks to overcome, or at least put aside for the moment, through music.

Seasonal labels can lead listeners to find things in music that may resemble what the composer specifically had in mind – if, indeed, there was anything specific, rather than just a general sense of how the music seemed to sound, at least to that composer on that day. So

Respighi and Debussy both react to the same famous painting of spring, Hanson spends the summer by the seaside, Delius recalls autumn in the North of England, and Torke remembers his childhood paper route on a winter day.

Some might suggest that such labels are unnecessary. Music, they attest, should just speak for itself. Often, it can do so, whether tenderly or determinedly, and abstract music has a time-honored place in the creative canon. However, one cannot – and ought not – discount the effectiveness of directing listeners' attention. That's what all the composers included here have sought to do, to varying degrees. Certainly, that has been the goal of this survey. The only remaining task is yours: to listen closely enough as to notice what the music seems to suggest to you: not necessarily everyone universally, just you. A wealth of musical adventure awaits discovery. Let the flowers, the breezes, the leaves, and the frosts launch that journey.

♫♫♫♫♫

Notes

Appendix One: Vivaldi's *Four Seasons* poems

La Primavera

Giunt'è la Primavera e festosetti
la salutan gl'Augei con lieto canto,
e i fonti allo Spirar de' Zeffiretti
con dolce mormorio Scorrono intanto.

Vengon' coprendo l'aer di nero amanto
e Lampi, e tuoni ad annuntiarla eletti;
indi facendo questi, gl'Augelletti
iornan' di nuovo al lor canoro incanto.

E quindi Sul fiorito ameno prato
al caro mormorio di fronde e piante
dorme l'Caprar col fido can' a lato.

Di pastoral Zampogna al Suon festante
danzan Ninfe e Pastor nel tetto amato
di primavera all' apparir brillante.

    Spring

    Spring has arrived with joy,
    Welcomed by the birds with happy songs,
    And the brooks, amidst gentle breezes,
    Murmur sweetly as they flow.

    The sky is caped in black, and
    Thunder and lightning herald a storm.
    When they fall silent, the birds
    Take up again their delightful songs.

    And in the pleasant, blossom-filled meadow,
    To the gentle murmur of leaves and plants
    The goatherd sleeps, his faithful dog beside him.

    To the merry sounds of a rustic bagpipe,
    Nymphs and shepherds dance in their beloved spot
    When Spring appears in splendor

- Translations by this author; all rights reserved.

L'Estate

Sotto dura staggion dal sole accesa
Langue l'huomo, langue 'l gregge, ed arde il Pino;
scoglie il Cucco la Voce, e tosto intesa
Canta la tortorella e 'l gardelino.

Zeffiro dolce spira, má contesa
muove Borea improvise al Suo vicino;
e piange il Pastorel, perche Sospesa
Teme fiera borasca, e 'l suo destino;

Toglie alle membra lasse il Suo riposo
il timore de' Lampi, e tuoni fieri
e de mosche, e mossoni il Stuol furioso!

Ah che pur troppo i Suoi timor Son veri
tuona e fulmina il Ciel e grandinoso
tronca il capo alle Spiche e a grani alteri.

    Summer

    Under the merciless sun of the season
    Languishes man and flock, the pine tree burns,
    The cuckoo begins to sing and at once
    Join in the turtledove and the goldfinch.

    A gentle breeze blows, but Boreas
    Is roused to combat suddenly with his neighbor,
    And the shepherd weeps because overhead
    Hangs the fearsome storm, and his destiny.

    His tired limbs are robbed of rest
    By his fear of the lightning and the frightful thunder
    And by the flies and hornets in furious swarms.

    Alas, his fears come true:
    There is thunder and lightning in the heavens,
    And the hail cuts down the tall ears of grain.

-    Translations by this author; all rights reserved.

L'Autunno

Celebra il Vilanel con balli e canti
del felice raccolto il bel piacere
e del liquor di Bacco accesi tanti
finiscono col sonno il lor godere.

Fa ch'ogn'uno tralasci e balli e canti
l'aria che temperate dà piacere,
e la Staggion ch'invita tanti e tanti
d'un dolcissimo sonino al bel godere.

I cacciatore alla nov' alba à caccia
con corni, Schioppi, e canni escono fuore;
Fugge la belua, e seguono la traccia;

Già Sbigottita, e lassa al gran rumore
de'schioppi e canni, ferita minaccia
languida di fuggir, mà oppressa muore.

    Autumn

    The peasant celebrates with dancing and singing
    The pleasure of the rich harvest,
    And full of the liquor of Bacchus
    They end their merrymaking with a sleep.

    All are made to leave off dancing and singing
    By the air which, now mild, gives pleasure
    And by the season which invites many
    To find their pleasure in a sweet sleep.

    The hunters set out at dawn, off to the hunt
    With horns and guns and dogs they venture out.
    The beast flees, and they are close on its trail.

    Already terrified and wearied by the great noise
    Of the guns and dogs, and wounded as well,
    It tries feebly to escape, but is bested and dies.

-    Translations by this author; all rights reserved.

L'Inverno

Aggiacciato tremar trà nevi algenti
al Severo Spirar d'orrido Vento,
correr battendo i piedi ogni momento;
e pel Soverchio gel batter i denti;

Passar al foco i dì quieti e contenti
mentre la pioggia fuor bagna ben cento
caminar sopra 'l giaccio, e à passo lento
per timor di cader gersene intenti;

Già forte, Sdruzziolar, cader à terra
di nuovo ir Sopra l' giaccio, e correr forte
sin ch'il giaccio Si rompe, e Si disserra;

Sentir uscir dale ferrate porte
Sirocco, Borea, e tutti I venti in Guerra –
quest'è 'l verno, mà tal, che gioja apporte.

    Winter

    Frozen and shivering in the icy snow,
    In the severe blasts of a terrible wind
    To run stamping one's feet each moment,
    One's teeth chattering through the cold.

    To spend quiet and happy times by the fire
    While outside the rain soaks everyone,

    To walk on the ice with tentative steps,
    Going carefully for fear of falling.

    To go in haste, slide and fall down to the ground,
    To go again on the ice and run,
    In case the ice cracks and opens.

    To hear leaving their iron-gated house Sirocco,
    Boreas and all the winds in battle –
    This is winter, but it brings joy.

-    Translations by this author; all rights reserved.

Appendix Two: Selected Vocal Texts and Translations

Most of these texts are in the public domain, though composer Lori Laitman gave approval to reproduce copyrighted texts for her songs, with appropriate acknowledgement. Alas, *Carmina Burana* and *Knoxville: Summer of 1915* are still under copyright.

To prevent doubling the size of this book, only selected movements of Haydn's *Jahreszeiten* are included. Most readily comprehensible English texts are omitted, also for the sake of space. Amongst the digital source list is an online site where nearly all of the texts for items in this book, even many in the public domain, are available.

- Morley: *Now is the Month of Maying*

Now is the month of maying,
When merry lads are playing.
Fa la la...
Each with his bonny lass
Upon the greey grass.
Fa la la...

The spring, clad all in gladness,
Doth laugh at winter's sadness.
Fa la la...
And to the bagpipe's sound,
The nymphs tread out their ground.
Fa la la...

Fie the! Why sit we musing,
Youth's sweet delights refusing?
Fa la la...
Say dainty nymphs, and speak,
Shall we play barley-break?
Fa la la...

- Morley: *April is in my mistresses' face*

April is in my mstress' face,
And July in her eyes hath place.
Within her bosom is September,
But in her heart a cold December.

- Morley: *It was a lover and his lass*

It was a lover and his lass,
With a hey, and a ho, and a hey nonino,
That o'er the green cornfields did pass.
When birds do sing, hey ding a ding a ding;
Sweet lovers love the spring.

This carol they began that hour,
With a hey, and a ho, and a hey nonino,
How that a life was but a flower
In the springtime, the only pretty ring time,
When birds do sing, hey ding a ding a ding;
Sweet lovers love the spring.

Then, pretty lovers, take the time
With a hey, and a ho, and a hey nonino,
For love is crowned with the prime
In the springtime, the only pretty ring time,
When birds do sing, hey ding a ding a ding;
Sweet lovers love the spring.

- Vivaldi: "Dell'aura al sussurrar," from *Dorilla in Tempe*

    Dell'aura al sussurrar, dell'onda al mormorar,
    Cantiamo con piacer fra il dolce, e bel goder
    Della nuova stagion l'onore, e il vanto.
    E sia di primavera d'ogni gioir foriera il nostro canto.

    Senti quell'usignolo su la nascente fronda,
    Come il piacer l'innonda e qual d'amor favella.
    Spiegando lieto il volo ei cerca fido il nido
    Al bel piacer ch'attende.
    E in noi di primavera d'amor
    Lieta foriera i voti accende.

    Ride il colle, e ride il prato fra viole, e gigli,
    E rose, e amorose l'aure spirano d'intorno.
    La Fedele rondinella lieta anch'ella
    Per goder fa a noi ritorno.

    Quest'è la bella stagion novella,
    Che dando vita all'erbe, ai fiori
    Ai nostri cuori Spiega l'amore.
    Ella gradita di nevi, e brine dilegua
    Al fine l'aspro rigor.

Translation:

>As the breeze whispers and the waves murmur,
>Let us sing with pleasure amidst the sweet delights,
>The honor and praise of the new season.
>Let our song be of spring, proclaiming its joys.
>
>Hear the nightingale on the new branches,
>How delight fills him as he sings of love.
>Delightedly, he flies off to his nest
>Seeking there the pleasure that awaits him.
>He stimulates our passion for spring,
>Announcing its approach.
>
>
>The hills and meadows smile, amidst
>Violets, lilies, roses and loving breeze.
>The faithful little swallow returns,
>Finding delight in our joy.
>
>Here is the new and lovely season,
>In giving us the grass and the flowers,
>Reveals love to us.
>She mitigates the severe rigors
>Of the snows and frosts.

- Translations by this author; all rights reserved.

- Haydn: *Die Jahreszeiten* – "Komm holder Lenz"

> Komm, holder Lenz, des Himmels Gabe, komm!
> Aus ihrem Todesschlaf erwecke die Natur!
>
> Ernaher sich, der holde Lenz;
> Schon fühlen wir den linden Hauch,
> Bald lebet alles wieder auf.
>
> Frohlocket ja nicht allzufrüh!
> Oft schleicht, in Nebel eingehüllt,
> Der Winter wohl zurück und streut
> Auf Blüt' und Keim sein stares Gift.
>
> Komm, holder Lenz, des Himmels Gabe komm!
> Auf unsere Fluren senke dich, komm, holder Lenz,
> O Komm! Und weile länger nicht!

Translation:

> Come, fair spring, gift of heaven, come!
> Awaken nature from its death-like sleep.
>
> Fair spring draws near;
> Already, we feel its soft breath,
> Soon, all will come to life once more.
>
> Do not rejoice too soon!
> All too often, wrapped in mists,
> Winter slips back and spreads
> Its cruel poison on blossoms and seeds.
>
> Come, fair spring, gift of heaven, come!
> Descend over our fields, come, fair spring,
> O come! Stay away no longer!

- Translations by this author; all rights reserved.

- Haydn: *Die Jahreszeiten* – "Welcher Labung"

    Welche Labung für die Sinne!
    Welch' Etholung für das Herz!
    Jeden Aderzweig durchströmet
    Und in jeder Nerve bebt erquickendes Gefühl.

    Die Seele wachet auf
    Zum reizenden Genuß,
    Und neue Kraft erhebt
    Durch milden Drang die Brust.

Translation:

    Such a balm for the senses!
    Such comfort for the heart!
    Through every vein and every nerve
    Streams feelings of refreshment.

    The soul awakes
    To stimulating pleasures,
    And new strength fills
    The breast with gentle force.

-    Translations by this author; all rights reserved.

- Haydn: *Die Jahreszeiten* – "Der Wein ist da"

    Juhe! Juhe! Der Wein ist da,
    Die Tonnen sind gefüllt.
    Nun laßt uns fröhlich sein, und juhe!
    Aus vollen Halse schrein.

    Laßt uns trinken! Trinket, Brüder!
    Laßt uns fröhlich sein.
    Juhe, juh! Es lebe der Wein!

    Es lebe das Land, wo er uns reift!
    Es lebe das Faß, das ihn verwahrt!
    Es lebe der Krug, woraus er fließt!

    [Etc...]

    Nun tönen die Pfeifen und wirbelt die Trommel.
    Hier kreischet die Fiedel, da schnarret die Leier,
    Und dudelt der Bock.

    Schon hüpfen die Kleinen, und springen die Knaben;
    Dort fliegen die Mädchen im Arme der Burschen
    Den ländlichen Reih'n.

    [Etc.....]

    Jauchzet, lärmen, springet, tanzet, lachet, singet!
    Nun fassen wir den letzten Krug!

    Und singen dann im vollen Chor
    Dem freudenreichen Rebensaft!
    Heisa, hei, juhe, juh!
    Es lebe der Wein, der edle Wein,
    Der Grillen und Harm verscheucht!
    Sein Lob ertöne laut und hoch
    In tausendfachem Jubelschall!
    Heida, laßt uns fröhlich sein!
    Und juhe, juhe, juh, aus vollem Halse schrein!

Translation:

> Hooray! Hooray! There is the wine!
> The vats are full,
> Let us be joyful, and shout 'hooray'
> At the top of our lungs!
>
> Let us drink! Drink, brother!
> Let us be joyful!
> Hooray, hooray! Long live wine!
>
> Long live the land where it ripens!
> Long live the vat where it's stored!
> Long live the jug, from which it pours!
>
> [Etc....]
>
> The pipes sound, the drums beat,
> The fiddle screeches, the hurdy-gurdy moans,
> The bagpipes wail.
>
> Already the children jump and the youths leap;
> There the girls are flying into their fellows' arms
> In peasant dances.
>
> [Etc....]
>
> Rejoice, shout, leap, dance, laugh, sing!
> Let us now open the last jug!
>
> Together, let us sing as a full choir
> The praises of the joy-filled juice of grapes!
> Hooray, hooray, hooray!
> Long live wine, noble wine,
> That dries away all cares!
> Its praises ring loud and clear
> In a thousand-fold cheers!
> Hooray, let us be joyful!
> Call out hooray, hooray, at the top of our lungs!

- Translations by this author; all rights reserved.

- Haydn: *Die Jahreszeiten* – Spinning Chorus

Knurre, schnurre, knurre!
Schnurre, Rädchen, schnurre!

Drille, Rädchen, lang und fein,
Drille fein ein Fädelein
Mir zum Busenschleier!
Knurre, schnurre...

Weber, webe zart und fein,
Webe fein das Schleierlein
Mir zur Kirmesfeier.
Knurre, schnurre...

Außen blank und innen rein
Muß das Mädchens Busen sein,
Wohl deckt ihn der Schleier.
Knurre, schnurre...

Außen blank und innen rein,
Fleißig, fromm und sittsam sein,
Locket wack're Freier.

Translation:

> Whir, purr, hum, little wheel!
>
> Little wheel, spin a long, fine thread
> To make for me a shawl for my breast!
> Whir, purr, hum, little wheel!
>
> Weaver, weave a soft, fine veil
> For me to wear to the festival.
> Whir, purr, hum, little wheel!
>
> Clean and pure both outside and in
> Must the maiden's breast,
> For the veil to suit.
> Whir, purr, hum, little wheel!
>
> Clean and pure both outside and in,
> Busy, pious, and demure,
> That's how to attract a suitor.

- Translations by this author; all rights reserved.

- Mozart: *Schon lacht der holde Frühling*, K. 580

Schon lacht der holde Frühling auf blumenreichen Matten,
Wo sich Zephirs gatten unter geselligen Scherze,
Wenn auch auf allen Zweigen sich junge Blüten zeigen,
Kehrt doch kein leiser Trost in dieses arme Herz.

Da sitze ich und weine einsam auf der Flur,
Nicht um mein verlornes Schäfchen,
Nein, um den Schäfer Lindor nur.

Translation:

Already, fair spring laughs on the flowery doorstep,
Where breezes pair off amidst friendly jests,
As on every branch, young blooms show themselves,
Bringing no little comfort to this poor heart.

There I sit and weep alone on the landing,
Not weeping over my lost little sheep,
No, only for the shepherd Lindor.

- Translations by this author; all rights reserved.

- Mozart: *Sehnsucht nach der Frühling*, K. 596

> Komm, lieber Mai, und mache die Bäume wieder grün,
> Und laß mir an dem Bache die kleinen Veilchen blühn!
> Wie möcht ich doch zo gerne ein Veilchen wieder sehn,
> Ach, lieber Mai, wie gerne einmal spazieren gehn!
>
> Zwar Wintertage haben wohl auch der Freuden viel;
> Man kann im Schnee eins traben und treibt mach Abendspiel,
> Baut Häuserchen von Karten, spielt Blindekuh und Pfand;
> Auch gibt's wohl Schlittenfahrten auf's liebe freie Land.
>
> Ach, wenn's doch erst gelinder und grüner drauß wär!
> Komm, lieber Mai, wir Kinder, wir bitten dich gar sehr!

Translation:

> Come, dear May, and make the trees green again,
> And let the little violets bloom for me beside the brook!
> I so want to see a violet again,
> Ah, dear May, how gladly I'd go walking once more!
>
> Admittedly, winter also has many pleasures,
> One can tramp through the snow, play evening games,
> Build houses of cards, play blind-man's-bluff
> Also, there are sleigh-rides in the countryside.
>
> Ah, but if only it was fresh and green outside!
> Come, dear May, we children, we ask you so nicely!

- Translations by this author; all rights reserved.

- Schubert: *Frühlingsgesang*, D. 709

Schmücket die Locken mit duftigen Kränzen
Und folget der Freude beglückenden Drang,
Begrüßet den Frühling mit heiteren Tänzen,
Den Sieger, der Alles in Liebe bezwang.

Der Winter bedroht ihn mit schauriger Kälte,
Der Sommer verfolgt ihn mit flammenden Speer,
Aber er schwebt unterm blauen Gezelte
Sorglos und lächelnd auf Düften daher.

Und die treue Erde mit Liebes-Geberde
Eilt ihm entgegen, es heben und regen
Sich tausend Kräfte in ihrer Brust,
Und künden der Liebe selige Lust.

Es rieseln Quellen und Knospen schwellen,
Blumen erscheinen und in den Hainen
Singt Philomele aus tiefer Brust
Und kündet der Liebe selige Lust.

Drum schmücke die Locken mit bräutlichen Kränzen,
Wem schaffende Kraft noch den Busen durchdringt,
Und huld'ge dem Sieger in freudigen Tänzen,
Der Alles mit schaffender Liebe bezwingt.

Translation:

> Deck your hair with scented wreaths
> And follow the joys of happy longings
> Greet spring with lively dancing,
> The victor who conquers all with love.
>
> Winter threatens with shivering cold,
> Summer follows with piercing heat,
> But spring floats beneath a blue canopy
> Carefree and smiling on the breeze.
>
> And the faithful earth with loving gestures
> Hastens to meet him, a thousand forces
> Rise and surge in her breast,
> And kindle the blessed passions of love.
>
> Watery springs and buds swell,
> Flowers appear, and in the fields,
> The nightingale sings from the heart
> And kindles the blesses passions of love.
>
> Thus, deck your hair with bridal wreaths, from which
> The building strength in your bosom presses,
> And hail the victor with joyous dancing,
> He who conquers all with love.

- Translations by this author; all rights reserved.

- Schubert: *Horch! Horch! Die Lerch' im Ätherblau*, D. 889

    Horch! Horch! Die Lerch' im Ätherblau;
    Und Phöbus, neu erweckt,
    Fränkt seine Ross mit dem Thau,
    Der Blumenkelche deckt;

    Der Ringelblume Knospe schleußt,
    Die goldnen Äuglein auf;
    Mit allem, was da reizend,
    Du süße Maid, steh auf! Steh auf! Steh auf!

Translation:

    Hark, hark, the lark in the heavens;
    Apollo, newly wakened,
    Waters his steed with the dew from
    A flower-decked goblet.

    The flower buds unlock
    Their golden eyes;
    With all that is splendid,
    You sweet maid, arise! Arise! Arise!

- Translations by this author; all rights reserved.

Seasonal Music Insights: | 293
Vivaldi and Much More

This page intentionally left blank,
so texts and translations will
continue to appear on facing pages.

- Schubert: *An den Mond in einer Herbstnacht*, D. 614

Freundlich ist dein Antlitz, Sohn des Himmels!
Leis sind deine Tritte durch des Aethers Wüste,
Holder Nachtgefährte.

Dein Schimmer ist sanft und erquickend,
Wie das Word des Trostes von des Freundes Lippe,
Wenn ein schrecklicher Geyer an der Seele nagt.

Manche Träne siehst du, siehst so manches Lächeln,
Hörst der Liebe trauliches Geflüster,
Leuchtest ihr auf stillem Pfade, Hoffnung schwebt
Auf seines Strahle herab zum stillen Dulder,
Der verlassen geht auf bedorntem Weg.

Du siehst auch meine Freunde, zerstreut in fernen Landen;
Du gießest deinen Schimmer auch auf die frohen Hügel,
Wo als Knabe hüpfte, wo oft bei deinem Lächeln
Ein unbekanntes Sehnen mein junges Herz ergriff.

Du blickst auch auf die Stätte, wo meine Lieben ruhn,
Wo der Thau fällt auf ihr Grab, und die Gräser drüber
Wehn dem Abendhauche.

Doch dein Schimmer dringt nicht in die dunkle Kammer,
Wo sie ruhen von des Lebens Mühn',
Wo auch ich bald ruhen Werde!
Du wirst geh'n und wiederkehren, du wirst seh'n noch
Manches Lächeln, dann werd' ich nicht mehr lächeln,
Dann werd' ich nicht mehr weinen, mein wird man
Nicht mehr gedenken auf dieser schönen Erde.

Translation:

> Friendly is your visage, son of Heaven!
> Soft is your step across the barren ether,
> Fair nighttime companion!
>
> Your glow is soft and soothing,
> Like words of solace from the lips of a friend,
> When some horrid demon gnaws upon the soul.
>
> You see so many tears, and so many smiles,
> Hear the whispers of faithful love.
> You light the silent path, hope floats upon your beams
> Down to the one who suffers in silence,
> Who forsaken toils along the thorny path.
>
> You also see my friends, scattered in distant lands;
> Your shimmering light beams also upon the hill
> So joyous where youths frolicked, where often
> In your gaze, an unknown longing arose in my heart.
>
> You gaze also upon the place where my loved ones rest,
> The dew falling upon their graves,
> And the grass above waving in the evening breeze.
>
> But your glow does not penetrate the dark chamber
> Where they rest from the troubles of life,
> Where I, too, shall soon rest!
> You will go, and come again, and see more smiles.
> Then I will smile no more, I will weep no more,
> I will think no more of this lovely earth.

- Translations by this author; all rights reserved.

- Schubert: *Der Winterabend*, D. 938

Es ist so still und heimlich um mich,
Die Sonn' ist unter, der Tag entwich.
Wie schnell nun heran der Abend graut!
Mir ist es recht, sonst ist mir's zu laut.

Jetzt aber ist's ruhig, es bämmert kein Schmiede,
Kein Klempner, das Volk verlief, und ist müd;
Und selbst, daß nicht raßke der Wagen Lauf,
Zog Decken der Schnee durch die Gassen auf.

Wie tut mit so wohl der selige Frieden!
Da sitz' ich im Dunkel, ganz abschieden.
Nur der Mondenschein kommt leise
Zu mir in's Gemach herein.

Er kennt mich schon, und läßt mich schweigen,
Nimmt nur seine Arbeit, die Spindel, das Gold,
Und spinnet stille, webt und lächelt hold;
Und hängt dann sein schimmerndes Schleiertuch
Ringsum an Geräth und Wänden aus.

Ist gar ein stiller, lieber Besuch,
Macht mir gar keine Unruh' im Haus.
Will er bleiben, so hat er Ort,
Freut's ihn nimmer, so geht er fort.

Ich sitze dann stumm im Fenster fern',
Und schaue hinauf in Gewölk' und Stern.
Denke zurück, auch! Weit, gar weit,
In eine schöne, verschwund'ne Zeit.
Denk an Sie, an das Glück der Minne,
Seufze still', und sinne und sinne.

Translation:

It is so still and secret here around me,
The sun has set, the day has passed.
How quickly now the evening here grows gray!
I don't mind; otherwise, all seems too loud to me.

Now, however, it is peaceful; no smithy hammers,
No metalsmith, the people, weary, have gone;
And now, as the wagons no longer rattle on their way,
The lanes have a covering of snow.

This blessed peace pleases me so that I sit
In the dark, quite alone. Only the moonlight
Comes to me, softly, in my chamber.

He already knows me and lets me be silent,
Just takes up his work, spinning gold,
And quietly spins, weaves, and smiles sweetly;
Then hangs his shimmering veil around on the walls.

It is a quiet, dear visit,
Making no trouble in the house;
If he wishes to stay, there is room,
If it doesn't please him, he will go.

Then I sit silently in the distant window,
And gaze out at the people and the stars.
Thinking back! Far, very far,
In a lovely, forgotten world,
I think of you, the happiness of your blessing,
Sigh quietly, and muse and ponder.

- Translations by this author; all rights reserved.

- Berlioz: *Les nuits d'eté* – two selections

    - I. *Villenelle*

        Quand viendra la saison nouvelle,
        Quand auront disparu les froids,
        Tous les deux nous irons, ma belle,
        Pour cueillir le muguet aux boix;

        Sous nos pieds égrenant les perles
        Que l'on voit au matin trembler.
        Nous irons écouter les merles,
        Nous irons écouter les merles siffler.

        Le printemps est venu, ma belle,
        C'est le mois des amants béni,
        Et l'oiseau, satinant son aile,
        Dit des vers au rebord du nid.
        Oh! Viens donc sur ce banc de mousse
        pour parlet de nos beaux amours.
        Et dis-moi de ta voix si donce,
        Et dis-mois de ta voix si douce 'Toujours!'

        Loin, bien loin, égarant nos courses,
        Faisant fuir le lapin cache
        Et le daim au miroir des sources
        Admirant son grand bois penché;

        Puis chez nous, tout heureux, tout aises,
        En paniers enlaçant nos doigt,
        Revenons rapportant des fraises,
        Revenons rapportant des fraises des bois.

Translation:

When the new season arrives,
When cold departs,
We shall go together, my lovely,
Picking lily of the valley in the forest.

Beneath our feet, pearls of dew scamper,
They tremble in the morning.
We shall listen to the blackbirds,
We shall listen to the blackbird's song.

Spring is here, my lovely,
It is the month that lovers bless,
And the bird, grooming its wings,
Sings poetry beside its nest.
Oh, come with me to the mossy bank
To speak of our love so fair.
Tell me with your sweet voice
And tell me, with your tender voice, "always."

So very far away let us wander,
The hidden rabbit flees from us,
And the buck leans in to admire in the spring.
The reflection of his antlers.

Then to our home, happy, relaxed,
Our fingers wound around baskets,
We return with strawberries,
We return with wild strawberries.

- Translations by this author; all rights reserved.

- VI: *L'isle inconnue*

'Dites, la jeune belle,
Où voulez vous aller?
La voile enfle son aile,
La brise va souffler!

L'aviron est d'ivoire,
Le pavillon de moire,
Le gouvernail d'or fin;
J'ai pour lest une orange,
Pour voile une aile d'ange,
Pour mousse un séraphin.

Dites, la jeune belle,
Où voulez vous aller!
La voile enfle son aile,
La brise va souffler!

Est-ce dans la Baltique,
Dans la mer Pacifique,
Dans l'ile de Java?
Ou bien est-ce en NorvLEge
Cueillir la fleur de neige,
Ou la fleur d'Angsoka?

Dites, la jeune belle,
Où voulez-vous aller?'

'Menez-moi', dit la belle,
'a la rive fidèle,
Où l'on aime toujours.'

'Cette five, ma chère,
On ne la connaït guère
Au pays des amours.

Dites, la jeune belle,
Où voulez vous aller!'

Translation:

'Tell me, young beauty,
Where would you like to go?
The sail fills with wind,
The breeze rises!

The oar of ivory,
The flag of silk,
The helm of fine gold;
I have an orange as ballast,
An angel's wing as sail,
A seraph as cabin-boy.

Tell me, young beauty,
Where would you like to go?
The sail fills with wind,
The breeze rises!

Perhaps to the Baltic,
To the Pacific,
To the isle of Java?
Or to Norway
To pick snow-flowers,
Or the Angsoka bloom?

Tell me, young beauty,
Where would you like to go?'

The fair one replies, 'take me,
To the shore of faithfulness,
Where love is eternal.'
'That shore,' my dear,
Is still unknown
In the land of love.

Where would you like to go?
The breeze rises!'

- Translations by this author; all rights reserved.

- Mendelssohn: *Frühlingsahnung*, op. 48, no. 1

> O sanfter, süßer Hauch! Schon weckest du wieder,
> Mir Frühlingslieder, bald blühen die Veilchen auch.

Translation:

> O, soft, sweet breeze! Already you again wake me
> With spring songs; soon, the violets will also bloom.

- Translations by this author; all rights reserved.

- Mendelssohn: *Die Primel*, op. 48, no. 2

> Liebliche Blume, bist du so früh schon wieder gekommen?
> Sei mir gegrüßet, Botin des Frühlings!
>
> Leiser den alle Blumen der Wiese hast du geschlummert,
> Liebliche Primel, Botin des Frühlings!

Translation:

> Dearest blossom, have you come back again
> So soon? Let me greet you, messenger of spring!
>
> You have slept more silently than all the flowers of
> The meadow, dearest primrose, messenger of spring!

- Translations by this author; all rights reserved.

- Mendelssohn: *Frühlingsfeier*, op. 48, no. 3

>Süßer, goldner Frühlingstag! Inniges Entzücken!
>Wenn mir je ein Lied gelang, sollt' es heut nicht glücken?
>
>Doch warum in diese Zeit an die Arbeit treten?
>Lasst mich ruhn und beten!

Translation:

>Sweet, golden spring day! Inner enchantment!
>If I were ever to craft a song, ought it not be today?
>
>But why should work intrude upon this time?
>Let me rest and pray!

- Translations by this author; all rights reserved.

- Mendelssohn: *Lerchengesang*, op. 48, no. 4

>Wie lieblicher Klang! O Lerche! Dein Sang!
>Er hebt sich, er schwingt sich in Wonne.
>Du nimmst mich von hier, ich singe mit dir,
>Wir steigen durch Wolken zur Sonne.

Translation:

>Such a dear sound! O lark! Your song!
>It rises, it floats in bliss.
>You take me away from here, I sing with you,
>We rise through the clouds to the sun.

- Translations by this author; all rights reserved.

- Mendelssohn: *Morgengebet*, op. 48, no. 5

>O wunderbares, tiefes Schweigen,
>Wie einsam ist's noch auf der Welt!
>Die Wälder nur sich leise neigen,
>Als ging der Herr durchs stille Feld.
>
>Ich fühle mich wie neu geschaffen.
>Wo ist die Sorge nun und Not?
>Was gestern noch mich wollt erschlaffen,
>Des schäm ich mich im Morgenrot.
>
>Die Welt mit ihrem Gram und Glücke
>Will ich, ein Pilger, frohbereit
>Betreten nur wie eine Brücke
>Zu dir, Herr, über'n Strom der Zeit.

Translation:

>O wondrous, deep silence,
>How lonely it is still in the world!
>The woods bow softly,
>As if the Lord were passing through the field.
>
>I feel myself newly created.
>Where now is trouble and need?
>That which wore on me yesterday
>Shames me in the morning light.
>
>The world, with its sorrows and joys,
>Will I, a pilgrim, joyfully traverse like a bridge
>To Thee, Lord, through the river of time.

- Translations by this author; all rights reserved.

- Mendelssohn: *Herbstlied*, op. 48, no. 6

> Holder Lenz, du bist dahin,
> Nirgends, nirgends darfst du bleiben!
> Wo ich sah dein frohes Blühn,
> Braust des Herbsts banges Trieben.
>
> Wie der Wind so traurig fuhr
> Durch den Strauch, als ob er weine;
> Sterbeseufzer der Natur
> Schauern durch die welken Haine.
>
> Wieder ist, wie bald! Wie Bald!
> Mir ein Jahr dahingeschwunden.
> Frägend rauscht es durch den Wald:
> 'Hat dein Herz sein Glück gefunden?'
>
> Waldesrauschen, wunderbar
> Hast du mire das Herz getroffen!
> Treulich bringt ein jedes Jahr
> Neues Laub wie neues Hoffen.

Translation:

> Fair spring, you've gone away.
> Nowhere, nowhere do you remain.
> Where I saw your early blooms,
> Now roar autumn's grim forces.
>
> The wind drives so sorrowfully
> Through the brush, as if it wept;
> The death-sigh of nature
> Shudders through the faded fileds.
>
> It comes again, so soon! So soon!
> A year has gone by for me.
> The query rushes through the forest:
> Has your heart found happiness?

- Translations by this author; all rights reserved.

Strauss Jr.: *Frühlingsstimmen*

Die Lerche in blaue Höh entschwebt,
Der Tauwind weht so lau;
Sein wonniger milder Hauch belebt
Und küßt das Feld, die Au.
Der Frühling in holder Pracht erwacht,
Ah, alle Pein zu End mag sein,
Alles Leid, entflohn ist es weit!
Schmerz wird miler, frohe Bilder,
Glaub an Glück kehrt zurück;
Sonnenschein, ah, dringt nun ein,
Ah, alles lacht, ach, ach, erwacht!

Da strömt auch der Liederquell,
Der zu lang dort wieder rein und hell
Süße Stimmen aus den Zweigen!
Ah, leis' läßt die Nachtigall
Schon die ersten Töne hören,
Um die Kön'gin nicht zu stören,
Schweigt, ihr Sänger all!
Voller schon klingt bald ihr süßer Ton. Ach, ja bald, ah, ah...

O Sang der Nachtigall, holder Klang, ah ja!
Liebe durchglüht, ah, ah...
Tönet das Lied, ah, und der Laut,
Süß und traut, scheint auch Klagen zu tragen,
Ah, wiegt das Herz in süße Träumerein, ah, leise ein!
Sehnsucht und Lust, ah, woht in der Brust,
Ah, wenn ihr Sang lockt so bang funkelnd
Ferne wie Sterne, ah, zauberschimmernd
Wie des Mondes Strahl, ah, wallt durchs Tal!
Kaum will entschwinden die Nacht,
Lerchensang Frisch erwacht,
Ah, Licht kommt sie künden, schatten entschwinden! Ah!

Ah, des Frühlings Stimmen klingen traut,
Ah ja, O süßer Laut, ah, ah... ach ja!

Translation:

> The lark rises into the blue heavens,
> The soft wind blows gently;
> Its mild and blessed breath enlivens
> And kisses the fields, the meadow.
> Spring awakes in splendor,
> Ah, all misery shall end,
> All suffering is far away.
> Pain lessens, cheerful visions,
> Belief in happiness returns;
> Sunshine penetrates, ah,
> Everything laughs and awakes.
>
> A wellspring of songs pours out
> That has been too long silent;
> One hears it ringing out pure and light,
> That sweet voice in the brush!
> Ah, softly, the nightingale allows
> Us to hear that first note, softly
> So as not to disturb the queen,
> All other singers, fall silent!
> Soon, that sweet tone rings out more fully, ah...
>
> Oh, nightingale's song, fair sound, ah, yes,
> Beaming with love, ah, ah...
> The song rings forth, ah, and its sound,
> Sweet and intimate, seems to carry sorrow,
> Ah, the heart rocks in sweet reverie, ah, softly!
> Longing and passion, ah, dwell in the breast,
> Ah, if the song lures me so anxiously,
> Sparkling star-like in the distance,
> Ah, ringing through the valley!
> The night has scarcely passed,
> And the lark's song awakes anew,
> Ah, it promises light shall come and shadows vanish! Ah!
>
> Ah, the voices of spring ring out familiarly,
> Ah, yes, oh, sweet sound, ah... ah, yes!

- Translations by this author; all rights reserved.

- Fauré: *Dans la forêt de Septembre*, op. 85, no. 1

Ramure aux rumeurs amoillies,
Troncs sonores que l'âge creuse,
L'antique forêt douloureuse
S'accorde à nos mélancolies.

Ô sapins angriffés au gouffre,
Nids deserts aux branches brises,
Halliers brûlés, fleurs sans rosées,
Vous savez bien comme l'on souffre!

Et lorsque l'homme, passant blême,
Pleure dans le bois solitaire,
Des plaints d'ombre et de mystère
L'accueillent en pleurant de même.

Bonne forêt! Promesse ouverte
De l'ecil que la vie implore,
Je viens d'un pas alerte encore
Dans ta profondeur encore verte.

Mais d'un fin bouleau de la sente,
Une feuille, un peu rousse, frôle
Ma tête et tremble à mon épaule;
C'est que la forêt vieillissante,

Sachante l'hiver, où tout avorte,
Déjà proche en moi comme en elle,
Me fait l'aumône fraternelle
De sa première feuille morte!

Translation:

> Foliage of deadened whispers,
> Trunks resonant, though hollowed by age,
> The ancient forest sorrows in accord
> With our melancholy thoughts.
>
> Oh, pines, clinging by the void,
> Abandoned nests in broken branches,
> Scorched thickets, dewless blossoms,
> You know well how one might suffer!
>
> And when man, a pale passerby,
> Weeps in the lonely woods,
> Lamenting shadows and mystery,
> Greet him with like tears.
>
> Good forest! Open promise
> Of the exile sought by life,
> With a still-lively step, I arrive
> In your still green depths.
>
> But from a slender birch beside the path,
> One leaf, barely red, brushes
> My head and shivers on my shoulder;
> For the aging forest,
>
> Aware that winter, when all is stillborn,
> Is as close for me and for her,
> Awards me with the brotherly alms
> Of the first fallen leaf!

- Translations by this author; all rights reserved.

- Fauré: *Automne*, op. 18, no. 3

>Automne au ciel brumeux, aux horizons navrants.
>Aux rapides couchants, aux aurores pâlies,
>Je regarde couler, comme l'eau du torrent,
>>Tes jours faits de mélancolie.
>
>Sur l'aile des regrets mes esprits emportés,
>> -   Comme s'il se pouvait que notre âge renaisse! –
>
>Parcourent, en rêvant, les coteaux enchantés,
>>Où jadis sourit ma jeunesse!
>
>Je sens, au clair soleil du souvenir vainqueur,
>Refleurir en bouquet les roses deliées,
>Et monter à mes yeux des larmes, qu'en mon couer,
>>Mes vingt ans avaient oubliées!

Translation:

>Autumn of misty skies and distressing horizons,
>Of quick sunsets, of pale dawns,
>Your melancholy days I watch pass by
>>Like a rushing stream.
>
>Wings of regret carry off my thoughts
>- as if our time could ever be reborn! –
>Dreaming, they wander the enchanted hillsides
>>Where once my youth smiled
>
>I feel, in the bright light of victorious memory,
>Scattered roses reborn into bouquets
>And tears rise in my eyes, tears already
>>Forgotten by my heart at twenty years!

- Translations by this author; all rights reserved.

- Fauré: *Le bonne chanson* – VII. *Un clair jour d'eté*

>Donc, ce sera par un clair jour d'été
>Le grand soleil, complice de ma joie,
>Fera, parmi le satin et la soie,
>Plus belle encore votre chère beauté.
>
>Le ciel tout bleu, comme une haute tente,
>Frissonnera somptueux à long plis
>Sur nos deux fronts qu'auront pâlis
>L'émotion du bonheur et l'attente.
>
>Et quand le soir viendra, l'air sera doux
>Qui se jouera, caressant, dans vos voiles,
>Et les regards paisibles des étoiles
>Bienveillamment souriront aux époux.

Translation:

>>And so it shall be on a clear summer day,
>>The great sun, complicit in my joy,
>>Amidst satin and silk, shall
>>Make your beauty even lovelier yet.
>>
>>The bluest sky, like the highest canopy,
>>Shall ripple luxuriously in long creases
>>Upon our foreheads, pale with joy
>>And anticipation.
>>
>>And when evening arrives, the soft breeze
>>That toys with your scarves shall be sweet
>>And the restful gaze of the stars
>>Shall fall tenderly on the lovers.

- Translations by this author; all rights reserved.

- Fauré: *Le bonne chanson* – IX: *L'hiver a cessé*

L'hiver a cessé: la lumière est tède
Et danse, du sol au firmament clair.
Il faut que le couer le plus triste cede
À l'immense joie éparse dans l'air.

J'ai depuis un an le printemps dans l'âme
Et le vert retour du doux floréal,
Ainsi qu'une flame entoure une flame,
Met de l'idéal sur mon ideal.

Le ciel bleu prolonge, exhausse et couronne
L'immuable azur oû rit mon amour.
La saison est belle et ma part est bonne
Et tous mes espoirs ont enfin leur tour.

Que vienne l'été! Que viennent encore
L'automne et l'hiver! Et chaque saison
Me sera charmante, ô Toi que décore
Cette fantaisie et cette raison!

Translation:

> Winter has ended: the soft light dances
> From the sun to the clear heavens.
> The most sorrowful heart must yield
> To the immense joy that suffuses the air.
>
> I have long held spring in my soul
> And the returning green of sweet blooms,
> Like a flame near a flame,
> Crowning my image with something perfect.
>
> The blue sky expands, exalts, and crowns,
> The unchanging azure where my love laughs.
> The season is lovely, my part of it good
> And all my hopes at last have their chance.
>
> Let summer come! And then afterward
> Autumn and winter! Each season enchants me,
> Ah, Thee who has adorned
> These dreams and thoughts!

- Translations by this author; all rights reserved.

- Mahler: *Das Lied von der Erde* – II. *Der Einsame im Herbst*

Herbstnebel wallen bläulich überm See;
Vom Reif bezogen stehen alle Gräser;
Man meint', ein Künstler habe Staub vom Jade
Über die feinen Blüten ausgestreut.

Der süße Duft der Blumen is verflogen;
Ein kalter Wind beugt ihre Stengel nieder.
Bald werden die verwelkten, goldnen Blätter
Der Lotosblüten auf dem Wasser ziehn.

Mein Herz ist müde. Meine kleine Lampe
Erlosch mit Knistern; es gemahnt mich an den Schlaf.
Ich komm zu dir, traute Ruhestätte!
Ja, gib mir Ruh', ich hab Erquickung not!

Ich weine viel in meinen Einsamkeiten.
Der Herbst in meinem Herzen währt zu lange.
Sonne der Liebe, willst du nie mehr scheinen,
Um meine bittern Tränen mild aufzutrocknen?

Translation:

> Autumn mists make blue waves over the lake;
> Grass stands erect with fog;
> One might suppose an artist had
> Strewn jade dust over the delicate blooms.
>
> The sweet breathe of flowers is gone;
> A cold wind bows their stems low.
> Soon will the wilted, golden leaves
> Of the lotus blossoms be scattered on the water.
>
> My heast is tired; my little lamp
> Sputters out, urging me to sleep.
> Familiar place of rest, I come to you!
> Yes, give me rest, I need comfort.
>
> In my loneliness, I weep much,
> Autumn has lasted too long in my heart.
> Love's sun, will you not shine again
> To gently dry my bitter tears?

- Translations by this author; all rights reserved.

- Mahler: *Das Lied von der Erde* – V. *Der Trunkene im Frühling*

Wenn nur ein Traum da Leben ist,
Warum den Müh und Plag?
Ich trinke, bis ich nicht mehr kann,
Den ganzen, lieben Tag!

Und wenn ich nicht mehr trinken kann,
Weil Kehl' und Seele voll,
So tauml' ich bis zu meiner Tür
Und schlafe wundervoll!

Was hör ich beim Erwachen? Horch!
Ein Vogel singt im Baum.
Ich frag ihn, ob schon Frühling sei,
Mir ist als wie im Traum.

Der Vogel zwitschert: 'Ja! Der Lenz
Ist da kommen über Nacht!'
Auf tiefstem Schauen lauscht' ich auf,
Der Vogel singt und lacht!

Ich fülle mir den Becher neu
Und leer ihn bis zum Grund
Und singe, bis der Mond erglänzt
Am schwarzen Firmament!

Und wenn ich nicht mehr singen kann,
So schlaf' ich wieder ein,
Was geht mich den? Der Frühling an
Laßt mich betrunken sein!

Translation:

> If life is just a dream,
> Then why misery and worry?
> I drink 'til I can drink no more,
> The whole, blessed day!
>
> And when I can drink no more,
> My belly and soul being full,
> Then I take myself back to my door
> And sleep most wonderfully!
>
> What do I hear upon waking? Listen!
> A bird sings in the tree.
> I ask him if spring has already come,
> To me it's all a dream.
>
> The bird twitters, "Yes, spring
> Is here, it arrived overnight!'
> With the greatest intensity, I listen.
> The bird sings and laughs!
>
> I fill my stein afresh
> And empty it in one gulp
> And sing, until the moon beams
> In the dark heavens!
>
> And when I can sing no more,
> Then I sleep again.
> What is springtime to me?
> Let me be drunk!

- Translations by this author; all rights reserved.

- Delius: *Midsummer Day*

> On midsummer day, we'll dance and we'll play
> And we'll wander and stray through the words. La-la-la...
>
> We'll dance and we'll kiss
> whilst it's youth, love and bliss,
> And the night is not far away. Heigh-ho!

- R. Strauss: *Frühling*

> In dämmrigen Grüften träumte ich lang
> Von deinen Bäumen und blauen Lüften,
> Von deinem Duft und Vogelgesang.
>
> Nun liegst du erschloßen in Gleiß und Zier
> Von Licht übergoßen wie ein Wunder vor mir.
>
> Du kennst mich wieder, du lockest mich zart,
> Es zittert durch all meine Glieder
> Deine selige Gegenwart.

Translation:

> In darkening vaults, I dreamed long
> Of your trees and blue breezes,
> Of your fragrance and bird song.
>
> Now you lie revealed, gleaming and adorned
> Bathed in light, as a wonder to me.
>
> You know me again, you beckon me sweetly.
> All my limbs tremble
> With your blessed presence.

- Translations by this author; all rights reserved.

- R. Strauss: *September*

    Der Garten trauert,
    Kűhl sinkt in die Blumen der Regen,
    Der Sommer schauert
    Still seinem Ende entgegen.

    Golden tropft Blatt um Blatt
    Nieder vom hohen Akazienbaum.
    Sommer lächelt erstaunt und matt
    In den sterbenden Gartentraum.

    Lange noch bei den Rosen
    Bleibt er stehen, sehnt sich nach Ruh.
    Langsam tut er die
    Műdegewordenen Augen zu.

Translation:

        The garden mourns,
        Coolly, rain drops on the flowers.
        Summer shudders quietly
        To its close.

        Golden leaves fall one on another
        Down from the tall acacia tree.
        Summer smiles, astonished and weak
        In the dying dream of the garden.

        Long by the roses it remains
        Standing, longing for rest.
        Slowly it closes its weary eyes.

-    Translations by this author; all rights reserved.

The superb LiederNet website has the following extensive texts available for online reading; please make a contribution to the site if you choose to access it with any frequency. It is not this author's website, just one well deserving of support.

- Vaughan Williams texts

http://www.lieder.net/lieder/assemble_texts.html?SongCycleId=5711

- Orff text

http://www.lieder.net/lieder/assemble_texts.html?SongCycleId=7237

Of Barber's *Knoxville: Summer of 1915*:

The text comes from the prologue to James Agee's Pulitzer Prize winning biographical novel *A Death in the Family*. Both its publication (1957) and the prize (1958) came posthumously. The novel is still under copyright and no extensive portion of it can be reproduced here, a fact that most websites also acknowledge. However, if one were resourceful, one could likely uncover it. Also, many recordings of the Barber work include it, at least in part, though one would need to purchase one to have that data at hand.

Reproducing the full text here complete would be in violation of coyright laws. The few phrases that appear in Chapter Seven serve to hint at the moods Barber is seeking to capture.

- Laitman: *Dear March*

> Dear March – Come in –
> How glad I am –
> I hoped for you before –
>
> Put down your Hat –
> You must have walked –
> How out of Breath you are –
> Dear March, how are you, and the Rest –
> Did youleave nature well –
> Oh March, come right up stairs with me –
> I have so much to tell –
>
> I got your Letter, and the Birds –
> The Maples never knew that you were coming – til I called
> I declare – how Red their Faces grew –
> But March, forgive me – and
> All those Hills you left for me to Hue –
> There was no Purple suitable –
> You took it all with you –
> Who knocks? That April
> Lock the Door –
> I will not be pursued –
> He stayed away a Year to call
> When I am occupied –
> But trifles look so trivial
> As soon as you have come
>
> That Blame is just as dear as Praise
> And Praise as mere as Blame –
>
> – text by Emily Dickinson

- Laitman: *The Apple Orchard*

> You won't remember it – the apple orchard
> We wandered through one April afternoon,
> Climbing the hill behind the empty farm.
>
> A city boy, I'd never seen a grove
> Burst in full flower or breated the bittersweet
> Perfume of blossoms mingled with the dust.
>
> A quarter mile of trees in fragrant rows
> Arching above us. We wlaked the aisle,
> Alone in spring's ephemeral cathedral.
>
> We had the luck, if you can call it that,
> Of having been in love but never lovers –
> The bright flame burning, fed by pure desire.
>
> Nothing consumed, such secrets brought to light!
> There was a moment when I stood behind you,
> Reached out to spin you toward me..., but I stopped.
>
> What more could I have wanted from that day?
> Everything, of course. Perhaps that was the point –
> To learn that what we will not grasp is lost.

"The Apple Orchard" © 2003 by Dana Gioia.
First published in *The Hudson Review* (Spring 2003 issue).
Used by permission of the poet.

- Laitman: *Early Snow*

Amazed I looked
Our of the window and saw
The early snow coming down casually,
Almost drifting, over

the gardens, then the gardens began
To vanish as each white, six-pointed
Snowflake lay down without a sound with all
The others. I though, how incredible

were their numbers. I thought of dried
leaves drifting spate after spate
out of the forests,
the fallen sparrows, the hairs of all our heads,

as, still, the snowflakes when on pouring softly through what
had become dusk or anyway flung
a veil over the sun. And I thought
how not one looks like another

though each is exquisite, fanciful, and
falls without argument. It was now nearly
evening. Some crows landed and tried
to walk around then flew off. They were perhaps

laughing in crow talk or anyway so it seemed
and I might have joined in, there was something
that wonderful and refreshing
about what was by then a confident, whitd blanket

carrying out its
cheerful work, covering ruts, softening
the earth's trials, but at the same time
there was some kind of almost sorrow that fell

over me. It was
the loneliness again. After all
what is Nature, it isn't
kindness, it isn't unkindness. And I turned

and opened the door, and still the snow poured down
smelling of iron and the pale, vast eternal, and
there it was, whether I was ready or not:
the silence; the blank, white, glittering sublime.

"Early Snow" © 2001 by Mary Oliver.
From <u>What Do We Know</u>, Da Capo Press.
Used with permission of the Molly Malone Cook Literary Agency.

- Whitacre: *Winter*

Text under copyright, but Mr. Whitacre has it on his website.

https://ericwhitacre.com/music-catalog/satb-choral/winter

Appendix Three: Pronunciation Guide

Albeniz, Isaac	al-BAY-nez, EE-sock
Alfven	ALF-vain
Bax	baax [NOT "box"]
Beethoven	BAY-toh-van
Berlioz	BAIR-lee-ohs
Bloch	[one syllable; soft "ch", like "h" in "hue"]
Boulanger	boo-lawn-ZHEY
Chaminade	chahm-ih-NAHD
Costé	COAST-eh
Delius	DEE-lee-us
Debussy	deb-you-SEE
Dohnanyi, Erno	DOCH-nan-yee, AIR-noh
Ernst, Heinrich	AIRNst, HIGHn-rik
Fibich, Zdenek	FIB-itch, zh-DEN-yek
Fauré	fah-RAY
Fučik	FEW-chik
German, Edward	GAIR-mahn
Glazunov	GLAHZ-ooh-nov
Glinka	GLEENK-ah
Haydn	HIGH-din
Honegger, Arthur	OHN-nah-gair
Humperdinck, Engelbert	HOOMP-er-dink, EN-gel-bairt
Ives	ives [NOT ee-VAY]
Kabalevsky	KA-bih-LEV-ski
Kodaly, Zoltán	koh-DIE-ee, ZOL-tahn
Laitman	LATE-man
Malipiero Gian-Francesco	MAL-ih-pee-AIR-oh, jon fran-CHES-koh
Mendelssohn	MEN-del-son
Milhaud, Darius	mee-YOH, DAH-ree-oos
Mozart, Wolfgang	MOAT-zart, VULF-gahng
Piazzolla	PEE-aht-ZOLL-ah
Puccini, Giacomo	pooh-CHEE-nee, JAH-co-mo
Rautavaara, Einojuhani	RAU-ta-vaara, AIN-no-yu-hahn-ee
Respighi, Ottorino	res-PEE-gee, OH-toh-REE-noh
Rimsky-Korsakov	RIM-ski KOR-sa-kov
Rodrigo, Joaquin	rod-REE-go, wah-KEEN
Roussel, Albert	roo-SELL, al-BAIR
Schickele	SHI-kell-ee

Spohr, Louis	s-POUR, lou-EE
Strauss	SHTRows
Suk, Josef	SOOK [NOT "suck"]
Tchaikovsky	chai-KOFF-ski
Vasks	[rhymes with "tasks"]
Vaughan Williams, Ralph	Rafe [NOT "Ralph"]
Vivaldi	viv-ALL-dee
Waldteufel	WALD-toy-fell
Webern	VAY-bairn
Ysaÿe, Eugene	eee-SIGH, ooh-ZHAIN

Appendix Four: Glossary

- **A cappella** – voices without instruments; original meaning was "in the style of the chapel," as in the Renaissance, church music was performed in this fashion
- **Adagio** - a rather slow tempo; from the Italian word for "slowly"
- **Allegro** – a brisk tempo; from the Italian word for "cheerful"
- **Andante** – a moderately slow tempo; from the Italian word for "current" (as in a stream)
- **Aria** – a portion of an opera scored for solo voice with instrumental accompaniment, and very occasionally choral interruptions as commentary; arias generally serve to provide insight into the personality of a particular character
- **Arpeggio** – playing the several notes of a chord sequentially, rather than simultaneously
- **Art song** – a short musical setting of a poem, generally for one singer and one pianist, though some art songs may add more accompanying instruments; synonym of "lieder"
- **Attacca** – to move from one movement to the next without any intervening pause
- **Avant garde** – the radical, progressive, cutting-edge of music, a term especially in use since the beginning of the 20th century

- **Baroque Era** – a time in European history,1600–1750, in which the royal courts were supremely powerful and music tended to be highly detailed

- **Cadenza** – a totally solo portion of a concerto in which the orchestra waits while the soloist plays on; in the 1700s and 1800s, the soloist was expected to improvise
- **Canon** – a pattern for composition in which a single melody is varied and expanded, each new version of the theme appearing over a simultaneous restatement of the basic theme; a popular technique of counterpoint
- **Cantabile** – a song-like melody or mood
- **Cantata** – a multi-movement composition for chorus and orchestra usually intended for liturgical use in the Protestant Church; especially identified with JS Bach
- **Chamber music** – music for small groups of players (duets, trios, quartets, etc.) playing "one to a part," so that each player makes a unique contribution to the composition
- **Classical Era** – a time from 1750-1820 or so, when the royal courts were declining in influence and composers were increasingly composing for general audiences; music tending to be simpler in structure than formerly
- **Classical music** – technically, music deriving from the Classical Era; more generically, fine music (as distinct from pop music, folk music, etc.) composed according to the artistic standards of a particular time in history; also called art music
- **Chanson** – a short, French-language musical setting of a poem, generally for one singer and one pianist, though some art songs may add more accompanying instruments; synonym of "art song"
- **Character piece** – a solo piano piece, perhaps somewhat free-form in nature, that is meant to convey an image or a mood to the listener; see also "lyric piece"
- **Coda** - the final minutes or moments of a composition (or of one of its constituent movements) that serve to bring it to a close
- **Coloratura** – a very high singing voice, either male or female, nimble enough to be able to sing many different pitches quickly; usually applied to sopranos

- **Commission** – a request to a composer that he/she write a composition in return for payment, usually requesting a particular type of music for a particular occasion
- **Concert overture** – a one-movement piece of program music
- **Concerto** – a multi-movement instrumental composition in which a soloists (perhaps more than one) contrasted with a full orchestra; formally, the plural is "concerti," though "concertos" is also used
- **Contralto** – a particularly low women's singing voice; sometimes just "alto"
- **Counterpoint** – techniques for combining diverse melodies for simultaneous performance; especially important in music of the Renaissance and Baroque Era
- **Countertenor** - a naturally very high male singing voice, often into the female soprano range
- **Cycle** – a series of individual pieces or short movements, perhaps related in some fashion; see also "song cycle"

- **Dodecaphonic music** – emphasizing all twelve notes of the octave (white keys and black ones) equally; a distinctly modernistic idea first attracting attention in the early 20th century
- **Dotted rhythms** – a manner of alternating long and short notes – perhaps a quarter note and an eighth note – so as to produce a sort of skipping pattern
- **Double-stops** – a string playing technique in which the bow is drawn across two adjacent strings at once, so that two notes are heard at the same time
- **Dynamics** – how loud or soft the music is played

- **Etude** – a short solo piece, often for piano, intended as a learning experience and usually designed to focus upon a particular performing technique

- **Fantasia** – a musical term implying that the composer intends to follow his or her own inclinations as to how the music will proceed, rather than adhering to strict structures

- **Fugue** – a compositional form in which several simultaneous and equally prominent melodies are combined into a single tapestry of sound; especially associated with the Baroque Era, though not unknown in later years

- **Harmony** – combinations of simultaneous notes, often as accompaniment to a melody; the three-dimensional aspect of music
- **Harpsichord** – a keyboard instrument popular in the Baroque Era and before the piano; keys are laid out the same as a piano, but the mechanism inside the instrument plucks the strings, rather than striking them with a hammer, leading to a more delicate soun
- **Impressionism** – a movement of the late 1800s/early 1900s emphasizing softer, subtler edges and structures in music; related to the artistic movement of the same name
- **Improvisation** – spontaneous creation of music, even in front of a live audience; although much identified with jazz, it was a skill much admired in earlier days, and both Mozart and Beethoven were known for their improvisatory abilities
- **Incidental music** – a set of short pieces to accompany performance of a play

- **Key** – the central set of notes upon which a composition is based, giving it a particular character; "major" keys generally sound bright and cheerful, "minor" keys dark and somber

- **Larghetto** – a somewhat leisurely tempo
- **Libretto** – the text of an opera or operetta
- **Lied** – a short, German-language musical setting of a poem, generally for one singer and one pianist, though some art songs may add more accompanying instruments; synonym of "art song;" the plural is "lieder"
- **Lyric Piece** – a solo piano piece, perhaps somewhat free-form in nature, that is meant to convey an image or a mood to the listener; see also "character piece"

- **Mallet instruments:** pitched percussion instruments played with mallets, including xylophone, marimba, glockenspiel, et al
- **Measure** – in musical notation, a portion of the written music (likely lasting just a few seconds) in which there is a set number of beats before the next measure, the next one likely due to have the same set number of beats
- **Meter** – the pattern of accented and unaccented beats in a composition. For example, 1-2-3, 1-2-3 (a waltz), as opposed to 1-2, 1-2, 1-2 (a march)
- **Mezzo-soprano:** a moderately low female singing voice, generally more in tenor range than soprano
- **Minimalism** – a musical style of the late 20th century in which a hypnotically steady beat is prominent, with small, subtle changes to melodic fragments; especially identified with Philip Glass
- **Minuet** – originally a triple-meter (1-2-3, 1-2-3) ballroom dance of the 1700s; becomes a popular form for composition in the late 1700s
- **Motif** – a fragment of a melody upon which larger musical structures may be built; one exceptionally famous motif is represented in the first four notes of Beethoven's Symphony no. 5
- **Movement** – a self-contained chapter of a more extended composition, usually contrasting in mood and intensity with the composition's other movements

- **Neo-Classical** – a movement in the early 1900s in which some ideas of the late 1700s were revived, though perhaps with more modern harmonies and a different selection of instruments
- **Neo-Romantic** – a movement in the early 20th century that sought to continue use of the grand melodic moods of late 19th century music

- **One to a part** – each player makes a unique contribution to the composition, with no simultaneous duplication whatsoever

- **Opera** – a musical drama with singers and orchestra; almost wholly lacking in spoken dialog
- **Operetta** – light opera with spoken dialog; a predecessor of modern musical theater
- **Oratorio** – a multi-movement composition for singers and orchestra, generally telling a Biblical story, though without sets or costumes, so not an opera; especially associated with Handel
- **Overture** – an instrumental introduction to a large-scale stage work, such as an opera; distinct from a "concert overture"

- **Parlor Songs** – short works for solo voice and piano, generally not too demanding in technique, and intended for amateur performers
- **Partita** – an instrumental composition often using dance rhythms in its various movements; particularly popular in the Baroque Era
- **Pas de deux** – literally "steps for two": a scene for two ballet dancers, usually a man and a woman
- **Pastoralism** – usually applied to early 20th century British composers fond of expressing the beauty of nature in their music; the adjective term is "pastoral" or "pastoralist"
- **Pitch** – the highness or lowness of a sound
- **Pizzicato** – plucking of the strings on an instrument
- **Pointillism** – as in art, a style in which the substance of the creation is made up of many tiny dots – here, of sound; largely identified with Anton Webern
- **Polyphony** – the practice of having several simultaneous and equally important melodies; especially important in the Baroque Era, though not unknown in later times; various techniques of "counterpoint" are used to create it; adjective form "polyphonic"
- **Program music** – instrumental music with a story to tell or a scene to paint; includes "tone poems," "symphonic poems," and "concert overtures"
- **Presto** – an extremely fast tempo

- **Renaissance Era** – after the Medieval Era but before the Baroque Era, therefore about 1600- 1750; increasing power of the royal courts and a greater tendency toward secular music
- **Rhythm** – patterns of long and short notes from which music may derive its forward motion
- **Romantic Era** – a time from 1820 to 1890 or so, in which music was moving away from the expectations of the Classical Era, generally (though not always) becoming bigger, more dramatic, and more personal in its expression
- **Rondo** – a form for composition with several alternating and contrasting melodies

- **Scherzo** – a form for composition having a quick tempo, a forceful triple meter (**1**-2-3, **1**-2-3) and usually two distinct melodies; one heard at the beginning and again at the end, the other in the middle
- **Score** – all the notes of a composition, with all its many parts, on the printed page
- **Siciliana** – a light and graceful dance-derived pattern for composition in which there are (usually) two groups of three notes per beat to each measure (**1**-2-3, **1**-2-3)
- **Sixteenth notes** – musical notation, very short, rapid notes, four to each beat, therefore often sixteen to each measure
- **Sonata** – a chamber work for one or two players, generally including a piano
- **Song Cycle** – a set of related art songs, perhaps all by the same poet or all on the same literary theme
- **Staccato** – short and separated notes, whether sung or played on instruments
- **Sturm und Drang** – an artistic movement just before and after 1800 that led to stronger, more dramatic compositions; especially associated with Beethoven; German for "storm and stress"
- **Suite** – an instrumental composition (either orchestra or solo keyboard) in several short movements, often portraying different portions of a story; a "suite" may also be several movements extracted from a larger work, such as *The Nutcracker Suite*

- **Symphonic poem** – a one-movement piece of program music, using instruments (not voices or dancers) to tell a story or paint a scene; roughly interchangeable with "tone poem"
- **Symphonic suite** – a multi-movement piece of program music, using instruments (not voices or dancers) to tell a story or paint a scene; sometimes called "program symphony," though "symphonic suite" is more common
- **Symphony** – a multi-movement instrumental composition distinct from a concerto in that a symphony has no featured soloist

- **Tempo** – how fast or slow the music is played
- **Timbre** – the general quality or color of a sound, whether vocal or instrumental
- **Tone poem** – a one-movement piece of program music, using instruments (not voices or dancers) to tell a story or paint a scene; roughly interchangeable with "symphonic poem"
- **Transcription** – the process of rewriting a musical work for different performers than were originally intended
- **Treble** – a boy soprano
- **Tremolo** – a string instrument technique in which the player alternates quickly between two repeated tones, especially tones that are at a very close interval to one another
- **Trill** – a wind instrument (especially woodwinds) technique in which the player alternates quickly between two repeated tones, especially tones that are at a very close interval to one another

- **Variations** – taking a basic melody and steadily changing it (perhaps its rhythm or its key) so as to create different views of that original melody
- **Vivace** – a quite lively tempo

Appendix Five: Sources

Print

- Altmann, Dr. Wilhelm. *Richard Wagners Briefe*. Breitkopf und Härtel. 1905.

- Bailey, Kathryn, editor. *Webern Studies*. Cambridge University Press: Cambridge. 1996.

- Bernstein, Leonard; edited by Jack Gottlieb. *Young People's Concerts*. Anchor Books/Doubleday. New York. 1970/1992. Originally Simon and Schuster 1962.

- Carr, Jonathan. *Mahler: A Biography*. Overlook Press: Woodstock and New York. 1997.

- Davies, Laurence. *César Franck and His Circle*. Barrie and Jenkins: London. 1970.

- Deutsch, Otto Erich. *Schubert: Erinnerungen von seine Freunden*. Breitkopf und Härtel: Leipzig. 1958.

- Grimley, Daniel M. *Carl Nielsen and the Idea of Modernism*. Boydell Press. Woodbridge, Suffolk, UK. 2010

- Hanslick, Eduard. *Musikkritiken*. Philipp Reclam: Stuttgart. 1972.

- Hildesheimer, Wolfgang. *Mozart*. Suhrkampf Verlag: Frankfurt am Main. 1977.

- Hilmes, Oliver. *Cosima Wagner: The Lady of Bayreuth*. Translation by Stewart Spencer. Yale University Press: New Haven and London. 2010.

- Honolka, Kurt. Translated by Anne Wyburd. *Dvořák*. Haus Publishing Limited: London. 2004

- Kennedy, Michael. *Master Musician: Britten*. Dent: London 1981.

- Kennedy, Michael. *Richard Strauss: Man, Musician, Enigma*. Cambridge University Press: Cambridge and New York. 1999.

- Mahler, Alma. *Gustav Mahler: Erinnerungen und Briefe*. [*Reminiscences and Correspondence*] Verlag Allert de Lange: Amsterdam. 1940.

- Massie, Susanne. *Land of the Firebird: The Beauty of Old Russia*. Simon and Schuster: New York. 1980.

- McVeagh, Diana. *Gerald Finzi: His Life and Music*. Boydell Press, Woodridge, Suffolk, UK. 2005.

- Mendelssohn Bartholdy, Paul und Dr. Carl. *Briefe aus den Jahren 1830 bis 1847 von Felix Mendelssohn Bartholdy*. Zusammengestellt von Dr. Julius Rieß. Leipzig. Dr. Hermann Mendelssohn. 1863.

- Morgenstern, Sam. *Composers on Music: An Anthology of Composers' Writings from Palestrina to Copland*. Pantheon Books: New York. 1956.

- Mozart, Wolfgang Amadeus. *Briefe*. [*Letters*] Philipp Reclam: Stuttgart. 1987.

- Newman, Ernest: translator. *Memoirs of Hector Berlioz from 1803 to 1865*. Dover Publications: New York. 1932.

- Nichols, Roger: translator and editor. *Debussy Letters*. Faber and Faber: London and Boston. 1987.

- Orlova, Alexandra. *Tchaikovsky: A Self-Portrait*. Oxford University Press: London. 1990.

- Pleasants, Henry: translator and editor. *Hanslick's Music Criticisms*. Dover Publications: New York. 1950.

- Prokofiev, Sergei. *Prokofiev by Prokofiev: A Composer's Memoir*. Doubleday and Company: New York. 1979.

- Sadie, Stanley, editor. *Grove's Dictionary of Music and Musicians*. MacMillan Publishers: London. 1980. 2001.

- Schindler, Anton. *Beethoven As I Knew Him*. Donald W. MacArdle, editor; Constance S. Jolly, translator. Dover Publications: New York. 1996. [Originally 1860]

- Schmidt, Dr. Leopold, editor. *Beethoven-Briefe.* Wegweiser Verlag: Berlin. 1922. Reprint available from University of California Libraries.

- Schonberg, Harold C. *The Great Pianists: From Mozart to the Present.* Simon and Schuster: New York. 1987.

- Secrest, Meryl. *Leonard Bernstein: A Life.* Alfred A. Knopf: New York. 1994.

- Selden-Goth G. *Felix Mendelssohn: Letters.* Elek Publishers: London. 1946.

- Seroff, Victor Ilyich. *Dmitri Shostakovich: The Life and Background of a Soviet Composer.* Books for Libraries Press: Freeport and New York. 1970.

- Slonimsky, Nicolas. *Lexicon of Musical Invective: Critical Assaults on Composers since Beethoven's Time.* University of Washington Press: Seattle and London. 1953. 1994.

- Solomon, Maynard. *Beethoven.* Schirmer Books: New York. 1998.

- Solomon, Maynard. *Mozart: A Life.* Harper Collins: New York. 1995

- Spaething, Robert. *Mozart's Letters, Mozart's Life: Selected Letters Edited and Newly Translated.* Norton and Company: New York and London. 2000.

- Stravinsky, Igor. *Igor Stravinsky: An Autobiography.* W.W. Norton and Company: New York and London. 1936.

- Tchaikovsky, Modest. *The Life and Letters of Peter Ilyich Tchaikovsky.* Translated by Rosa Newmarch. Vienna House: New York. 1973.

- Thomas, Nancy G. and Jaffe, Jane Vial, editors. *Kurt Oppens on Music: Notes and Essays for the Aspen Music Festival 1957 – 1995.* Science/Art Press: Aspen, Colorado. 2009.

- Vaughan Williams, Ursula. *R.V.W: A Biography of Ralph Vaughan Williams*. Oxford University Press: London. 1964.

Correspondence with Composers – and One Guitarist

Eric Ewazen
Jennifer Higdon
guitarist Sharon Isbin
Lori Laitman
Libby Larsen
Mark O'Connor
Michael Torke
Joan Tower
Pēteris Vasks (via his Publisher, Schott,
 and his daughter, Gundega Vaska)
Eric Whitacre (via his publisher, Music Productions, Ltd.)

Digital

Boosey and Hawkes publishers – In business since 1930 and formed from a partnership of two publishers of 18th and 19th century vintage, Boosey and Hawkes maintains catalogs and biographical information for a vast array of composers, both vintage and current – https://www.boosey.com

Boston Symphony digital archives –
https://www.bso.org/brands/bso/about-us/historyarchives/archival-collection.aspx

Clarke Society – Dedicated to the life and works of Rebecca Clarke – https://www.rebeccaclarke.org/

Gramophone Magazine – In print since 1923, and a fine source of first-hand composer information, including interviews both with current and with now long-departed composers. – https://www.gramophone.co.uk/search/node/archives

LiederNet Archives – texts and often translations for over 100,000 songs and choral works – http://www.lieder.net/

Naxos Music Library – over two million tracks of audio recordings from dozens of top labels – https://www.naxosmusiclibrary.com

New York Philharmonic digital archives – http://archives.newyorkphil.org

Petrucci Music Library, aka International Music Score Library Project [IMSLP] – several hundred thousand public domain music scores – https://imslp.org/wiki/Main_Page

Schott Music – In business since the year of Beethoven's birth and based in Germany, Schott maintains catalogs and biographical information for an immense number of composers, both vintage and current – https://en.schott-music.com/

Sullivan Society – Dedicated to the life and works of Sir Arthur Sullivan – http://www.sullivansociety.org.uk/

Universal Edition AG (Vienna-based music publishers since 1901) – https://www.universaledition.com

Appendix Six:
Acknowledgements and Author Information

Thank you to graphic artist Wayne Rigsby of Gearbox Creative for designing the covers for all of my books.

Thank you to composer RJ Miller for converting my chapter headings into print-worthy form, and for providing insights into how composers go about their craft.

Thank you to my countless performing colleagues who have shared their thoughts about playing one work or another.

Thank you to Rick, who not only tolerates my habit of identifying virtually all music that passes by in movies, but also supports the fact that I can happily spend hours each day typing away about music.

This book is for Ferdi.

♪♪♪♪♪

Music historian Betsy Schwarm spent a dozen years on the air at the vintage KVOD 99.5fm, "The Classical Voice of Denver," and served long on the music faculty at Metropolitan State University of Denver. She gives pre-performance talks for symphonies, opera companies, and chamber music presenters, and has written literally thousands of program notes on works from the Medieval Era to the present day. Over 200 of her articles are available on Encyclopædia Britannica online. Additionally, she writes for performing arts organizations and presenters throughout the US and abroad, including Opera Colorado, the summer season of the Cleveland Orchestra and many other clients.

Her websites:

> www.classicalmusicinsights.com
> www.rubyhillpublishing.com

Her Amazon author page:

> www.amazon.com/Betsy-Schwarm/e/B00DXFZJOQ

Ms. Schwarm's other titles:

- *Classical Music Insights: Understanding and Enjoying Great Music* (2011)
- *Operatic Insights: Understanding and Enjoying Great Music for the Stage* (2012)
- *More Classical Music Insights: From Mozart to Muhly and More* (2013)
- *Classical Music Insights: If All Else Fails, Play Mozart* (2014)
- *Classical Music Insights: Getting to Know Ludwig* (2015)
- *Classical Music Insights: A Star-Spangled Survey* (2016)
- *Classical Music Insights: Bach and Beyond* (2017)

Appendix Seven: Index

Agee, James: 249, 250

Albany Symphony: 267

Albéniz, Isaac: 30-31

Aldeburgh Festival: 265

Alfven, Hugo: 188-119

Alwyn, William: 166-167, 174

Anderson, Leroy: 205-206

Ashmore, Lawrence: 48-50

Aspen Music Festival: 53

Bach, Johann Sebastian: 40, 52

Barber, Samuel: 168, 172, 173
- *Knoxville: Summer of 1915*: 249-251

- *Summer Music*: 133-134

- *Vanessa*: 6

Barbirolli, Sir John: 165, 166

Barratt, Carol: 256

Bartók, Béla: 123, 211

Bax, Sir Arnold: 102, 174
- *November Woods*: 160-161

- *Spring Fire*: 94-95

Beecham, Sir Thomas: 157

Beethoven, Ludwig van: 18, 32, 40, 49, 62, 70, 77, 127, 238, 270, 271
- "Spring" Sonata: 63-66

- Symphony no. 3, "Eroica": 70

- Symphony no. 5 in c minor: 62

- Symphony no. 6, "Pastorale": 104-107

Berg, Alban: 159

Berg, Nathanael: 61

Berkshire Festival of Chamber Music: 89, 126

Berlioz, Hector: 228-231

Bernstein, Leonard: 1, 39, 97, 130, 168

Bizet, Georges: 150

Bloch, Ernest (composer): 200-201

Bloch, Ernst (philosopher): 200

Boston Pops: 168, 205

Boston Symphony: 39, 130, 155, 250

Böttger, Adolf: 68

Botticelli, Sandro: 82, 88, 89, 90

Boulanger, Lili: 97-98

Boulanger, Nadia: 46, 97

Brahms, Johannes: 25, 32, 135, 159, 198

Brandman, Margaret: 176

Bridge, Frank: 90-91, 138, 175

Britten, Benjamin: 5, 263-265

Bunch, Kenji: 215

Büsser, Henri: 82

cadenza: 54, 269

Carmen: 108, 150

Castelnuovo-Tedesco, Mario: 270

Chaminade, Cécile: 150-152

Chopin, Frederic: 144

Christmas: 6, 10, 20, 22, 30, 50, 74, 177, 187, 210, 214, 219, 246, 256

Cincinnati Symphony: 189

Clarke, Rebecca: 125-126

Coates, Eric: 102

Colorado Symphony: 136

Coolidge, Elizabeth Sprague: 89

Coolidge, Peggy Stuart: 168-169

Copland, Aaron: 46, 97, 98-100

Coste, Napoléon: 143-144

counterpoint: 41, 144, 219

Crane, Hart: 98-99

Curtis Institute of Music: 172

Czerny, Carl: 145

Daughtery, Michael: 208-209

Debussy, Claude: 3, 8, 157, 159, 272
- *Children's Corner*: 194
- Preludes for Piano: 193, 194
- *Prelude to the Afternoon of a Faun*: 82
- *Printemps*: 81-83, 89
- *Rondes de Printemps* (from *Images*): 83
- winter pieces: 193-195

Deck the Halls: 219

Delius, Frederick: 60, 102, 174, 272
- *Midsummer Song*: 241
- *North Country Sketches*: 157-158
- *Songs to be Sung of a Summer Night on the River*: 242
- *Summer Night on the River* (orchestra): 115

Desyatnikov, Leonid: 47

Detroit Symphony: 131

Dickinson, Emily: 252

Dohnányi, Erno von: 198-200

Dvořak, Antonín: 77, 78, 86, 120, 195, 238

Eichendorf, Joseph von: 243

Ellington, Duke: 57

Ellisor, Conni: 211-214

Ernst, Heinrich: 110-111

Esch, Edward: 254

Fachiri, Adira: 126

Fantasia (film): 13

Fauré, Gabriel: 235-238

Fenby, Eric: 60

Ferguson, Howard: 165

Fibich, Zdenek: 77-78

Fiedler, Arthur: 205

Finzi, Gerald: 174
- *Fall of the Leaf*: 165-166

- *New Year's Music*: 203-204

Flotow, Friedrich van: 109

Flynn, Errol: 201

Foerster, Josef: 78-80

Forman, Miloš: 140

Franck, Cesar: 189

Fučik, Julius: 195-196

fugue: 17, 75, 109

Gardel, Carlos: 46

Gauld, Tom: 63

Gautier, Théophile: 228

Genée, Richard: 234

German, Edward: 32-33

Gershwin, George: 57

Gilbert, William S.: 73

Ginastera, Alberto: 98

Gioia, Dana: 252

Glass, Philip: 53-54

Glazunov, Alexander: 9, 10, 34-36

Glinka, Mikhail: 107-108

Gluck, Christoph: 181

Gogol, Nicolai: 76

Gounod, Charles: 265

Graham, Martha: 98-99

Grainger, Percy: 175

Grieg, Edvard: 102, 149-150, 157

Guanren Gu: 103

Hadley, Henry: 39-41

Hallé Orchestra: 165, 166

Handel, George Frideric: 14

Hanslick, Eduard: 234

Hanson, Howard: 132-133, 163, 272

Harvard University: 70, 130, 205

Haydn, Joseph: 14-17, 142

Heindl, Victor: 199

Heine, Heinrich: 243

Hensel, Wilhelm: 20

Hepburn, Katharine: 67

Higdon, Jennifer: 134, 172-173

Holst, Gustav: 196-197

Honegger, Arthur: 128-130

Humperdinck, Englebert: 113-114

Ibsen, Henrik: 115

Impressionism/Impressionist: 37, 81, 85, 115, 126, 130, 157, 158, 193, 199, 215

Ippolitov-Ivanov, Mikhail: 80-81

Isbin, Sharon: 206, 207

Ives, Charles: 3, 10, 41-44

Jenkins, Karl: 256

Juilliard School: 53, 169, 211

Kabalevsky, Dmitri: 100-101

Kodaly, Zoltán: 123-124

Koechel, Ludwig: 181

Korngold, Erich: 201-203

Koussevitzky, Serge: 169, 250

Kreisler, Fritz: 40

Laitman, Lori: 251-253

Lamb, Charles: 203, 204

Larsen, Libby: 136-137

Larsson, Lars Erik: 259, 266-267

Leighton, Kenneth: 215

Leipzig Gewandhaus Orchestra: 67

Leitner, Karl: 227

Lenau, Nikolaus: 232

Liszt, Franz: 24, 34, 124, 153, 154
- *Transcendental Etudes*: 145-146

Lyapunov, Sergei: 153-154

Ma, Yo-Yo: 57

MacDowell, Edward: 154-156

Mahler, Gustav: 102, 202, 238-240

Malipiero, Gian Francesco: 44-45

Marx, Joseph: 159-160

May Day: 5

McDuffie, Robert: 53-54

Melartin, Erkki: 138

Mendelssohn, Felix: 5, 18, 20, 67, 116, 258-259, 263, 270
- Fantasia on "The Last Rose": 108-109

- *A Midsummer Night's Dream*: 5, 260-262

- *Sechs lieder im Freien zu singen*, op. 48: 231-233

Mendelssohn Hensel, Fanny: 20-22

Mendès, Catulle: 236

Milhaud, Darius: 95-97

Minnesota Orchestra: 136

Moeran, EJ: 286

Moore, Thomas: 109

Morley, Thomas: 49, 217, 218-220

Moscheles, Ignaz: 77

Moscow Conservatory: 153, 184

Mozart, Leopold: 3
- *Musical Sleighride*: 179-181

- Sinfonia da caccia, "The Hunt": 140-141, 181

Mozart, Wolfgang: 3, 57, 65, 138, 139, 140, 179, 205
- Piano Concerto no. 27, K. 595: 224
-
- German Dances, K. 605: 181-182

- String Quartet no. 17, "The Hunt", K. 458: 139, 141-143

- *Schon lacht der holde Frühling*, K. 580: 222-223

- *Sehnsucht nach dem Frühling*, K. 596: 223-224

Muczynski, Robert: 138

Mussorgsky, Modest: 88

Myrick, Julian: 43

Napoleon: 4

Nashville Chamber Orchestra: 212

Neoclassical: 37, 96, 267

New England Conservatory: 40, 168

New York Philharmonic: 39, 100

New Yorker Magazine: 63

Nielsen, Carl: 116, 255

Nietzsche, Friedrich: 115

Nijinsky, Vaclav: 91

O'Byrne, Dermot: 160

O'Connor, Mark: 57-60

Oliver, Mary: 253

Orchestra Iowa: 208

Orff, Carl: 3, 247-248

Ostrovsky, Alexander: 190

Oswald, James: 178-179

Overbeck, Adolf: 224

Pachelbel, Johann: 51

Paderewski, Ignacy: 40

Paganini, Nicolò: 110

Paine, John Knowles: 69-72

Paisiello, Giovanni: 221

Palmgren, Selim: 61

Paray, Paul: 131

Paris Conservatoire: 97, 111, 129, 150

Paris Opéra: 22

Pastoralism/Pastoralist: 158, 166, 174, 256

Pears, Peter: 263

Peterson-Berger, Wilhelm: 116-118

Petipa, Marius: 35

Pi Kappa Lambda: 172

Piazzolla, Astor: 10, 46-48

Piston, Walter: 130-131

Popper, David: 175

Prague Conseratory: 78, 86

Prokofiev, Sergei: 34, 61
- *Autumnal Sketch*: 162
- *Alexander Nevsky*: 4
- *Peter and the Wolf*: 127
- *Summer's Day*: 127-128
- Symphony no. 5: 128
- *War and Peace*: 4, 127

Puccini, Giacomo: 6, 202, 264

Pulitzer Prize: 163

Purcell, Henry: 60

Rachmaninoff, Sergei: 34

Raff, Joachim: 24-27

Rautavaara, Einojuhani: 169-171

Ravel, Maurice: 130, 201

Respighi, Ottorino: 3, 83, 87-89, 256, 272

Richardt, Christian: 149, 150

Rimsky-Korsakov, Nicolai: 32, 34, 88

- *Capriccio espagnole*: 75

- *May Night*: 75-76

- *Scheherazade*: 32, 75, 88, 114

- *Snow Maiden*: 190-192

Rodrigo, Joaquin: 3, 61, 134-136

Rosetti, Dante Gabriel: 167

Rossini, Gioacchino: 227

Roussel, Albert: 10
- *Pour une fete de printemps*: 85

- Symphony no. 1, "La poeme de la foret": 36-38

Royal College of Music: 32, 160, 197, 245

Royal Conservatory of Music: 125

Rubinstein, Nicolai: 184

Russian Revolution: 4, 76

Rutter, John: 257

Ryom, Peter: 14

St. Petersburg Conservatory: 34, 162

Salerno-Sonnenberg, Nadja: 57

San Francisco Symphony: 39

scherzo: 21, 22, 29, 49, 66, 69, 71, 106, 186, 261

Schickele, Peter: 51-52

Schnaufer, David: 212

Schoenberg, Arnold: 116

Schreiber, Aloys: 227

Schubert, Franz: 225-228, 238

Schulze, Ernst: 226

Schumann, Clara: 67

Schumann, Robert: 67-69, 198

Shakespeare, William: 5, 49, 58, 60, 68, 214, 220, 258-266, 268, 270
- *As You Like It*: 58, 220
- *Cymbeline*: 226
- *A Midsummer Night's Dream*: 5, 258-265
- *A Winter's Tale*: 5, 214, 259, 266-270

Shankar, Ravi: 53

Shostakovich, Dmitri: 34

Sibelius, Jean: 84, 116, 169

Silvestre, Armande: 236

Simon and Garfunkel: 49-50

sitar: 53, 254

Smetana, Bedrich: 7

Songwriters' Hall of Fame: 205

Sousa, John Philip: 195

Sowerby, Leo: 163-164

Spohr, Louis: 18-19

Steber, Eleanor: 250

Stenhammar, William: 137

Still, William Grant: 176

Stoltzman, Richard: 48

Strauss, Eduard: 147, 234

Strauss, Johann Jr.: 111-112, 144, 147-148, 196, 234-235, 244

Strauss, Johann Sr.: 147, 234

Strauss, Josef: 147-148, 214, 235

Strauss, Richard: 120, 124, 159, 202, 243-244, 251

Stravinsky, Igor: 63, 64, 91-94

Suk, Josef: 86-87, 120-122, 270

Sullivan, Sir Arthur: 5, 72-75

Sviridov, Georgy: 215

Symbolism: 79

symphonic poem: 77, 101, 159

Tchaikovsky, Peter: 35, 107, 153, 177, 191, 192, 214
- *Eugene Onegin: 191*
- *The Nutcracker*: 177, 187-188
- *The Seasons*: 27-30
- *Sleeping Beauty*: 35
- *Symphony no. 1, "Winter Dreams"*: 184-186

Tennyson, Lord Alfred: 115, 217

Thanksgiving: 3, 42, 43

Thomas, John: 175

Thomson, James: 14

Thoreau, Henry: 166

Tolstoy, Leo: 127

Torke, Michael: 2, 138

- *December*: 138, 210-211

- *A Winter's Tale*: 267-269

Toronto Symphony: 53

Tower, Joan: 206-208

Twichell, Edward: 43

Uhland, Ludwig: 232

Vanderbilt University: 51

Vasks, Pēteris: 55-56

Vaughan Williams, Ralph: 174, 211, 245-247

Verdi, Giuseppe: 22-24, 265

Verlaine, Paul: 237

Vivaldi, Antonio: 1, 3, 7, 44, 47, 53, 63, 84, 90, 96, 129, 134, 135, 173, 217
- "Dell'aura sussurrar": 220-221
- *The Four Seasons*: 9-14

Wagner, Cosima: 113

Wagner, Richard: 113, 197, 234

Wagner, Siegfried: 113

Waldteufel, Emil
- *Les Patineurs*: 182-183

- *Soirée d'ete*: 111-112, 183

Walter, Bruno: 239

Webern, Anton: 124-125, 159

Weill, Kurt: 113

Whistler, James: 81

Whitacre, Eric
- *October*: 173-174

- *Winter*: 253-255

Whitman, Walt: 115

Wille, Bruno: 125

Williams, John: 129

Wincenc, Carol: 206

Wood, Grant: 209, 210

Wordsworth, William: 270

Ysaÿe, Eugene: 189-190, 215

Zemlinsky, Alexander: 202

Ziehrer, Carl Michael: 137

Notes

Notes